The
Weekend Builder

The
Weekend Builder

A practical guide to major home improvements and extensions

Edited by Julian Worthington

ORBIS PUBLISHING · London

Acknowledgments

Aristocast Ltd 38, 58; Blacknell Buildings Ltd 129, 135–8 (photos); Brick Development Association 26, 28 (photo), 32 (photo), 107 (photo); Brightlife Ltd 1, 105–6; British Gypsum Ltd 51–2 (photos), 70 (photo), 73 (photos), 74, 78–9 (photos); Burlington Slate Ltd 111; Celuform Ltd 93; Cement & Concrete Association 2, 8, 10–11, 12, 15, 16–17, 18 (photos), 81, 99–101 (photos), 109 (photo), 121; Calvin Evans 24 (artwork); Eugene Fleury 9, 13–14, 19–20 (artwork); Halls Homes & Gardens Ltd 133 (photo); Hayward Art Group 21–3 (artwork), 27, 28–31 (artwork), 32–5 (artwork), 39–43, 54–7, 59–63, 82–6, 88–92, 94–8 (artwork), 99–103 (artwork), 107–10 (artwork), 112–5 (artwork), 122 (artwork), 123, 125 (artwork), 127, 131–4 (artwork), 136–7 (artwork), 140–3; London Brick Buildings Ltd 130, 134 (photo); Marley Buildings Ltd 116–20 (photos), 122 (photos), 126 (bottom photo); Orbis/Dudley Reed 139; Orbis/Terry Trott 21 (photo), 24–5 (photo), 36–7 (photo), 48–9, 87, 96–7 (photo); Harry Smith Horticultural Photographic Collection 19 (photo), 110 (photo), 112–4 (photos); Studio Briggs 18 (artwork), 44–7, 51 (artwork), 64–7, 117–9 (artwork); Venner Artists 68–73 (artwork), 75–80 (artwork), 104; Peter Weller 36 (artwork); Willian Home Improvements 124–5 (photos), 126 (top photos), 128.

First published in Great Britain
by Orbis Publishing Limited, London 1981
© Orbis Publishing Limited 1981
Reprinted 1982, 1983

Printed in Czechoslovakia
ISBN: 0–85613–337–X
50141/3

Contents

Introduction

Move or extend? There are probably few property owners who have not at some time in their life had to face up to this question, the answer to which is never that simple. So many factors are involved in a decision of this kind. Which can we afford? Do we really want to move? Is there anywhere really suitable that we like? Will the family mind the change? What about switching schools in midstream? Is it going to be convenient for work – or will we have to find work somewhere else? The list could go on. But in the end the decision has to be reached on the basis of many different personal factors, none of which can reasonably be considered in a book of this kind.

What this book does do is to discuss what is involved in extending an existing property and the amount of work you can tackle yourself, which is, of course, of fundamental importance if budget is a major consideration. Naturally this involves the heavier, dirtier side of DIY work, but it is one which probably brings the greatest reward in terms of achievement. And it could be that this alone may be sufficient to answer that all-important question.

Because of the size and importance of this type of work – and with it the considerations of cost and time – sound and thorough planning is crucial. To change the structure or size of a property includes much more than the job itself. Local authorities have to be consulted and plans submitted for approval; this will always involve Building Regulation controls; depending on the work you want to do, planning permission may not necessarily be required. If you have borrowed money for the purchase of the property, the body concerned – be it a building society, local council or bank – will have to be consulted as well. The golden rule when considering structural work in or around your property is to check first. If you do not, the consequences can be expensive and soul-destroying; you can even be ordered to pull down what you have painstakingly put up.

In this book the different aspects of work likely to be required are covered separately. The first two chapters deal with the techniques of working with concrete and bricks, two essential ingredients in any job of this kind. You may not, of course, regard yourself as a competent bricklayer; but you can save a lot of money by doing the 'labouring' – digging the foundations, mixing mortar, carrying bricks, etc – and employing just one brickie.

Naturally no set of plans is necessarily going to be the same as any other and the information in this book is there as a guide to the various techniques involved, as well as details on certain specific tasks you may need to do or decide you would like to do. Having put up the walls of your extension, for example, you will need to know how to line them. Plastering is a skilled operation, but one which you can master with practice. You may decide to use plasterboard for the internal walls, particularly if you want to divide a large room into two smaller rooms – and so there is a section on the types of timber stud partition and how to put them up. The techniques of removing a disused fireplace to create more space are also discussed.

You will certainly want some access to the new areas and there is information on how to make a wall opening and on RSJs and lintels, in certain cases crucial to provide support for such openings. There are also details on the construction of timber staircases, in the event of you having a two-storey extension and wishing to create access within the extension to the upstairs. Whether or not you are building on to the existing property, you may decide for reasons of space – or just for the effect – to make internal arches between rooms rather than hang doors; the techniques for doing this are also covered.

Whether or not you are extending your property, there is work you may want to do outside the house – to improve facilities or just to enhance or protect your property. Porches give added protection to the home, as well as keeping it warmer; these can be bought prefabricated or you can build them to your own design. Depending on their size, however, planning permission may be needed. Garages and carports may not be top priority, but if space allows they will help protect another valuable possession – the car – as well as providing cover or storage for a lot of other bits and pieces.

Fences and gates are not only important as boundary markers but also provide a degree of privacy for your property. They can be essential, too, if you have a family or pets and live on a busy road. With the techniques covered in this book you can put up more permanent structures such as walls or landscape the garden with paths or steps. If you have a garage, you will, of course, want a suitable drive to provide access from the road. If space allows, a patio or terrace can make an attractive and useful feature, particularly in the warmer months, and you can organise access from a ground floor room by installing patio doors.

The more you look around your property, the more you will find to do to improve the facilities and – in many cases – increase its value. Again this may influence your decision on whether it is worth the time and effort to work on your existing home rather than look for another more suitable one.

Archtects may not be cheap, but money spent at the initial planning stage, which will be minimal in terms of the overall costs, will be well spent if the end result meets your expectations. Today there are many prefabricated constructions which are worth considering if they suit your style of property. Firstly they are generally fully approved in that they meet current Building Regulations; and they are usually easier and cheaper to put up. However, they may not meet your requirements, so do not be tempted by these considerations alone if the structure is not what you want.

This book will not be of value just to the keen DIY person who is prepared to tackle much of the heavier work, thus reducing the costs of experienced labour. It will also help those who want to cost the job in terms of time and work required and the amount of materials needed, as well as the problems to be overcome. Whether you decide to do it yourself or pay someone else to do it for you, it will be invaluable if you know what is required and can check that it is being done properly. This alone could save you a great deal of time and money and ensure that the work is done to the standard and specification you want.

Concrete

Working with concrete is not such a daunting task as you may think; it has been made very much easier by ready-mix material, to which you only have to add water. When using large quantities you may find it more convenient to buy the individual ingredients and mix them yourself or buy it ready mixed in bulk if you are laying concrete over a large area. The secret of successful concreting is to prepare for the work thoroughly and have the right equipment available. Some of the tools needed you may already have; others you can make up yourself; the rest – particularly if you are only doing the odd job – you can hire.

Mixing concrete

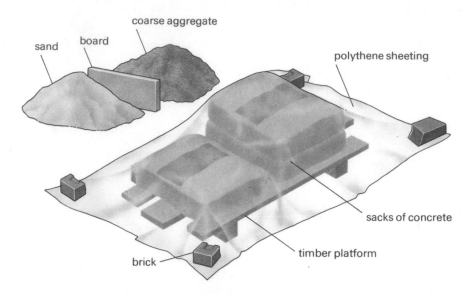

Concrete is widely used in both the home and garden; you can buy it in pre-packed dry-mix form for small jobs, mix your own ingredients for medium size work or have ready-mixed concrete delivered in bulk, ready to lay, when tackling large areas. The basic concrete mix is Portland cement, sand, stones and water. The cement is normally grey but other colours, including white, are available for decorative work, although all are more expensive than the standard grey. If using colouring, you may have difficulty achieving a uniform effect.

The sand and stones (called aggregate) are bonded by the cement as it reacts with water to form a mineral glue which, helped by the aggregate, gains in strength as it hardens. Only sharp, washed sand should be used; soft sand is mainly used for mortar, when laying bricks. The type of aggregate varies according to the type of job. For foundations or other large jobs, use a coarse aggregate: gravel, crushed gravel or crushed stone between 5 and 20mm ($\frac{3}{16}-\frac{3}{4}$in) in diameter. For finer jobs, such as making window sills or slabs, use a coarse sand or a mix of sand and fine shingle not more than 10mm ($\frac{3}{8}$in) in diameter. Coarse aggregate mixed with sand (known as a combined aggregate or ballast) is generally the most convenient way of buying the material from a builder's merchant – but make sure you are sold washed ballast.

Water Always use clean tap water and add only enough to make the concrete workable, usually about half a bucket for each bucket of cement. If you add too much water, the mix will be sloppy and will shrink on drying; too little and the mix will be difficult to work and small air pockets will appear in the finished work. Both of these defects cause weakening of the finished concrete. Mixing becomes easier if you add a proprietary wetting agent or some washing-up liquid to each bucket of water.

Lime A handful of hydrated lime added to each mix will slow the setting time and the concrete will be less likely to shrink and crack.

PVA The mixing becomes smoother if you add PVA (builders' merchants stock several proprietary brands) to the water; this also helps to reduce the dust when the concrete has set. Neat PVA brushed onto existing concrete helps to bond a fresh layer.

Above right Keep materials separate and store cement bags clear of the ground
Right Use our graph to estimate what quantity of concrete you will need. Find the area to be concreted on the vertical scale; read across the lines of the graph until you reach the desired thickness and then down to the horizontal scale to find the volume of concrete. You will find how much of each ingredient you need for the different volumes by reading across the bottom scales. The shaded area indicates when ready-mix concrete is more economical

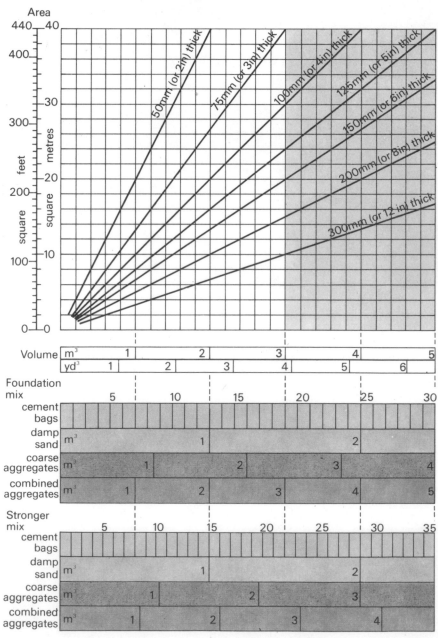

Ready-mix concrete
There are several companies who will deliver ready-mixed concrete to your home and will advise you on the best mix for a particular job. Before you order, decide whether the site is accessible, if you can get the preparatory work done by your delivery date and whether you can organize enough volunteer labour among your friends to help you lay the concrete before it becomes unworkable. The smallest economic load is about 3cu m (4 cu yds).

Pre-packed concrete
Bagged in various sizes and grades, pre-packed mixes are an expensive way of buying concrete for anything other than small jobs – but, if storage is a problem they are useful and do save time in proportioning materials.

Storing materials
If you are storing cement outdoors, keep the bags clear of the ground and cover them with water-proof sheeting. Bagged aggregate is easier to store than loose material, but is more expensive. If you are storing more than one type of loose aggregate, you must put a board between each one to keep them separate. Never store materials on earth.

Warning If you are leaving materials overnight in the road outside your house, you must place red warning lamps alongside and should not obstruct the pavement.

Estimating quantities
Using our easy-to-check graph decide how much concrete you want for each task and how much of each material you need. Wastage is not allowed for, but add an extra ten percent for cement and round up your aggregate requirements to the next half or whole cubic measurement.

First work out the area you are concreting and relate this to the desired thickness of concrete; this gives you the volume you require, so you can establish the quantities of each ingredient. Determining the area of a rectangle (one side multiplied by the adjacent side) is simple, so is a triangle

1 When mixing concrete by hand, tip the ingredients into a neat pile
2 Make a crater in the middle, pour in water and turn in material from the outside
3 Add more water as necessary, using a watering can to regulate the amount
4 Turn the pile with a shovel to mix the materials thoroughly
5 When using a machine, mix half the water with half the aggregate, then add the cement and the remainder of the water and aggregate
6 After a few minutes the concrete will be of workable consistency and is ready for use

(half one side multiplied by the perpendicular height from that side). For other areas with straight sides, break them down into squares, rectangles and triangles and add them together.

Basic mixes

There are four basic mixes. For foundations etc. where the thickness of the concrete is 75mm (3in) or more, you need one part cement, two and a half parts damp sand and four parts coarse aggregate. A stronger mix more suited to small units or thin sections will be made from one part cement, two parts damp sand and three parts coarse aggregate. Normal strength blockwork and rendering mortar is made from one part cement, one part lime and six parts soft (builder's) sand. For lightweight blockwork use one part cement, two parts lime and nine parts soft sand. Bedding mortar consists of one part cement to five parts sharp (concreting) sand.

Most supplies of sand and aggregate will be delivered damp due to washing at the quarry or being left uncovered. If in hot weather your supplies are delivered dry, you will need to reduce your sand or ballast content and increase the water content accordingly. After a little experience you will get the feel of the right texture for each mix and should not have any problems achieving the correct balance every time.

Mixing the concrete

If you are mixing the concrete yourself, you can do it by hand – using a shovel, buckets and a watering can – or you can hire a cement mixer. The mixers run on either petrol or mains electricity; some can be powered by an electric drill. Also available is a manual roller mixer which turns the concrete as you roll it along. Bear in mind petrol-driven machines are noisy; if you are using one for prolonged periods, you may disturb the neighbours.

If concreting is likely to take some weeks, it may be worth buying a second-hand mixer and selling it when you have finished.

Because concrete hardens quickly, you should not mix more than you can lay while it remains workable. Never allow concrete to harden in a mixer; wash the mixer out with water and a stiff brush before it sets, otherwise you will have to spend a lot of time with a hammer and chisel before you can return the mixer to the hire firm or use it again.

Mixing by hand Work on a firm, dry surface. Using buckets, measure out the sand and the aggregate and form it into a compact heap with a crater in the middle. Add the cement and turn the heap until the materials are uniform in colour. If using a pre-packed mix, turn the materials over until the colour is consistent.

Pour water into the crater and turn in dry material from the outside; keep mixing and adding water until the whole pile is of a consistent form and colour.

Machine mixing Make sure the machine is level. Place half the aggregate and half the water in the machine and mix them for a short time. Add the cement and the remainder of the aggregate and water until you achieve the correct consistency. Mix for about two minutes, but not for much longer. The concrete should fall cleanly off the blades in the drum without being too soupy.

Warning Don't wash surplus cement into drains since it will set at the bottom and cause a blockage.

Laying a slab of concrete

Although the principles of laying concrete are the same whether you are working on large or small areas, the techniques do vary and you should follow instructions carefully in each case. We start the series with concrete slabs for which, as with all concrete, the right preparation is vital.

Site conditions and the finished thickness of your concrete base determine the depth of subsoil you must remove and the amount of hardcore to be rammed in before you lay any concrete. For a small job a base of 75mm (3in) deep is usually sufficient, unless the soil is very soft clay when the thickness should be 100mm (4in). The subsoil should be firm and fairly level and if you are digging into a well-compacted subsoil you should stop approximately 125–150mm (5–6in) below the finishing level of the concrete. If you are working on recently laid top-soil, dig out to a depth of at least 225mm (9in) and then compact the soil with the back of a shovel or a punner or ramming tool.

Warning You must dig out topsoil, vegetation and roots over an area that extends 150mm (6in) on all sides of the planned base.

Making formwork
Now make a formwork to the required level and dimensions of your base. Use 25mm (1in) thick timber of the same width as the depth of your intended finished base, with lengths cut to the appropriate size. Sharpen one end of each of the timber pegs to a point and drive the pegs partway into the ground about 1m (or 39in) apart. Check each corner for squareness with a builder's square and drive the pegs into the ground until the proper level is reached. Nail the outer edges of the timber to the pegs, with the tops of the pegs flush with the top of the edging timber.

Planning drainage
If a drainage slope is required, a fall of 1:60 is usually sufficient, as long as the surface of the concrete is flat and smooth. You can achieve this drop by gently hammering one end of the form-work deeper into the ground than its opposite end. To check whether you have the right fall, place a board across the formwork in the direction of the required slope and a 15mm ($\frac{5}{8}$in) shim under the lower end of a 900mm (3ft) spirit level. When the bubble shows dead centre, you will have achieved the correct fall. Make the test at both sides and in the middle of the formwork.

Making hardcore base
Spread coarse hardcore inside the formwork on top of the firm subsoil base. Broken brick, broken concrete or stonework is ideal. Keep the smaller grade hardcore or clinker and spread this between the larger pieces to bring up the level to the bottom edges of the formwork. Tread it down firmly or force it down with a ramming tool or punner.

Damp proofing
Concrete is a porous material and will allow moisture to rise through it from the base. If you want a dry concrete floor, in a shed for example, place a damp proof membrane of plastic sheeting over the base before laying the concrete.

Make sure the base is well compacted and level off sharp corners of the hardcore to prevent it ripping the membrane; for added protection, place sharp sand on top of the base and level it carefully. Lay a sheet of 1000-gauge plastic sheeting over the sand, turning it up the sides of the formwork. If necessary, overlap the sheets by at least 150mm (6in). Then lay concrete on top.

Above Successful concreting depends on the right base, of which hardcore is an essential ingredient
1 Make sure your site is firm and level and clear an extra 150mm all round
2 Set out the formwork, using a builder's square to ensure the corners are at right-angles
3 If you need a slope for drainage, hammer one side of the formwork further into the ground. To check the fall is accurate, place a spirit level on a board across the formwork in the direction of the required slope and put the correct size shim under one end of the level. When the bubble is dead centre, you will have the right fall

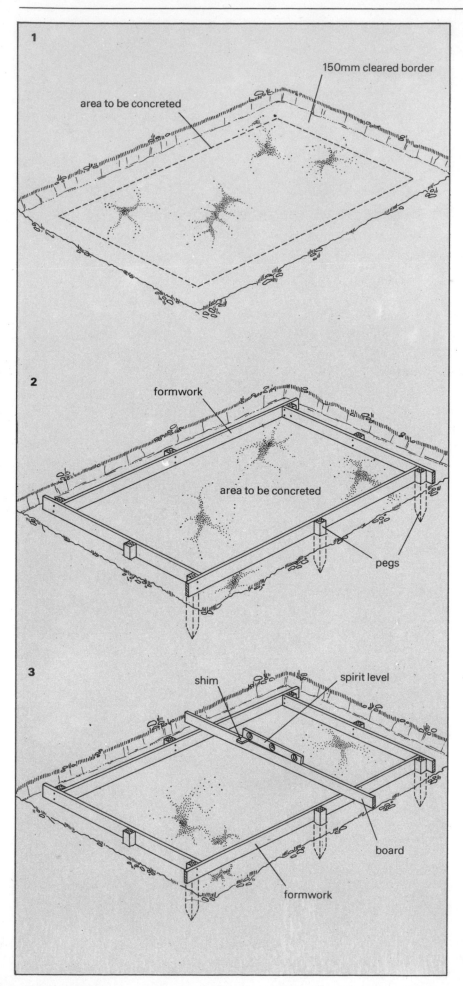

1

area to be concreted

150mm cleared border

2

formwork

area to be concreted

pegs

3

shim

spirit level

board

formwork

Laying concrete

Now the concrete can be spread on top of the hard-core. Mix your concrete as near to the base as possible to reduce the distance you have to carry the heavy wet mix. Make sure you have a firm, clean mixing surface – a solid path is ideal since this can be washed down after the mixing is finished. If this is any distance away from the site, use a wheelbarrow to transport the wet mix.

Wheelbarrow plank It might be necessary to carry concrete down steps. You can overcome this hazard by laying a builder's deal plank, which should never be less than 32mm (1¼in) thick, across the steps. Spike the top end in place and hammer in pegs each side at the bottom to prevent it moving sideways. This type of plank should never span more than 2m (6ft 6in) unsupported. The alternative is to use a builder's bucket and carry the wet mix to the site, depositing it in mounds within the formwork.

Use the rake to spread the concrete level and about 10–15mm (⅜–⅝in) above the edges of the formwork.

Finishing methods

The concrete is now ready for compacting. This is an important stage which will give the finished job strength and durability. Any small voids in the mix are closed and the air is expelled by tamping down the surface with the edge of a timber plank – or a timber tamping board if you have help, with one person on each side of the formwork.

Tamping involves a chopping action and you should move the timber along the concrete, about half the thickness of the timber each time. Do this twice and any high or low spots will show. These surface deviations should be eliminated when you make one final pass along the entire surface with a sawing motion that will leave the surface ready for the finishing operation. If any low spots remain, add extra concrete and make another sawing pass. Various finishes can be applied to the surface, although the rippled effect left by the final sawing action is ideal for a drive or an incline where a grip might be required in icy conditions. This finish is generally too coarse for a floor base and is difficult to sweep.

Brushed finish A light brushing with a soft broom will remove the rippled effect and produce a smoother finish. The effect will vary, depending on how long the concrete is allowed to set before you start brushing. Test a small area at various stages until the desired finish is achieved, then complete the entire area.

If you leave the brushed effect until the concrete is quite firm, you can make another light brushing, having sprinkled water on the concrete through a fine rose on a watering can. This will expose the aggregate, giving a smooth but stony effect to the surface. Timing is crucial as the aggregate can be washed out if the water is applied too soon – and the surface will be ruined.

Wood float finish A lightly textured finish can be achieved by rubbing a wood float (using a light circular motion) across the surface soon after tamping down.

Steel float finish After the wood float has been applied, a steel float will polish out the texture left by the wood float and provide a really durable finish. Don't use the steel float too soon after tamping or it may cut into the concrete. Wait long enough for the concrete to begin to harden at the top before working on the finish.

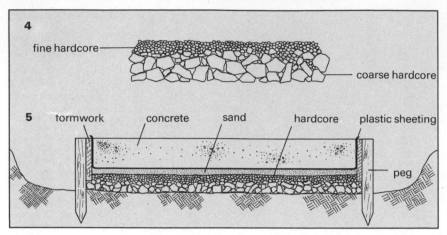

4

fine hardcore — coarse hardcore

5 tormwork concrete sand hardcore plastic sheeting

peg

Curing concrete

When you are satisfied with the concrete finish, it is important you cure the concrete properly. This is one reason why you are advised against laying concrete in frosty conditions, since frost is concrete's biggest enemy. If frosts are likely (and they can occur even in May), protect the surface with a thick layer of straw under a sheet of polythene. If this is not available, cover the surface with a thick layer of sand or earth once the concrete is firm.

The concrete must be prevented from drying too quickly in hot weather. This can be done by covering the surface with sheet polythene or dampened hessian or sacking. Weight down the covering along the edges to prevent the wind lifting it. If sacking is used, keep it dampened for up to four days before removing it. In normal weather concrete takes a

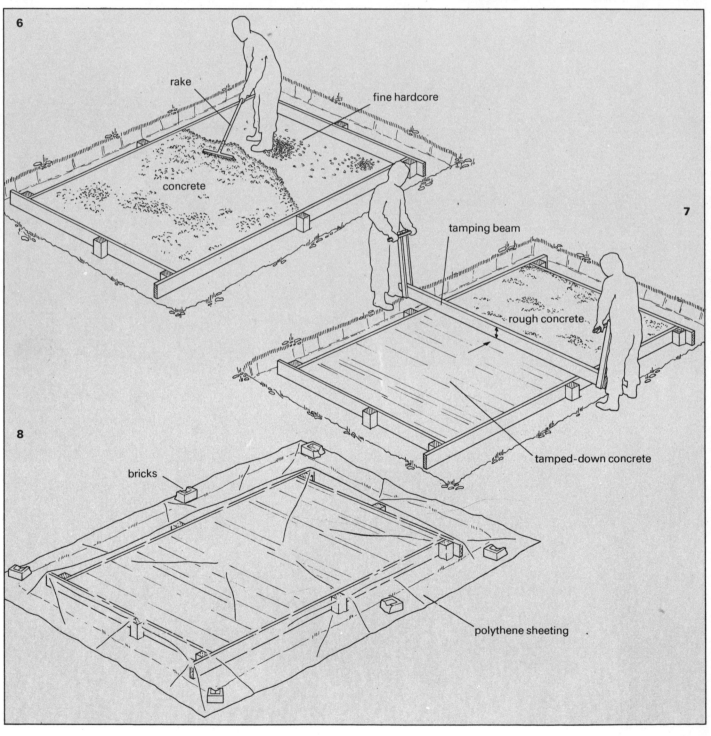

6

rake

fine hardcore

concrete

7

tamping beam

rough concrete

tamped-down concrete

8

bricks

polythene sheeting

4 Lay large grade hardcore packed with smaller pieces
5 Before laying a damp proof course, place sand over the hardcore
6 Rake the concrete level
7 Compact the concrete with a tamping beam
8 Cover finished concrete with polythene sheeting
9–12 Finishing techniques
9 Brush out ripples
10 Lightly dampen the surface for a smoother finish
11 Make a lightly textured finish with a wood float
12 For a really smooth finish, use a steel float

week to cure (ten days in cold weather), during which time the covers should be retained. The floor can be used as soon as the curing period is over.

Take precautions to keep children and animals off the new surface, since footprints and pawmarks are difficult to remove from a hardening surface.

Removing formwork Once the concrete is cured, you can uncover the surface and lever the formwork out of the ground. Dismantle the timber carefully, remove the nails from the board and pegs and store the timber in a dry place for future use.

For formwork
timber 25mm (1in) thick, 75 or 100mm (3 or 4in) wide
timber pegs 50 × 50mm (2 × 2in)
builder's square
measuring tape
spirit level, wood shim
club hammer
50mm (2in) galvanized wire nails

For finish
rake, tamping beam
punner or ramming tool
soft brush, wood and steel floats
polythene sheeting, hessian or sacking, straw (for protection)

equipment

Concrete block paving

If you use concrete blocks you will find laying an area of paving a fairly easy task. More traditional types of paving involve mixing a considerable amount of mortar and handling numerous paving slabs, some of which can be extremely heavy. Concrete blocks are comparatively easy to handle, both when stacking and using them, and do not require the use of a cement mix when you are bedding them into position.

Suitable for patios, paths and driveways, these blocks are strong enough to carry very weighty objects, such as a heavy fuel-delivery lorry, immediately after they have been put down. Area for area they are similar in price to any top quality coloured slab paving and are available in a variety of colours and shapes in sizes similar to house bricks – about 65mm (or 2½in) thick. The range of colours and interlocking shapes means you can choose from a wide selection of patterns for use in contrasting areas for herringbone, zigzag and chequered effects, as well as for plain infills and borders.

Preparing the surface

The area to be paved must have a firm base, preferably consisting of well rammed hardcore. Make sure the overall surface of the base follows the required fall of the finished paving. It is important to remember the completed paving will be almost entirely impervious to water and you should consider this when setting out your levels. Puddles will form in any depressions remaining on the surface after laying has been completed.

Edge restraint You should provide an edge restraint around the outer perimeter of the area to be paved. Place 25mm (1in) thick profile boards at the outer edges and fix them with 25mm (1in) thick wood stakes driven well into the ground. Make sure the timber is well creosoted before fixing and set the top edge of the profile boards at the level the finished surface of the paving will reach. You do not need to place edge profiles against brick walls or the side of the house, but make sure the completed paving surface will be at a level at least one brick below the damp proof course and that there is a suitable fall-away from the house to carry off rain water.

Completing the base Spread a layer of washed, sharp sand over the entire area to be paved and level it by drawing a long timber straight-edge across the surface between the profile boards. The sand should be 65mm (or 2½in) thick and when the concrete blocks are placed on it their top surface should be about 13mm (½in) above the top edge of the profile board.

Laying the blocks

Once you have decided on the pattern you wish to follow, lay the concrete blocks as close to each other as possible across the width of the paving for about 1m (or 1yd). Cut to size any blocks which might be required at the ends to complete the section. To cut blocks you can use a sharp brick bolster with a club hammer; aim firm blows along a

Left Concrete blocks laid to a pattern make an interesting driveway; they are available in a range of shapes and colours (**inset**).
1 Levelling the sub-base with a timber straight-edge. **2** Laying the blocks.
3 Using a hydraulic guillotine to cut blocks to fit

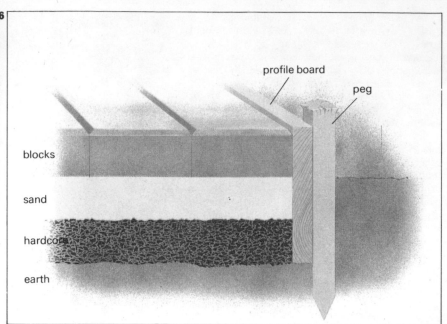

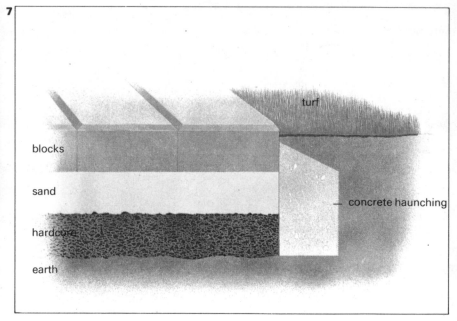

line marked on the top surface of the block with the block placed on a firm surface to make cutting as easy as possible. Alternatively, if you have a lot of cutting to carry out, hire a hydraulic guillotine.

Vibrate the first section down into the sand by passing a petrol-driven vibrating machine or plate vibrator over the surface. You can hire one of these from your supplier at not too much cost and, though it requires two people to lift it, it will fit easily into the boot of an average-sized family saloon car. The sand is compressed and forced up between the blocks so the paving level corresponds with the top edge of the profile boards.

When the first section is bedded into position, complete the second metre (or yard) using the same process of laying, cutting and vibrating and continue until the entire area is finished. Brush a thin layer of sand over the surface of the paving and follow up with the vibrating machine to drive fine grains of sand down between the blocks to complete the locking process.

Keep the profile boards around the outer edges of the paving in position after the job has been com-

pleted since the edge blocks will fall away if not supported. Alternatively, you can lift the boards and support the outer blocks with a concrete haunching, afterwards putting turf down on top of the haunching to butt up close to the blocks.

Lifting blocks If it is necessary to lift blocks after they have been laid, you should start at a point on the outer edge. Break away the concrete haunching or lift the board. Once the outer blocks have been taken up, you will find it comparatively easy to lift others. You can then carry out any service repairs below paving level and, when these are completed, replace the blocks following the same procedure as for laying. If you are lifting areas of block for planting purposes, remember it will be necessary to use profile boards or concrete haunching on the internal faces of the finished area to prevent blocks falling into the flower bed.

Cleaning and drainage To keep the surface of the blocks in good order you simply have to sweep them lightly fairly regularly. If the falls have been set accurately, rain will run from the surface to suitable drainage points.

4 Use a vibrator several times over the blocks to level the surface
5 Sweep fine sand over the surface and go over it with the vibrator to force the sand into the joints
6 Leave the supporting profile boards in place to prevent the edge blocks falling away
7 Alternatively remove the boards, laying in their place a concrete haunching covered with turf

Laying a concrete path or drive

The method of laying a concrete path or drive is fairly straightforward and, if you follow the right procedure, the surface will last indefinitely.

Laying concrete over a long narrow area, such as a drive or a path, involves the same basic techniques as laying a concrete slab, but there are certain extra things to be taken into account. The level along the length must be accurately plotted to avoid puddles collecting in the middle, a fall should be provided to allow for drainage and joints must be made along the length to prevent cracking. The procedure for laying a drive is the same as for laying a path, but the mix, depth of concrete and distance between joints will differ.

Paths Use a mix of one part cement, two parts sand and three parts coarse aggregate; lay the concrete 75mm (3in) thick and on a good base – firm soil is usually sufficient, but use fine, clean hardcore or hoggin where there is clay or the soil is poor.

Drives Use cement, sand and coarse aggregate in the proportions of $1:1\frac{1}{2}:3$. For a drive to be used by cars and light vans, lay concrete 100mm (4in) thick on firm subsoil; 125mm (5in) thick concrete should be laid on soft clay or poor subsoil. Increase the thickness by 50mm (2in) if the drive is to be used regularly for parking heavy vehicles. Since the area of a drive is often several cubic metres, it is probably more economical to buy ready-mix concrete.

Preparing the site
Establish the line the path or drive is to take and clear away topsoil, plants and roots from the site.

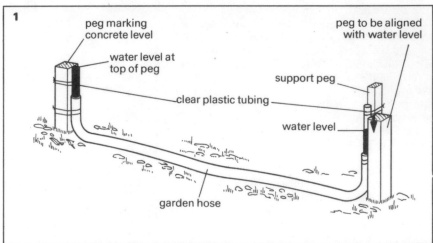

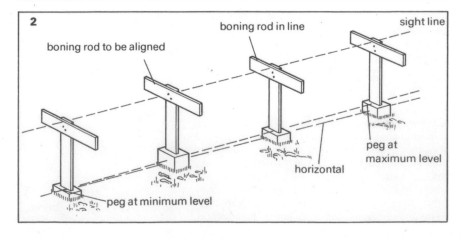

Dig to the proposed level of the base of the concrete, allowing up to 75mm (3in) extra depth for drives or where there is clay or poor subsoil. If the drive or path will be next to the house, the finished surface should be at least 150mm (6in) below the damp proof course.

Obtaining a level
Use the water method to set levels at each end of the site. Drive a peg into the ground to the level of the finished concrete. Insert a short length of clear plastic tubing in each end of a hose and fill the hose with water until all air bubbles are forced out. Attach one end of the hose to the peg and the other end to a temporary support at the other side of the site; adjust the water level so it aligns with the top of the peg and hammer in a second peg to the level of the temporary support.

To establish a fall along the length of the site, lower the appropriate end peg to the required level and ensure a constant fall with boning rods. These consist of two pieces of timber fixed squarely together to form a right-angled 'T' piece at the top. You will need three or four boning rods to set the fall accurately and they must be the same height from the top of the crosspiece to the base of the vertical.

Using boning rods Place pegs in the ground at equal distances along the site and, with someone to help you, place a boning rod on each. Look along the rods from one end and tap the intermediate pegs down until all the rods are in line.

Crossfall Allow for a fall of about 1 in 60 across the width of the site by lowering the pegs on one side. If the path or drive is next to the house, make sure the fall is away from the building.

The formwork
Using the pegs as guides, stretch a string line on each side of the site along its length and fix it at both ends. Make the formwork to the dimensions of the site, using the string lines as guides, and check with a spirit level and straight-edge that it is level with the pegs.

Curves You can produce curves in the formwork by making sawcuts part of the way through the timber, at about 250mm (or 10in) intervals, to enable it to be bent.

Making joints
Depending on the width of the site, joints should be made at 2–2.5m (or 6–8ft) intervals in paths and at 3m (or 10ft) intervals in drives. For joint boards use softwood battens the full depth of the concrete and about 12mm (½in) thick. Set the battens at the required intervals so they are at right-angles to the formwork and support them on one side with a strip of formwork timber pegged to the sub-base.

Lay the concrete right up to the exposed side of the batten and to within 50mm (2in) of the back of the supporting board. Remove the support board, leaving the batten in place; fill the resulting gap and compact the concrete well on both sides of the joint with a tamping beam.

Alternate section method If the site is next to a wall, so you cannot use a tamping beam in the normal way to compact the concrete, use the alternate section method to lay the path or drive. Lay a thicker batten at right-angles to the formwork where each joint is to be made and concrete every other section. Use the tamping beam across the battens over the section to compact the concrete.

When each section has set (after one or two days), remove the battens and concrete the remaining sections, making butt joints between each.

Curing the concrete
Cover the concrete with polythene sheeting and leave it to cure for about seven days (ten in cold weather). Keep the formwork in place during this time to protect the edges of the concrete against damage. Once the curing period is over you can use the path or drive, but don't allow heavy vehicles onto it for at least two weeks after laying.

1 Establish the level at each end of the site by the water method
2 Set the fall by lining up boning rods along the length of the site
3 To make a curved path, cut the formwork at intervals so it can be bent as needed
4 Form joints using battens and support boards: lay the concrete, remove the support boards and fill in the gaps
5 Where a path is right next to a wall, lay it in alternate sections

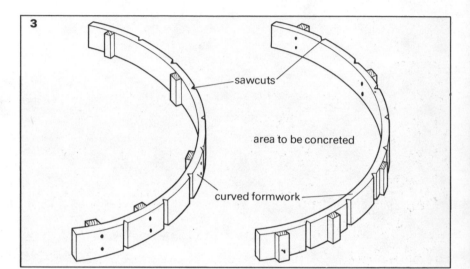

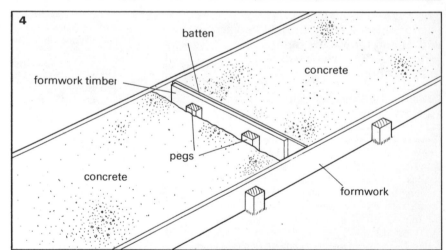

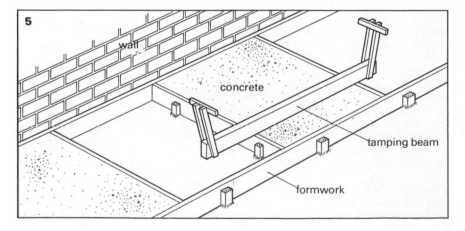

Concrete blocks

Concrete blocks can be used instead of bricks for most construction work. They are available in a wide range of sizes and types and either smooth or very coarse in texture. Some are load-bearing but others, while they look the same, are not. To ensure you select the right type of block for the job you have in mind, it is important to know about the range available and the uses to which each type may be put.

Types of block

There are three main types of concrete block, classified in BS 2028 as type A dense blocks, type B lightweight load-bearing blocks and type C lightweight non load-bearing blocks.

Type A These dense blocks are generally made of Portland cement, sand and gravel or blast furnace slag. Some have a rough surface which is rather unattractive, but provides a good key for rendering; others are smooth-faced and can be left exposed with the joints forming a feature. Some blocks are made of cement and crushed natural stone; the finished blocks are regular in size, but have the same colouring and a similar appearance to natural stone. Cast stone and dense aggregate blocks are often manufactured double size and split in two to produce standard size blocks with the split face revealing the aggregate.

These blocks are available in a wide range of sizes; measurements given here are nominal and include an allowance for one vertical joint and one horizontal joint. The most common are 450 × 229mm (18 × 9in) and 75–229mm (3–9in) thick. These blocks match standard brickwork with one block equal to three courses of brick in height and to two bricks in length. The most popular size for smooth-faced blocks is 400 × 200mm (16 × 8in).

Dense aggregate blocks are mainly used for external load-bearing walls above and below ground. They are heavier than lightweight blocks and have a lower thermal insulation value; but they are better sound insulators, are generally cheaper and can carry greater loads than lightweight blocks of the same size.

Type B These blocks are made from Portland cement with clinker, foamed slag, pulverized fuel ash, expanded clay or pumice used as aggregates. Solid autoclaved aerated concrete blocks are also available; in this case finely powdered aluminium is added to a slurry of cement and specially ground sand, pulverized fuel ash, shale or slag. Bubbles are generated in the concrete and are trapped as the

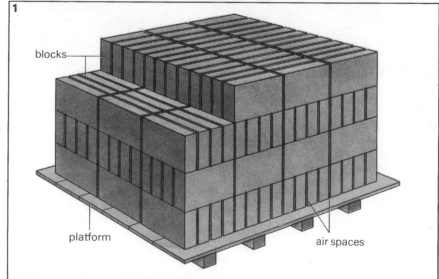

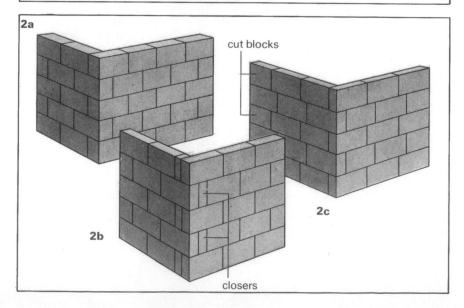

Top right Some of the wide range of concrete blocks available
1 Stacking concrete blocks; place them on a platform and leave spaces between the blocks to allow air to circulate
Three methods of bonding blocks.
2a When the block thickness equals half the length, use a normal stretcher bond
2b With thin blocks use a stretcher bond, but insert closers at the corners
2c Alternatively lay a normal stretcher bond and use three-quarters or two-thirds cut blocks at the wall ends

concrete sets. Precast aerated concrete blocks are autoclaved at high temperatures and under pressure; this is an essential part of the manufacturing process and can reduce the drying shrinkage as well as provide the compressive strength of the block.

Lightweight blocks have a better thermal insulation value than brick. They are generally used for the internal leaf of cavity walls and for load-bearing partitions. When used for external walls, a weatherproof finish is always applied.

Some lightweight blocks can be used below the damp proof course, but check with the manufacturer to ensure the blocks you have chosen have adequate resistance to frost and to damage from ground conditions.

Lightweight blocks may be solid or hollow with two or more cavities, depending on the size of the block; cellular blocks have similar cavities but these run only part-way through the block. Solid blocks at least 100mm (4in) thick with a compressive strength of 2.80N/sq mm can be used to carry the joists and floor loads of two storey buildings.

Sizes for type **B** blocks are 400–600mm (16–24in) long, 100–300mm (4–12in) high and 75–215mm (3–8½in) thick.

Type C These blocks are similar to type B, but are non load-bearing. They are of the same length and height, but are less than 75mm (3in) thick.

Using blocks

Concrete blocks are laid in much the same way as bricks and the rules for good bricklaying described later in the book apply also to blocklaying. There are, however, several points to bear in mind when building with blocks and these are outlined below. Manufacturers supply detailed information on the use of their blocks and you should always follow their instructions carefully.

Care of blocks

When storing blocks, make sure they are kept dry and protected against the effects of the weather. Stack them on edge in sets of four until the columns are about 2m (6½ft) high and cover them with plastic sheeting. When using the blocks, take care to ensure the corners are not damaged; this is particularly important if the wall is to be fair-faced with the blocks and joints exposed to view. After an exterior wall has been constructed – and during breaks in construction – it should be covered with plastic sheeting to protect it until the mortar is hard.

Bonding blocks

Most lightweight blocks are laid to a stretcher bond with a cut block or closer inserted at corners and openings. Half blocks are available for this purpose or you can cut the blocks yourself using an old saw or a bolster and club hammer.

Blocks used to build external walls should not be wetted before laying and should normally be given a full bed of mortar. However, when a single skin of hollow blocks is being built as an external wall, mortar is laid only on the edges of the inner and outer faces of the blocks. This gives greater resistance to rain penetration, but the wall will not be as strong as one built on a full bed of mortar.

Mortar For internal walls built of foamed mortar blocks, use a mortar mix of one part cement, two parts lime and nine parts clean sand. The same mix is suitable for exterior walls constructed of these blocks, unless they will be exposed to severe

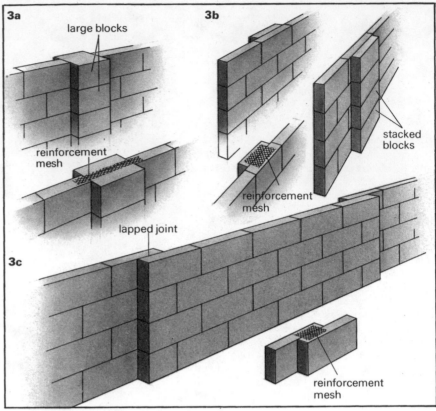

3a large blocks
reinforcement mesh
lapped joint
3b stacked blocks
reinforcement mesh
3c reinforcement mesh

weather conditions; in this case use a mix of one part cement, one part lime and six parts sand.

Blocks which are suitable for below ground level can be laid on a mix of one part cement and four parts sand; this can be made easier to use by adding lime to form a mix of two parts cement, one part lime and nine parts clean sand.

Lightweight aggregate blocks can be laid with a mortar mix of one part cement and nine parts of ready mixed lime/sand mortar. This ready mixed mortar should be of two parts lime and nine parts clean sand.

In all cases you should use soft or building sand and not the sharp sand generally used for concrete work. Whatever type of block is used, the mortar must be weaker than the block so any slight movement will cause cracks to follow the mortar joints instead of cracking the blocks themselves.

Building base walls

Where lightweight blocks are suitable for base walls they can be 255 or 150mm (10 or 6in) thick and 229 or 150mm (9 or 6in) high. These solid blocks are laid on the normal concrete foundation which is used for brick walls of the same dimensions. The blockwork is continued to one course below ground level, where the facing bricks can be commenced or the leaves of a cavity wall started.

Building cavity walls

Cavity walls of lightweight or aerated concrete blocks can be constructed to meet the Building Regulation requirements for sound and thermal insulation and structural stability. Because of the difference in the materials and processes used to make blocks, you should consult manufacturers' literature to ensure you use the right thickness and combination of blocks or blocks and bricks. For example a 103mm (4in) thick brick wall with a 50mm (2in) cavity and a 75mm (3in) thick auto-

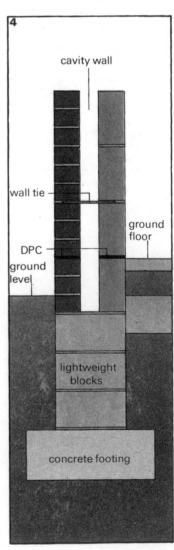

4 cavity wall
wall tie
ground floor
DPC
ground level
lightweight blocks
concrete footing

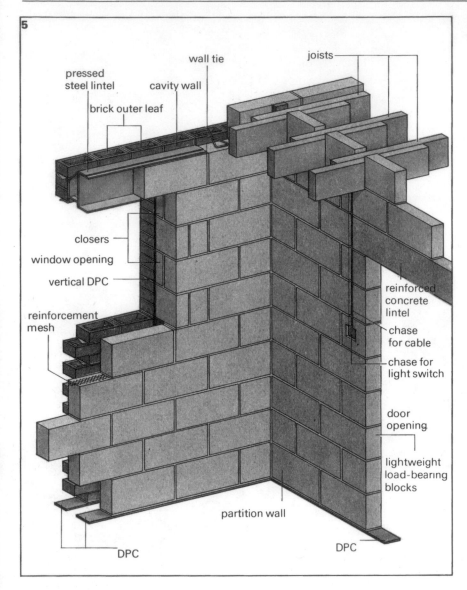

5

pressed
steel lintel

cavity wall

brick outer leaf

wall tie

joists

closers

window opening

vertical DPC

reinforcement
mesh

reinforced
concrete
lintel

chase
for cable

chase for
light switch

door
opening

lightweight
load-bearing
blocks

partition wall

DPC

DPC

Reinforcing walls

Extensive lengths of wall need some form of lateral bracing; this is supplied in buildings by cross walls and partitions, but free-standing walls such as those in a garden require piers at regular intervals. These intervals vary according to the height and length of the wall. As a general rule, walls built of 450×229mm (18×9in) blocks 100mm (4in) thick should not be built more than 900mm (3ft) high without piers. With piers the wall could be built to 1.2m (4ft) in height and the piers would be built at 2.4m (8ft) intervals. Piers should always be at least twice as thick as the walls they support; for walls over 2m ($6\frac{1}{2}$ft) high you should seek professional advice on the size and spacing of piers.

Besides being more stable, walls built with piers are more economical since the panels between can be thinner. There are various ways of constructing the piers which, when their width is less than half their length, cannot be bonded like bricks. One method is to overlap the wall panels by half a block and bond the two together with pieces of expanded metal mesh bedded in the horizontal mortar joints. Another method is to build a stack of blocks against the wall and bond this into the main work using expanded metal mesh in the bed joints. A third method is to build a separate pier using square blocks which are more than twice the wall thickness. The wall panels can then be bonded to the pier with strips of expanded metal mesh stretching right across the pier and at least 150mm (6in) into the wall panel at each side of the pier.

Chasing walls

A completed wall can be cut or chased for wires and pipes, but the depth of the cut should not normally be more than one-sixth of the thickness of the block; vertical chases can be up to one-third the thickness of the block. Don't carry out hand chasing on hollow or cellular blocks, since you will risk bursting through the cavity; use a mechanical chaser or an abrasive wheel on an electric drill.

Finishing walls

Where the wall is to be plastered or rendered you can leave the joints unpointed since this will help to provide a key for the first coat of render. Where fair-faced blocks are being used, so no other finish or a painted finish only is needed, you can give the joints a decorative appearance by hollowing them with a bucket handle or a piece of pipe; alternatively give them a weathered finish by bevelling them smooth with a trowel. Pointing is best done when the mortar has had time to set a little and can be worked to a smooth firm surface.

Rendering Where the blocks are to be rendered externally the mix applied must be durable and resistant to moisture. The standard mix to use is one part cement, one part lime and six parts sand; a plasticizer can be used instead of the lime or masonry cement and sand can be used. For internal plastering, lightweight materials such as Carlite Browning and Carlite finish are suitable.

Cladding When you are cladding a wall made from blocks such as foamed mortar, you will have to plug the blocks to take fixings; with orthodox lightweight aggregate blocks, however, you can nail into them without having to plug the wall first. Cut nails should be used and they must penetrate 50mm (2in) into the block. It is best to predrill any timber battens used for fixing the cladding material or the cut nails may split the timber.

Constructing piers:
3a Build a separate pier with large blocks and bond it to the wall with metal mesh
3b Build a stack of blocks against the wall and bond the two together with metal mesh
3c Overlap the wall panels by half a block and bond the two together with mesh
4 Using special quality lightweight blocks as the base for a cavity wall
5 Making a cavity wall with inner block and outer brick leaves and a partition wall

claved aerated concrete block inner leaf with a lightweight plaster finish would have a thermal insulation or 'U' value of 1.0 watts/sq m °C; if the wall were to be built with two leaves of 100mm (4in) thick blocks, the 'U' value would be 0.63 watts/sq m °C. Since the smaller the figure, the better the resistance, the latter construction would have the higher standard of thermal insulation.

As with brick cavity walls, metal ties used to link the two leaves of the wall must be placed clear of vertical joints. Where the outer leaf is built of clay bricks and the inner leaf of concrete blocks, it is better to use butterfly twisted wire ties than the ordinary galvanized wire ties. It is essential to keep the cavity clean and to prevent mortar droppings lodging on the wall ties. You can do this by attaching strings to a timber batten and laying it on the ties; the batten can be lifted out of the cavity when the next wall tie is inserted, cleaned and replaced to catch the next lot of mortar droppings.

The cavity is closed with cut blocks and a vertical damp proof course is built into the wall. At the head of openings, lintels are built-in to support the load above and to close the cavity; dpcs are either incorporated in the lintel or fitted separately above the lintel along its length. The ends of timber floor joists are built into the inner skin in the same way as for brick cavity walls.

Tools for working with concrete

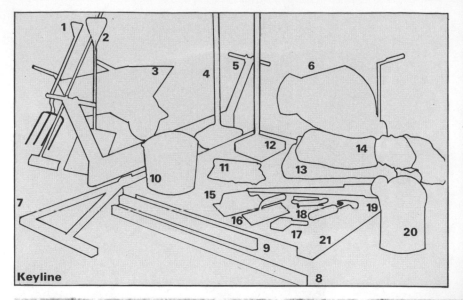

Keyline

You need a surprising number of tools for mixing and laying concrete; many of them you will probably have already, some you can make yourself and some you can hire. All equipment which comes into contact with concrete should be thoroughly scrubbed at the end of each work session to prevent the concrete setting.

1 Fork For digging out foundations. You will also need a spade to clear the site

2 Shovel & rake For shovelling the concrete into the formwork and spreading it slightly proud of the formwork timbers

3 Wheelbarrow A sturdy model is essential if the ballast and cement has to be carried from the storage area to the mixing site or if the mixing site is any distance away from the formwork. If the barrow has to be pushed over soft ground, lay down a line of strong planks

4 Ramming tool For compacting the subsoil or hardcore used in foundations, if a roller is not available. Fill a timber mould (about 200 × 150 × 100mm/8 × 6 × 4in) with concrete, insert a piece of iron pipe or a broom handle in the mould and keep it supported until the concrete has set. A punner (**12**) may also be used

5 Tamping beam For levelling drives and wider sections of concrete. Make it from 150 × 50mm (6 × 2in) timber. Strong handles help you move the tamper more easily

6 Hand-operated concrete mixer This comprises a mixing drum on a trolley. The cement, ballast and water are poured into the drum and the machine pushed along a hard, level surface to rotate the drum and mix the concrete. Electric, petrol and diesel-powered mixers are also available (all can be hired). Tipping stand facilitates pouring of concrete into barrow; while one load is being spread, another can be mixed

7 Builder's square To check the corners of the form for squareness. Make one by joining three lengths of wood with sides in the proportion of 3:4:5. A good size is 450 × 600 × 750mm (or 18 × 24 × 30in). Use an L-shaped bracket and screws to make rigid joints. If the proportions are accurate, the angle between the shortest sides will be 90 degrees

8 Spirit level For checking formwork and crossfall

9 Timber straight-edge For setting out fall of concrete if drainage is required. You

can also use it for levelling narrow sections such as paths; a 100 × 50mm (4 × 2in) straight-edge is sufficient

10 Bucket You will need two of these (both the same size) for measuring and two shovels (again of equal size) for mixing. Keep one bucket and shovel for measuring out and adding cement to the mix. The second bucket and shovel can be used for adding ballast and water and for mixing. Using equal sized buckets gives an easy guide to quantities; for example, a 1:5 mix needs one bucket of cement and five buckets of ballast

11 Coarse brush You can give a textured finish to concrete by sweeping the surface with a coarse brush fitted to a long handle

12 Punner This is used for compacting concrete in a trench. It may also be used for compacting the foundation. To make a punner, nail together several layers of timber and fix a broom handle vertically

13 Polythene sheeting Used to protect concrete from the elements while it is curing

14 Straw & sacking Either can be used to protect new concrete from frost

15 Wood float For giving a textured finish to concrete

16 Steel float Also for finishing concrete

17 Measuring tape For measuring out a large site or path

18 Pegs & string Use with the measuring tape to mark out the site

19 General purpose saw & claw hammer For making formwork

20 Watering can This is useful to control the rate at which water is added to the mix

21 Mixing platform Use where there is no suitable solid area for mixing concrete. Nail boards together for the base and add side pieces to keep the concrete on the platform. Or fix side pieces to a large sheet of 18 or 25mm (¾ or 1in) plywood

Bricklaying

Any brickwork will only be as good as the
foundations you lay. If these are not adequate, you
will find that in time the bricks may crack and the
wall you have built collapse. As important as the
foundations is the measuring. You should always
mark out the position of the brickwork accurately
and check continually that you are laying the bricks
square. There are many different ways of laying
bricks, so check carefully which design you want.
And when the wall is built, give it a neat finish by
pointing the mortar. The correct tools will make your
task that much easier.

Bricks and mortar

When you look around you will see there is an enormous variety of bricks available – but the most common type has an orange-brown colour and is extensively used for houses, garages and garden walls. Although these are called 'flettons', because they are made from fletton clay, they are more generally known as 'commons'.

Facing bricks are the only other type used extensively for domestic purposes. These are also made of fletton clay but have a more decorative appearance, formed by burning mineral granules or coarse sand into the clay. Facings can be obtained with all-round decorative faces or with just three decorative sides if only the outside face of a wall needs an attractive finish.

Bricks are sold in one size only – 225 × 112.5 × 75mm (9 × 4½ × 3in) – but the actual size is 10mm (or ⅜in) less all round. The reason for this is quite simple: since mortar is used to join the bricks, the thickness of each joint – a built-in allowance of 10mm (or ⅜in) – is added to all three dimensions. This makes it much easier to calculate accurately the number of bricks required.

The V-shaped indentation in one face – called a frog – allows plenty of mortar to lie in the brick, giving a firmer bond to the flat surface of the brick that will be laid above. Bricks can be laid with the frog facing downwards, but this makes it more difficult to control the thickness of the mortar.

Second-hand bricks

Builders' merchants not only sell new bricks but some also supply second-hand ones obtained from local demolition sites. In many areas you are positively welcome at demolition sites to buy old materials; and if you buy from such a site, you have a good chance of getting bricks to match the existing ones in your own property. Thus any new extension or garage will look the same as the original part of the house. Second-hand bricks have real visual appeal for garden walls, where the weathered appearance is more in keeping with the traditional 'country garden'.

The other obvious advantage of second-hand bricks is they are cheaper; but you must select them carefully. Choose bricks which have the least mortar on them, because this has to be chipped off with a bolster chisel and club hammer before the bricks can be used. Try to get those where the mortar looks sandy because this will crumble off easily with the help of a wire brush. Reject any cracked bricks and ones with very porous faces if they are to be used for weatherproof walls.

The right mortar

Mortar for general bricklaying is made by mixing one part Portland cement, one part hydrated lime and six parts clean builder's sand. If you want a stronger mix – for a garden wall, for example, which has to withstand more extreme elements – a mix of one part Portland cement to three parts sand should be used. This mortar will be more workable if a small amount of liquid plasticizer, available from builders' merchants, is added to the mix. Then use just sufficient clean water to make the mortar stiff but workable.

Estimating how much mortar to mix depends on how quickly you can lay bricks. This is important because mortar becomes useless within a couple of hours – and even earlier in really hot weather. So start by mixing small batches. You will soon learn how much you can use within the setting time. On no account should you add water to setting mortar because the mix will become too weak to support the weight of the bricks.

Professional bricklayers use a different system, which is worth following once you have gained enough experience. Soak the lime in water overnight. In the morning pour off the surplus water and mix the lime with sand in the proportions given earlier. Use only a small amount of water so a stiff consistency is achieved. The resultant mix is known as 'coarse stuff'. During a day's work you can add cement – in the proportion of 1:6 – to the 'coarse stuff' to give you small batches of mortar quickly as and when you need them. This means rather than having to stop and make a complete batch using all the ingredients, sufficient amounts can be made to last an hour or even just enough to fill in the last ten minutes before lunch. The 'coarse stuff' will stiffen from time to time, but if you sprinkle on some water and turn the mix over, it will keep it fresh.

Ready-mix

Many people doing a job requiring only a couple of hundred bricks prefer to use one of the proprietary mortar mixes. These are supplied in large bags and contain all the necessary ingredients: all you have to do is empty the bag and mix in water according to the instructions. A 20 kilogram (or 44lb) bag contains enough mortar for about 80 bricks. The only disadvantage is that for large jobs the cost is far greater than buying and mixing your own ingredients.

Below When estimating what quantity of bricks you require for a particular job, remember the stated size of the brick includes an allowance for the mortar on all sides; there is no need to calculate this yourself
Bottom Before using second-hand bricks, chip off any old mortar with a hammer and chisel

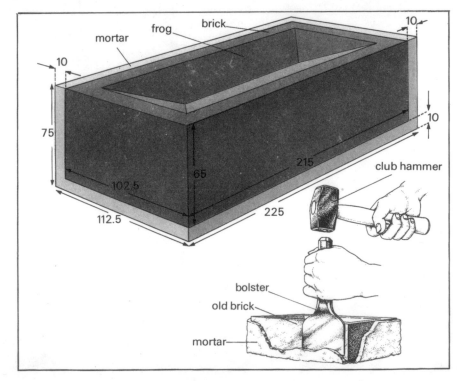

Basic brickbuilding

Accurate bricklaying on the correct foundations is vital for a professional finish – and a job that's permanent.

To ensure long-lasting brickwork pay particular attention to the foundations. If these are not adequate, in time the bricks may crack and the wall collapse. To support a brick wall you will need to make a level concrete strip foundation of a suitable depth and width for the proposed height of the wall. There are building regulations specifying the width, depth, thickness and reinforcements necessary for foundations, so consult your local building inspector for advice.

To make a concrete strip foundation first cut a trench in firm, previously undug ground. For a foundation which requires 225mm (or 9in) thick concrete and one course of 75mm (or 3in) thick brickwork below ground level you will need to dig a trench at least 300mm (or 12in) deep. If at this depth you have not reached a really firm surface, you will have to dig on until you do; then fill the extra depth to the trench bottom with well compacted hardcore (broken brick and concrete). If you dig to a depth of 600mm (or 24in), for example, you should have 300mm (or 12in) of hardcore at the bottom, then 225mm (or 9in) of concrete and finally 75mm (or 3in) of brickwork. For a single brick wall 1m (39in) high you will need a strip foundation of 100mm (or 4in) thick concrete, 300mm (or 12in) wide, in a trench of the same dimensions.

Preparing trench Using a builder's square to get accurate right-angles, set out the width and length of the trenches with lines fixed to pegs around each proposed corner and mark out the exact length at the corners with pins. To avoid having to cut bricks later it is worth positioning a row to make sure they fit exactly within the proposed length of the trench. Replace the pegs with profile boards supported by wood pegs driven into the ground. Use low grade timber to make the boards which should be about 25mm (or 1in) thick.

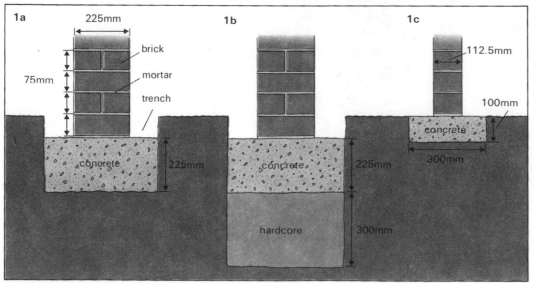

Above When that wall is finally up, put the finishing touches to it by pointing the mortar joints
Left No wall will stand up properly unless built on the right foundations
1a For a 225mm (9in) thick wall you must lay 225mm (9in) of concrete and one brick course in a trench at least 300mm (12in) deep
1b If the base of the trench is not really firm, you must dig deeper and fill the extra depth with hardcore
1c With a single brick wall you need only lay 100mm (4in) of concrete up to ground level

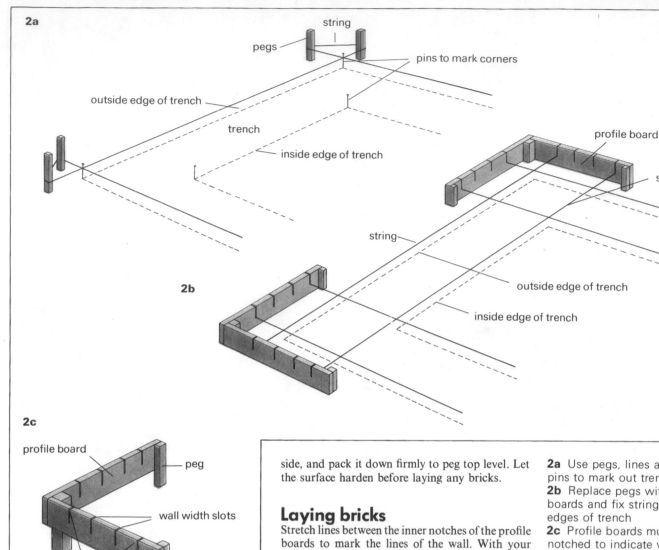

2a
string
pegs
pins to mark corners
outside edge of trench
trench
inside edge of trench
profile board
string
string
outside edge of trench
inside edge of trench

2b

2c
profile board
peg
wall width slots
trench width slots

100–175mm (or 4–7in) deep and 450mm (or 18in) long. Cut four notches into the top edge of each board: two outer notches to mark the width of the foundations and two inner notches to mark the thickness of the wall. Make sure the profile boards are level and of the same height and that they are set well back from the edge of the trench. Measure the diagonals to check they are of equal length to ensure the corners are true right-angles. Stretch lines between the outer notches of the boards; you can then dig the trench.

Laying concrete
Once the trench is dug to the required depth, drive a series of flat wood pegs into the trench so the tops of each are set at the proposed level of the finished concrete. This makes final levelling of the concrete a lot easier. The length of the pegs required will depend on the depth of the trench and an extra 100–150mm (4–6in) should be allowed for driving into the soil. Place any hardcore required around the pegs and across the trench, compacting each section thoroughly. Take care not to move any pegs out of level as you work. Then pour the concrete, which should be on the dry

side, and pack it down firmly to peg top level. Let the surface harden before laying any bricks.

Laying bricks
Stretch lines between the inner notches of the profile boards to mark the lines of the wall. With your mortar mix on a clean board close to the laying area, start from one end or corner and spread the mortar with a bricklayer's trowel. The mortar should form a bed about 16mm (or $\frac{5}{8}$in) thick, trowelled as level as possible, and should cover the greater part of the concrete with a clear border on each side. Using the line indicating the outer side of the wall as a guide, mark its position onto the mortar bed at suitable intervals using a spirit level vertically. Use the point of the trowel to score a line between these marks in the soft mortar to provide a guide for setting down the first course of bricks. Remove the profile lines and start building the corners of the walls.

2a Use pegs, lines and pins to mark out trench
2b Replace pegs with profile boards and fix string to mark edges of trench
2c Profile boards must be notched to indicate widths of trench and wall
3a & 3b Use pegs as guide to mark final concrete level

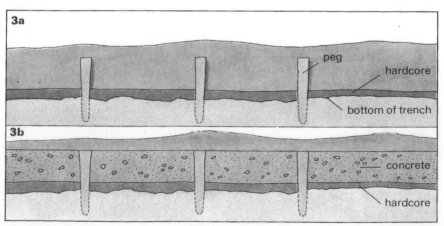

3a
peg
hardcore
bottom of trench
3b
concrete
hardcore

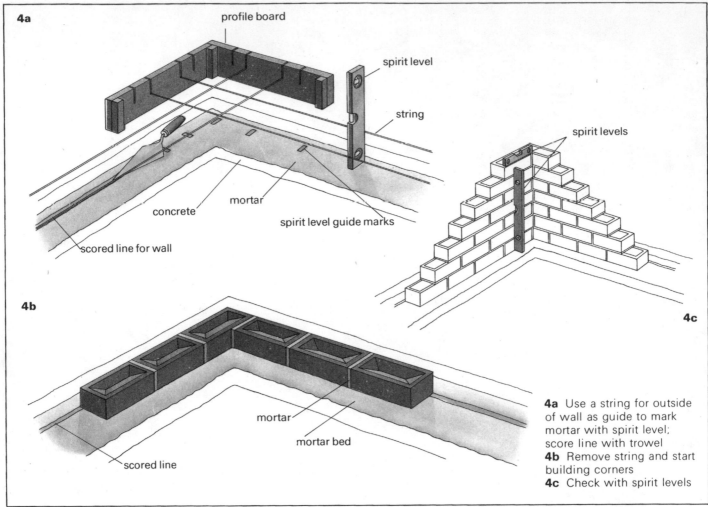

4a profile board
spirit level
string
spirit levels
mortar
concrete
spirit level guide marks
scored line for wall

4b
mortar
mortar bed
scored line

4c

4a Use a string for outside of wall as guide to mark mortar with spirit level; score line with trowel
4b Remove string and start building corners
4c Check with spirit levels

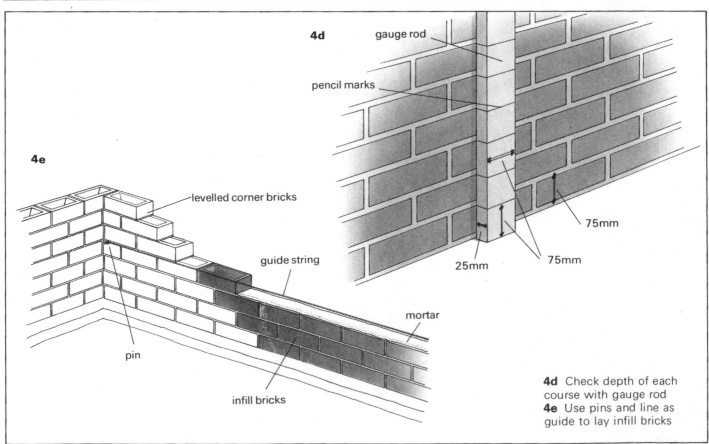

4d gauge rod
pencil marks
75mm
25mm
75mm

4e
levelled corner bricks
guide string
mortar
pin
infill bricks

4d Check depth of each course with gauge rod
4e Use pins and line as guide to lay infill bricks

The simplest method of joining or bonding bricks is called stretcher bonding. By this method every brick in a wall is laid lengthwise so the vertical joint between two bricks in one course lies in the centre of a brick in the courses above and below. To make corners in single thickness walls using this method you will not need to cut bricks, provided there are four corners.

Build up the corners to about six or seven courses high. Check with the spirit level to make sure each corner is a true vertical and place a gauge rod against it as each brick is added to check the thickness of your mortar bed. You can make a gauge rod from a piece of 75×25mm (3×1in) timber about 1m (39in) long. Mark clear lines across the face at 75mm (3in) intervals using a try square and pencil.

For accurate positioning of infill bricks (those bricks linking up the corners) you will need a fine string line and two steel pins. Push the pins into the mortar bed at each end directly above the line of bricks to be laid. With the string held taut by the pins, you will have a straight, level line against which to set the bricks. Move the pins and line up course by course until the corner height levels have been reached.

Trowelling mortar

Mix the mortar so it slides easily off the trowel but keeps its form when in place. Lift a small amount of mortar at a time and spread it as evenly as possible. Aim to spread it along a line from the centre of the bricks without losing too much over the edge.

Spread one end of each brick with mortar and place that end close to the brick previously laid, trying to keep an even mortar line to match the horizontal beds. Remember the recessed part of the brick, known as the frog, is placed face upwards. Use the handle end of the trowel to tap the brick into the mortar for any slight adjustment. Until you gain experience, it is best to use a spirit level at intervals to check the line both along and across the bricks. Remove surplus mortar by drawing the edge of the trowel along the bottom edge of the bricks, then use a rounded piece of metal or wood

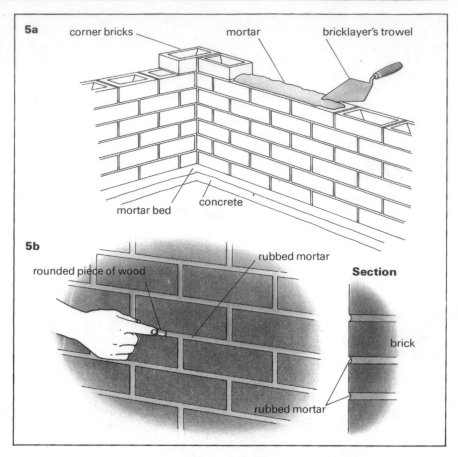

5a Spread even line of mortar along centre of bricks when infilling courses between corners
5b Simplest joint made by running round piece of metal or wood along mortar
6a Split bricks by marking cut line and tapping firmly with bolster and hammer
6b You can break bricks with edge of trowel

to form a rubbed joint between the bricks. This is the easiest finish for a beginner and leaves a slightly concave line in the mortar.

Cutting bricks

When a single brick wall exceeds 2.5m (or 8ft) in length, you will have to build piers into it. These consist of a double thickness of bricks which have to be bonded correctly to give the maximum support strength to the wall. This means cutting bricks in half and three-quarter lengths. You will have to carry out this process on other occasions, for example when the wall end is not a corner Clearly mark the cutting line and use a sharp brick bolster and club hammer to tap a surface cut along the line on all sides of the brick. (To sharpen a blunt bolster, file the edge at an angle from either side of the blade until a keen cutting edge is produced.) Once the groove has been cut, turn the brick (frog down) on a flat surface. Place the bolster into the groove on the flat underside of the brick and use the club hammer with a little more force. A clean break should result. As you gain experience, you will find you can cut most bricks by bringing down the side of the trowel with some force on each side in turn. Practise with a softer type of brick to get used to striking the brick at the same point with each blow. It should not take you long to perfect the technique.

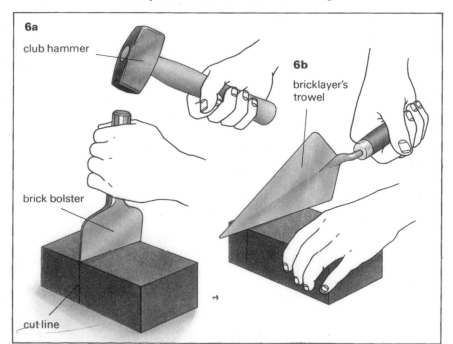

Bonding bricks

The strength of brickwork is based on the way each course (or horizontal line) is laid in relation to the courses above and below. This is known as the bond of the bricks. There are a number of variations all producing different patterns; but the common rule is that a mortar joint between two bricks must never appear above a joint in the course below because this would weaken the structure.

When a brick is laid with its long side visible, it is known as a stretcher; when laid with an end face showing it is called a header; when laid in a perpendicular (on end) fashion, for example as a door lintel, it is called a soldier. When a brick is cut across its width, the parts are known as bats – so you would have a quarter bat, half bat and three-quarter bat. These are used when building stopped ends and junctions.

For garden walls

The first bricklaying job an amateur is likely to attempt will probably be a garden wall consisting of a single thickness of brick, which is called half brickwork.

A continuous run of stretcher bonding is acceptable for a wall which is less than 2.4m (8ft) high or long. If these dimensions are exceeded, piers must be built into the brickwork to provide extra stability. These are pillars of double the wall thickness and project on one side only – usually the internal surface, for example, when building a garage. Piers can be placed at the ends of the wall and at intervals along it.

If you intend to use a single-thickness garden wall to support a load of soil behind it, you will need to back-fill with concrete and reinforcing steel rods, otherwise the wall will not stand the pressure for long. You will also need drainage holes and you should seek advice from your local authority

before implementing any plans to put up this type of wall in your garden.

Stretcher bonding is suitable for short-screen walling with open bonds – which is created by leaving a space equal to a quarter of a brick's length between every brick in each course. Brick sleeper walls, used in the foundation of a house to support timber floors, are usually open-bonded to allow for air circulation.

1 Part of a stretcher bond wall, the simplest form of brick bonding. Stretchers are bricks laid with the long side visible. This wall also shows part of a junction wall, stopped ends and a pier, which gives extra support to a length of wall

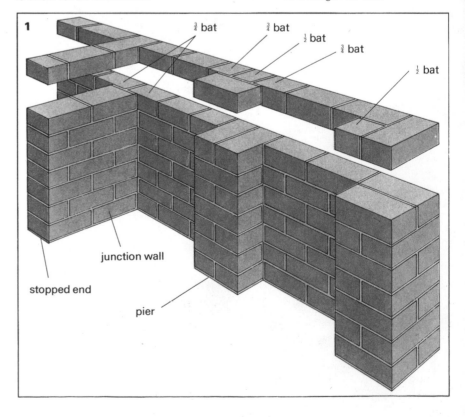

1

¾ bat ¾ bat ½ bat ¾ bat ½ bat

junction wall

stopped end

pier

For house walls

Stretcher bond is often used in modern houses, where cavity wall construction is employed. This means the outer skin of single brick can be laid with the minimum of bat-cutting. But the outer wall must be tied (with sheet metal, a wire butterfly or a plastic tie, for instance) to an inner skin, which may be brick, breeze block or similar type building block, or concrete blocks.

Different bonds

Producing a different type of bond does not necessarily mean you are reducing the strength of the construction. In many cases where you are extending an older house, it is often essential to match not only the bricks but also the method of bonding. Usually it simply means more brick-cutting is required.

The wide range of brick bonds has been developed over hundreds of years from the original solid wall constructions of 225mm (9in) thickness or more. Traditionally, the most common bonds were Old English and Flemish. The original Old English bond consisted of alternate courses of headers and stretchers and was in general use in the 15th Century. Flemish bond, which involved laying a header next to a stretcher in each course, was not introduced until the second quarter of the 17th Century.

Both styles have been rearranged and given new names by architects and builders in different places. Two are now more standard than others: English Garden Wall and Flemish Garden Wall, which, despite their names, are commonly used for building construction. English Garden Wall is formed by setting three courses of stretchers between a course of headers above and below. Flemish Garden Wall involves laying three stretchers set between two headers in each course. Both bonds mean careful cutting of bricks at junctions and corners to fill small closures.

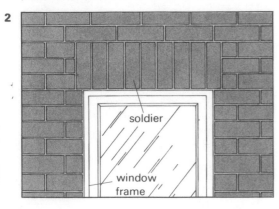

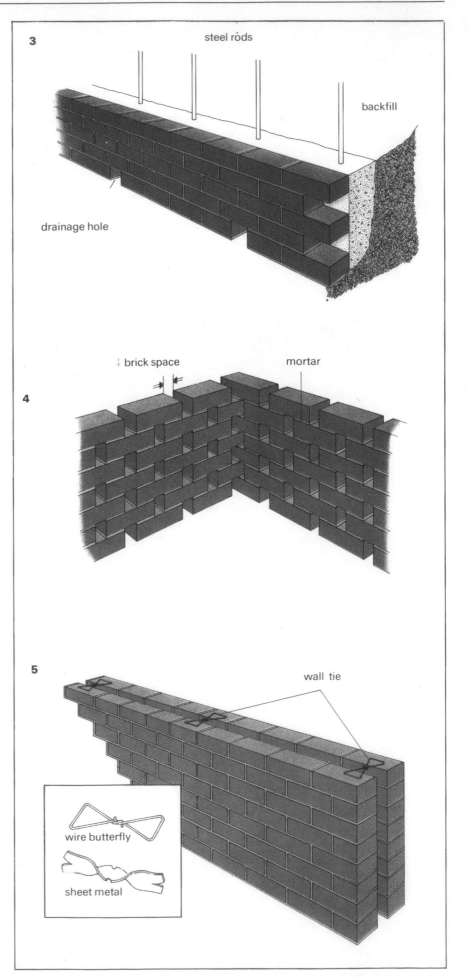

2 When bricks are laid in a perpendicular fashion they are known as soldiers. These you often find as a door or window lintel above the frame
3 For single thickness walls that will have to take heavy loads against them, back-filling with concrete and reinforcing rods will provide the extra strength, although it is vital to leave drainage holes at the bottom
4 Open bond gives a pleasant effect to a garden wall. This is done with stretchers, but with a quarter brick space between each
5 Stretcher bond is used for cavity walls, but you must tie the walls together

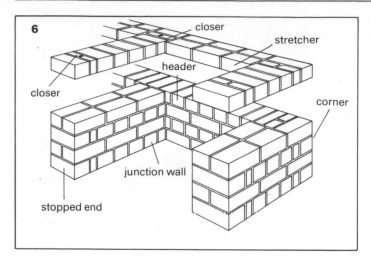

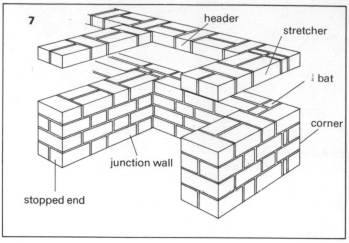

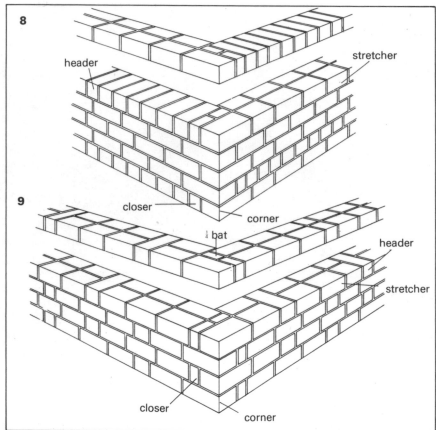

Patterns

Variations in the way bricks are laid inevitably results in a pattern being formed and this can be emphasized when using bricks of two or more different colours in a wall.

English Cross and Dutch Both are variations on the Old English bond.

Header Constructed entirely of headers. The contrast in alternate bricks gives a diagonal stepped effect.

Monk Creates a zig-zag pattern when two stretchers are placed each side of a header in every course.

Double English Consists of two rows of stretchers placed on top of two rows of headers throughout.

Modern Face Similar to Monk and consists of two stretchers set between headers in every row: but pattern differs because the headers are laid vertically above each other.

Chevron Formed by using three stretchers followed by a header in series along each row.

Diapers Popular in Victorian buildings, these can be complicated to construct. The simplest is obtained by setting two stretchers between headers on either side.

Reinforced brickwork

If decorative brickwork of exceptional strength is required, you should create cavities by laying bricks one-and-a-half deep and filling the cavities with fine concrete and steel rods. Flemish bond is a popular method and this was used frequently in building air raid shelters in World War II.

6 The Old English bond was widely used. It was made by alternating a course of stretchers with a course of headers (end face showing)

7 The Flemish bond was made by laying a stretcher next to a header in each course

8 The English Garden Wall bond – three courses of stretchers between a course of headers above and below

9 The Flemish Garden Wall bond – three stretchers between two headers in each course

10 The English Cross and Dutch bonds – variations on the Old English bond

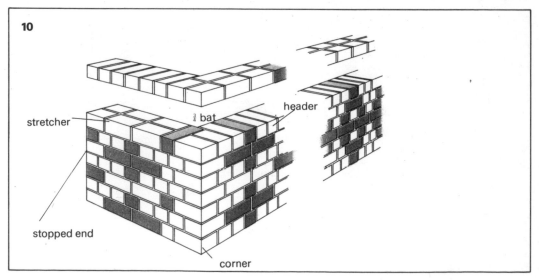

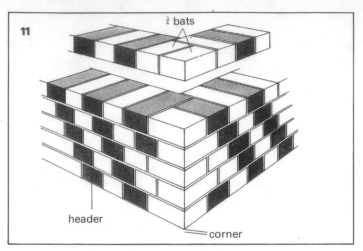

11

¾ bats

header

corner

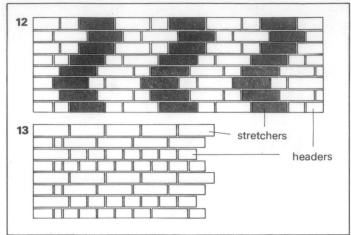

12

13

stretchers

headers

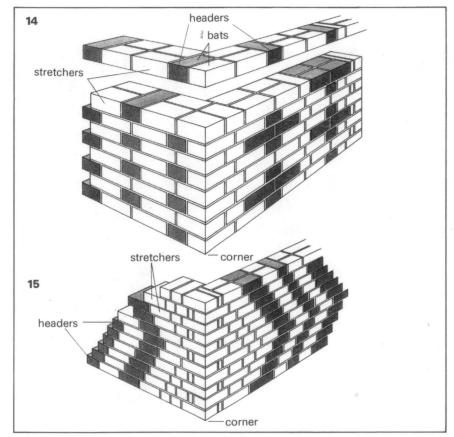

14

headers

¾ bats

stretchers

corner

15

stretchers

corner

headers

16

headers

stretchers

headers   stretchers

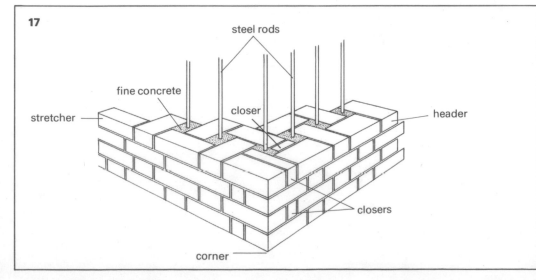

17

steel rods

fine concrete

closer

stretcher

header

closers

corner

11 The Header bond (all headers) has a stepped effect
12 The Monk bond makes a zig-zag pattern
13 Double English – two rows of headers, then two rows of stretchers
14 The Modern Face bond is like the Monk, but headers go vertically above each other
15 The Chevron bond has three stretchers then a header in sequence
16 Diapers – the simplest is when two stretchers are laid between headers
17 Reinforced brick bonding – achieved by laying bricks one and a half deep, filling in with concrete and rods

Tools for bricklaying

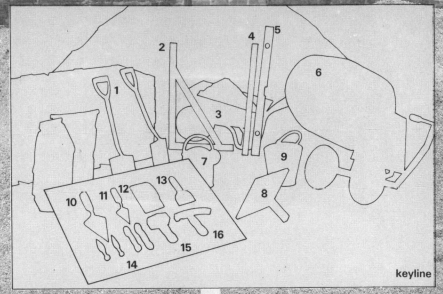

keyline

1 Shovels You need two – one for mixing the mortar and the other exclusively for shifting dry cement from the sack to the mix

2 Builder's square To check the first few courses of your wall are at right-angles to the concrete foundations

3 Wheelbarrow A sturdy model is essential for carrying bricks and mortar

4 Gauge rod Used to check the mortar joints are being kept to a uniform thickness. A 75 × 25mm (3 × 1in) softwood batten (about two metres or six feet long) will do. Mark the batten in 75mm (3in) graduations (the depth of a brick and its mortar). When checking with the gauge rod, each graduation should align with the top edge of a brick course

5 Spirit level A 1m (or 3ft) level is needed to check the bricks are being laid accurately – horizontally and vertically. A 150mm (6in) level is useful for the beginner for levelling each brick as it is laid against the previous one in the course

6 Cement mixer Many consider hiring one essential, especially for larger jobs. It all depends on your muscles and your money

7 Watering can Must be fitted with a fine rose for adding water to the mix

8 Mortar board or hawk For holding small quantities of mortar while working. Make it yourself from a 13mm ($\frac{1}{2}$in) thick piece of board with a 100mm (4in) length of broom handle screwed to it

9 Bucket You need two; keep one for cement only. If the buckets are the same size, it makes it easy to add the various ingredients to the mix in the correct proportions

10 Laying trowel For spreading mortar on the bricks

11 Pointing trowel For cleaning and shaping the mortar joints between the bricks. The joints can be flush with bricks or sloped to allow water to drain

12 Steel float If you want a really smooth finish on your concrete foundation, you can use a steel float

13 & 15 Bolster chisel and club hammer Use these together when you need to cut a brick in half. Lay the brick on a firm, level surface and make grooves on both sides of the 112.5mm ($4\frac{1}{2}$in) face. Place the bolster chisel at right-angles on the grooved line and tap gently with the hammer. Two more sharp blows with the hammer should leave you with a clean brick. Remember to practise first with some unwanted bricks. You can also use these tools to remove old mortar from second-hand bricks

14 Bricklayer's pins and string Use the line as a running guide in conjunction with a spirit level to ensure each course of bricks is laid horizontally. Knock the pins into the mortar course at each end of the wall and stretch the line taut between them. As you complete each course, reposition the line for the course above

16 Bricklayer's hammer Used for cutting bricks when only a small amount has to be trimmed. One end is shaped like a chisel.

Internal work

There are quite a few constructional jobs you can tackle inside the home. Learn about the different designs of timber staircase you can build. You may want to block off an unused fireplace; but remember to seal it off effectively and check it is properly ventilated. If you need to make more rooms, you can partition off areas with timber studs and plasterboard. With practice you can do your own plastering, make a hole in the wall or create an archway between rooms instead of a door. And if you need to support these openings, find out how to put in RSJs and lintels to avert disasters.

Timber staircases

Basically a staircase consists of two sloping pieces of timber, called strings, with treads fixed between them and a handrail. There is, however, a variety of ways in which these and other components are arranged and the form of the staircase will vary depending on the amount of space available and design of the house. The most common forms of timber staircase are the straight flight stair, the quarter-turn stair and the half-turn (or dog leg) stair. Where there is a space between the flights of a staircase, it is called an open-well staircase.

The type of staircase you have and its method of construction will govern the type of repairs that may be needed and whether you can do them yourself or need expert help.

Closed-riser staircases
Whatever form a staircase takes it will be constructed according to one of two basic patterns in that it will be either a closed-riser or an open-riser type structure. Traditionally, the staircases found in most homes are of a closed-riser type and it is therefore worth considering the construction of this type of staircase at the outset, while remembering that many of its components are the same as those of open-riser staircases and that repairs can often be carried out in a similar fashion.

Treads and risers In a closed-riser staircase the horizontal treads are connected by vertical risers, with a tread and a riser together forming a step. The protruding front edge of a tread is called a

1 Typical closed-riser staircase with cut outer string, close wall string and horizontal treads connected by vertical risers Ways in which bottom step of staircase may be shaped:
2a Bullnose
2b Curtail
2c Splayed

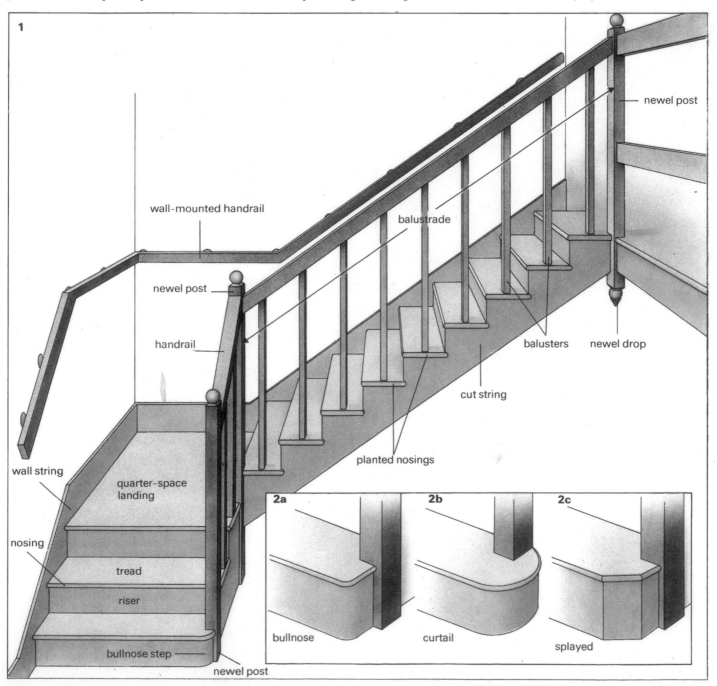

wall-mounted handrail

newel post

balustrade

newel post

handrail

balusters

newel drop

cut string

planted nosings

wall string

quarter-space landing

nosing

tread

riser

bullnose step

newel post

2a bullnose

2b curtail

2c splayed

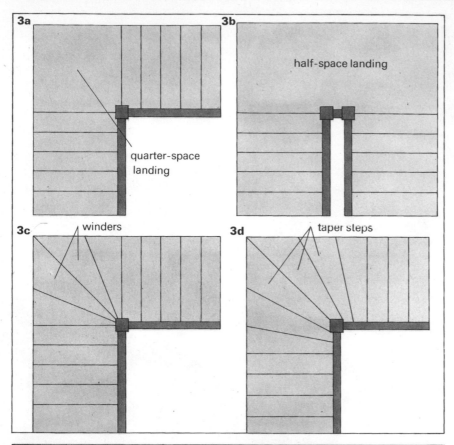

3a quarter-space landing

3b half-space landing

3c winders

3d taper steps

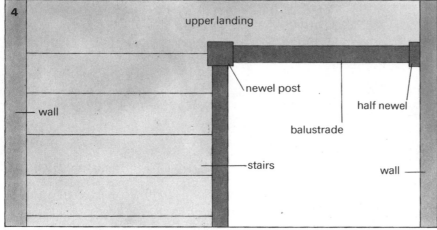

4

upper landing

newel post

half newel

balustrade

wall

stairs

wall

nosing; this usually has a rounded profile. Where the side edge of a tread is exposed a planted, or return, nosing is fixed. Usually the bottom step projects in front of the staircase and this step will be shaped in one of three ways. It may be a bullnose step, which is rounded, a curtail step, which is similar to a bullnose step except it projects to the side as well as to the front of the staircase, or a splayed step, which is more angular in design. When a staircase turns there will be either a quarter or half-space landing. Where space is restricted taper steps or winders may be used.

Strings Treads and risers are supported at each side by strings, which can take two forms: close strings and cut (open) strings. Normally a string against a wall (a wall string) is a close string with the top and bottom edges parallel and the string deeply grooved to secure the treads and risers. The outer string may also be a close string or it may be a cut string with the lower edge of the string parallel with the pitch line or slope of the stairs, while the upper edge is cut to accept the treads and risers. Cut strings are common in older closed-riser staircases, but are not found so often in modern ones since they are more costly to construct.

With close strings the treads and risers are glued and wedged in position; if both strings are the close type, repairs can be carried out only from beneath the stairs – which may be difficult if the underside of the staircase is boarded over or plastered and in this case it may be better to call in a professional.

Balusters These are the rails which give rigidity to the handrail and provide safety on the open side of the stairs. The balusters, and any infilling panels, together with the handrail and upper portions of the newel posts, form the balustrade.

Newel posts The outer strings and handrails are supported by newel posts at the top and bottom of the stairs; a newel post is also placed at every change of direction of a flight of stairs. Where a newel projects below a landing ceiling, the projecting portion, which is usually moulded or shaped at the end, is known as a newel drop. Half newels are often found on landings fixed to a wall to support the end of the landing balustrade away from the upper stair newel.

Spandrel This is the triangular surface between the outer string and the floor; it may be panelled with wood or plasterboard or made of building blocks and plastered.

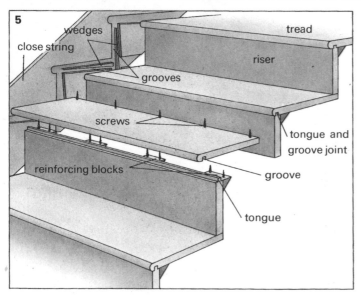

5 wedges, close string, grooves, screws, reinforcing blocks, tread, riser, tongue and groove joint, groove, tongue

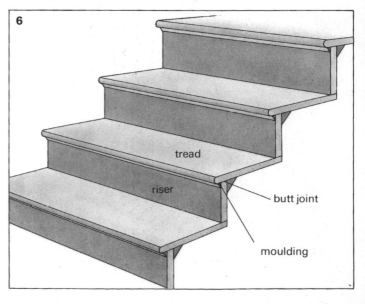

6 tread, riser, butt joint, moulding

3a & 3b Types of landing
3c Winders
3d Taper steps
4 Half newel supporting landing balustrade
5 How treads and risers are fixed
6 Moulding hiding joint between tread and riser
7 How outer string is fixed to newel post
8 Geometrical stair
Types of open-riser staircase:
9a Cut strings
9b Strings and blocks
9c Close strings

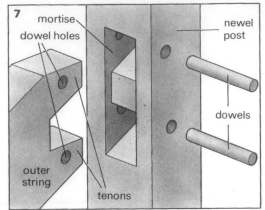

7 · mortise · dowel holes · newel post · dowels · outer string · tenons

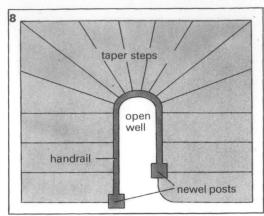

8 · taper steps · open well · handrail · newel posts

9a · balusters · tread · cut strings

9b · balusters · tread · blocks · strings

9c · balusters · blocks · tread · strings

10a

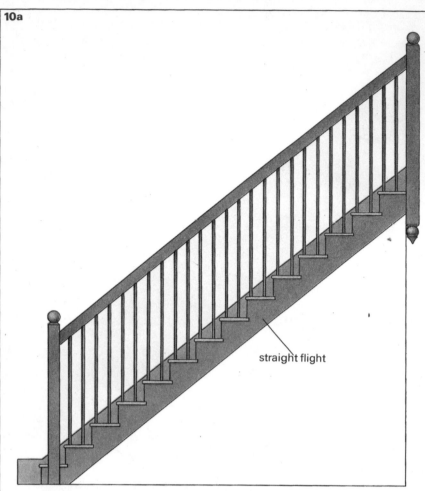

straight flight

Carriage There may be other hidden components in the construction which can further complicate staircase repairs. For example, there could be a softwood beam, called a carriage, fixed below a flight where the width of the stairs is 900mm (or 35in) or more. Wood support blocks (brackets) nailed to each side of the carriage support the treads. The bottom of the carriage beam is notched over a timber plate nailed to the floor and the top is fixed to a suitably placed supporting beam known as a landing trimmer or pitching piece. If the underside (soffit) of the stairs is to be plastered, then beams similar to the carriage beam are fixed at either side of the staircase.

When a close string staircase is fitted with a carriage, it is extremely difficult to replace treads or risers and such work should be left to the professional.

Fixing and joints Treads and risers are fixed into the grooves of close strings with adhesive and wedges are hammered home. With cut strings they are fixed with adhesive and nails and balusters are usually dovetailed to the treads, which may be given extra support with bearer blocks screwed to the inside face of the cut string. The exposed edge of the tread at the side will probably be finished with a planted nosing.

In well made stairs the tread and riser joints are likely to be tongued and grooved, but sometimes the treads and risers are simply butt-joined and a moulding often used to hide any gap between the riser and the tread above. The joint between the upper part of the riser and the tread is glued and may be nailed; it may also be reinforced with triangular blocks glued and nailed in place. The lower edge of the riser is fixed to the tread below

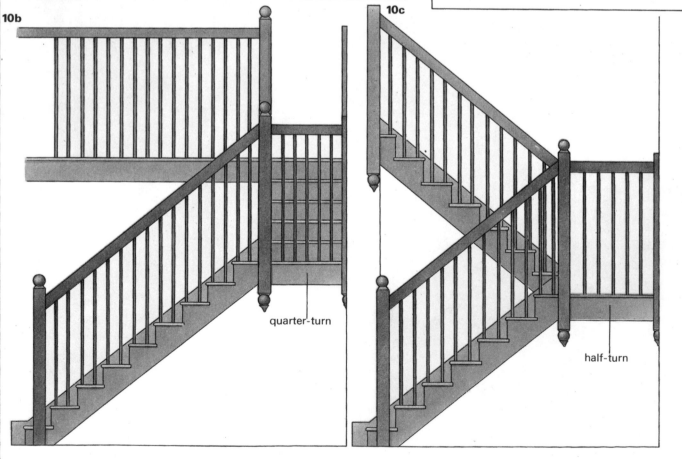

10b

quarter-turn

10c

half-turn

Flights of stairs:
10a Straight
10b Quarter-turn
10c Half-turn
11 Carriage provides extra support for wide staircases
12 Current Building Regulation requirements for staircases ('going' is horizontal distance between two adjacent risers)

with screws at least 32mm (1½in) long. On some stairs there are additional glued blocks to reinforce the joints between treads and strings.

Wall strings are fixed to the wall with screws and wallplugs. Outer strings are fixed to newel posts by tenons, which are usually secured with hardwood dowels; handrails are usually fixed in a similar way. Newels are mortised to receive the string and handrail; tenons are notched and bolted to a floor joist at the stair base and to a trimmer joist on the landing.
Geometrical stair This has a continuous outer string and handrail round an open well, tapered steps and newels at the top and bottom of the stairs; it is a complicated construction and all but the simplest repairs should be left to a professional to cope with.

Open-riser staircases

In new houses and with conversions it is common to find open-riser stairs which are economical in their use of timber, take up a minimum amount of space and have an airy appearance which is ideal for open-plan layouts. These staircases do not have risers and the treads must be thicker than normal so they do not bend in use – they range in thickness from 38 to 50mm (1½ to 2in). Because it is difficult to carpet

open-riser stairs apart from wrapping a short length of carpet round each tread, it is usual to use a timber which can be finished with a clear sealer. A hardwood such as mahogany may be used, or a strong, straight-grained softwood such as parana pine. Sometimes treads are made with a man-made board like plywood with an attractive hardwood for the outer veneer; usually the tread is finished with a hardwood lip.

With open-riser stairs in the home, close strings may be used although cut strings, with treads protruding beyond the strings, are more popular. Because of the size of the timber required, it is common for the strings to be made from laminated timber planks; these will look attractive when finished with clear sealer.

Sometimes the treads are mounted on hardwood blocks so the size of the timber required for the strings can be reduced. The blocks are fitted, usually with hardwood dowels, to the top edge of the strings, or screwed to the inside face of the strings. Whichever method is used for cut string construction, the treads are normally fixed with adhesive and screws; the screw heads are recessed into the treads and covered with wood plugs to give a neat finish.

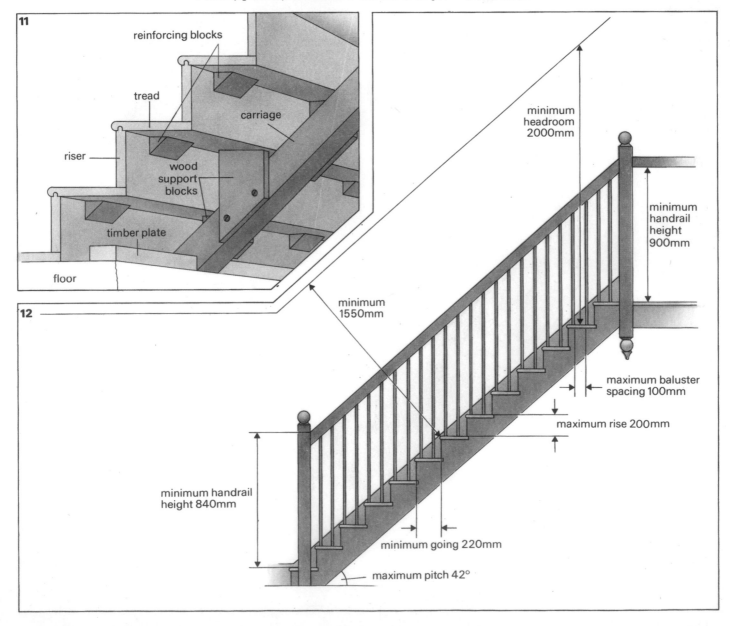

Removing a fireplace

Electricity, gas and oil have, to some extent, superseded solid fuel as a means of heating – and where fireplaces were originally planned for rooms in the home, these may have become obsolete, in which case they can be removed. The techniques involved are well within the capacity of the DIY person, as long as the necessary precautions are taken to seal off the original area and provisions made to install adequate ventilation to avoid problems of damp.

1

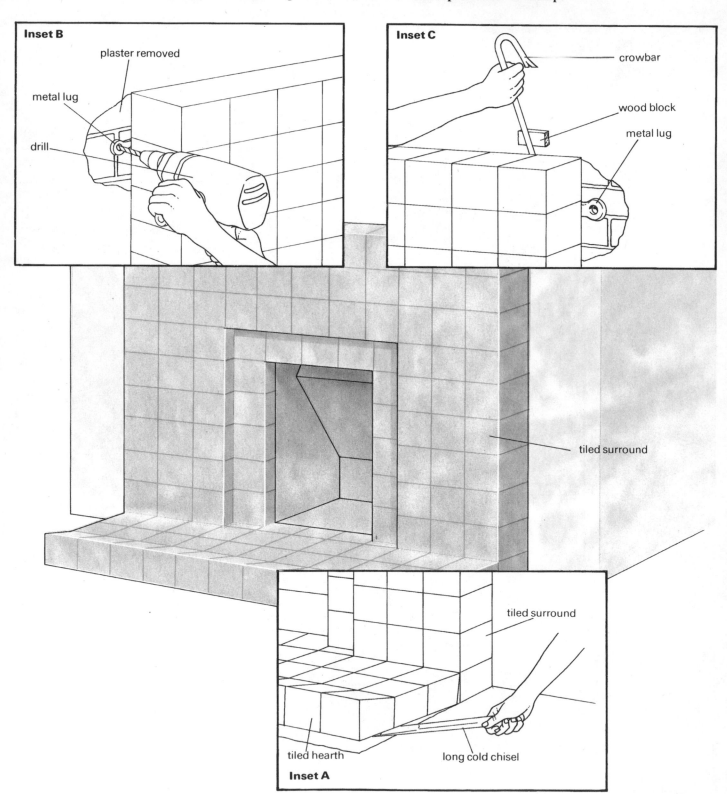

Inset B
plaster removed
metal lug
drill

Inset C
crowbar
wood block
metal lug

tiled surround

Inset A
tiled surround
tiled hearth
long cold chisel

A disused fireplace can be an eyesore and take up valuable space; it may also create a focal point which distracts from the room's decor. You can give a room a new look by removing the fireplace, blocking it up and blending in the area with the rest of the room.

If you tackle the job in easy stages, it is not as difficult as it may appear. Before starting any demolition work, check the chimney is thoroughly swept or you could have problems when it is blocked up and ventilated. Clear the room of as much furniture as possible and group the remainder in the middle of the room and cover the items with dust sheets. Lift the floor covering around the hearth, unless it is fixed tiling or parquet.

Taking out the fireplace

The hearth is usually laid after the surround has been fixed in position, in which case you should remove the hearth first. But if the surround has been placed on top of the hearth, which is rare, you will have to remove the surround first.

Removing the hearth

A tiled hearth is usually laid in one piece, whereas a stone hearth will probably have been bedded down in sections. In either case, drive the blade of a long cold chisel under one end of the hearth and lever it away from the floor, using the chisel as a crowbar.

A tiled unit is reinforced and you should be able to lift it in one piece without damaging the tiles. If you do not plan to keep it or sell it, you will find it easier to remove from the room if you break it up into pieces with a club hammer. Inset tiled hearths (usually in upstairs rooms) need not be removed, but can be brought level with the floorboards by using a screeding compound or by gluing hardboard directly to the tiles. If you have a stone fireplace, you may find it is worth selling. In this case, lift each stone carefully and mark with a number to indicate its position in the hearth.

The mortar on which the hearth was bedded may need patching up to leave a smooth surface for a floor covering; use a mix of one part Portland cement, one part hydrated lime and six parts clean builder's sand – or buy a small bag of ready-mix.

Removing the surround

The surround is usually fixed to the wall by screws or nails inserted through metal lugs, one on either side about 75mm (3in) from the top. Some larger surrounds have more than one fixing on each side. To locate the fixings, strip off any wallpaper; if

the positions of the fixings are not obvious after removing the wallpaper, tap the plaster lightly until you hear a change of sound and remove about 50mm (2in) of plaster around the lugs using a bolster chisel and club hammer. Remember that the less plaster removed, the easier the repair work will be.

Undo the fixing screws; if they are difficult to remove, drill out the heads using a drill bit the same size as the shank. Insert a crowbar behind the edges of the surround, using a block of wood to protect the wall, lever it forwards slowly and lower it to the ground. A ground floor fireplace might be too big and heavy to take out of the house in one piece; if so, use a club hammer to break it up into small sections, but cover it with sacking first.

Stone or brick A stone or brick surround is usually built like a wall to lie flat against the chimney-breast. Dismantle the surround piece by piece by setting a wide bolster chisel squarely against the mortar joint and tapping it gently with a club hammer. You should be able to remove most of the bricks intact and, since they will probably be in good condition, it is worth storing them for future

1 Initial stages in removing a fireplace: lifting the hearth with a cold chisel (**inset A**); drilling out rusted screws holding the surround to the wall (**inset B**); using a crowbar and block of wood to lever the surround away from the wall (**inset C**)
2 Construction of a brick fireplace. As you remove the bricks, you may find a steel plate supporting the bricks above the opening
3 Construction of a tiled fireplace with timber surround. Sometimes bricks are built end-on into the wall to tie the fireplace to the wall; chip off the protruding section of these bricks with a club hammer and bolster chisel

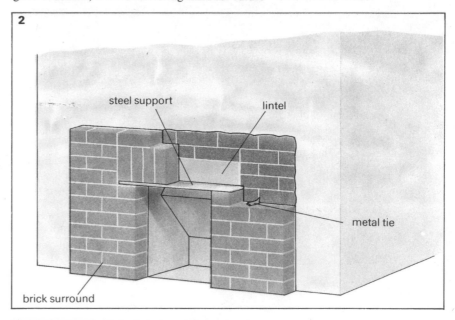

2

steel support   lintel

metal tie

brick surround

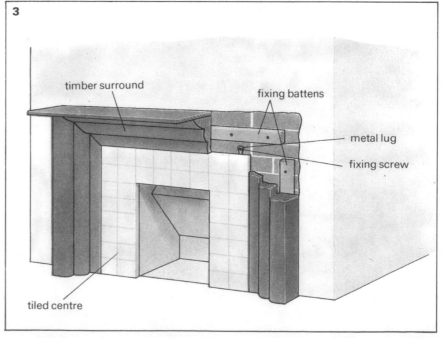

3

timber surround   fixing battens

metal lug

fixing screw

tiled centre

Basic items
long cold chisel, crowbar, bolster chisel club hammer, hacksaw (if needed)
bricks or lightweight building blocks, airbrick, mortar, plaster, expanded metal, nails (for bricking up)
50 × 25mm (2 × 1in) battens, countersunk screws 50mm (2in) long and wall plugs, asbestos or fire-retardant board, pad saw, hand or electric drill, scrim mesh, plaster (for panelling)
screeding compound or hardboard (for concrete floor)
joist and floorboards (for timber floor)

equipment

4

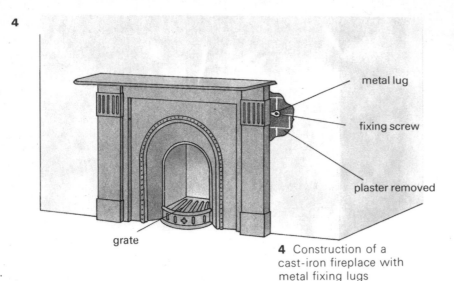

4 Construction of a cast-iron fireplace with metal fixing lugs

metal lug

fixing screw

plaster removed

grate

5

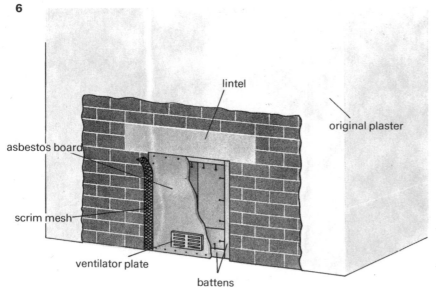

lintel

original plaster

masonry nails

existing bricks

expanded metal strip

airbrick

gap

5 Bricking up the opening: seal the gap with expanded metal and fit an airbrick

6

lintel

original plaster

asbestos board

scrim mesh

ventilator plate

battens

6 Fitting a panel over the opening; again a ventilator is essential

use. As you remove the bricks you should find metal ties inserted in the mortar; these help keep the surround in place. To release the ties, simply chip out the mortar.

Tiles Where the surround is made of tiles enclosed by wood, the timber might comprise a single unit or be a separate mantel and side pieces. In either case the timber is usually screwed to battens fixed to the chimney-breast wall. The screws in the surround will not be visible since they will have been sunk below the surface and covered with filler. They can usually be located by tapping lightly round the surround and listening for a change in sound. If not, the decorative finishing material – paint or varnish – will have to be stripped off to reveal the small patches of filler. Dig out the filler and release the screws.

The central tiled area could be fixed directly to the wall, in which case you will have to chip the tiles off, or fixed with metal lugs and screws.

Cast iron These are usually fixed to the wall by screws and lugs. Once the fireplace is away from the wall, you may find there is a separate section framing the opening; this will be secured at the back by nuts and bolts and it will probably be easier to undo the fixings and dismantle the fireplace before taking it out of the room. It is best to apply a little penetrating oil to the fixings and leave this to seep into the joints before you try to remove the fixings. Alternatively saw off the heads of the bolts with a hacksaw.

Interior After removing the surround and hearth, knock out the fireback, the sloping throat above and the side cheeks with a club hammer or lever them out with a crowbar. Remove the pieces and the rubble backfilling.

Skirting board If the fireplace is set in a projecting chimney-breast wall, remove the two short pieces of skirting board on either side of the opening. To do this, hammer the bolster behind the boards and lever them off, protecting the wall behind the bolster with scrap wood. If the fireplace is in a long unbroken wall, leave the skirting board in position since it is easier to fill the gap with a matching length later.

Blocking up the opening

With the hearth and surround out of the way, you can now block up the opening. There are two ways of doing this: with bricks or with a panel; the latter is preferable since you can remove the panel should you wish to reopen the fireplace at any time.

Bricking it up

If there is a draught or ash box space below the level of the hearth you will have to form a concrete plinth as a foundation for the brickwork. As a precaution, lay a damp proof course to join up with the existing one.

Using bricks or lightweight building blocks, brick up the opening with a single skin wall; the courses should align with the existing courses either side of the opening (if they do not, first lay the relevant depth of concrete to bring the bricks to the correct level); the front face of the new brickwork should lie flush with the existing brickwork round the opening. Incorporate an airbrick in the centre of the brickwork above skirting level to ensure an adequate flow of air to the flue.

Complete the job by plastering over the bricks – but not the airbrick – to leave the new surface flush with the surrounding plaster. First rake out the joints between the bricks to a depth of about 13mm ($\frac{1}{2}$in) to provide a good plaster-to-brick key and ensure the plaster is well forced into the joints as work proceeds. If a gap of more than about 13mm ($\frac{1}{2}$in) is left at the edges where the new bricks meet the existing walls, nail strips of expanded metal over the gap to serve as a backing for the plaster. When the plaster is dry, screw a metal or plastic ventilator plate to the wall over the airbrick.

Fitting a panel

Screw a simple framework of 50×25mm (2×1in) battens to the wall inside the opening as a support for a sheet of asbestos or fire-retardant board. Recess the battens from the front of the opening by a distance equal to the thickness of the board being used; this ensures the surface of the board will lie flush with the existing bricks on either side of the opening. Before screwing the board in position, cut a hole in it with a pad saw; a ventilator plate should be fitted over this to stop damp forming. The hole should be about 100×50mm (4×2in); mark its position on the board and drill a hole at one corner; insert the saw in the hole and cut along the guide-lines. Fix a length of scrim mesh to cover the joins of the board and the bricks before replastering.

Completing the flooring

You will need to bring the hearth area up to the level of the existing floor. This is a fairly easy job in the case of a solid floor, but it entails a little more work if you have a timber floor with foundations below, since you must fit a new joist.

Solid floor

Remove any loose rubble infill to a depth of 150mm (6in) and pack in fresh concrete, tamping it well down to about 25mm (1in) below the existing concrete level. When this is dry, lay a screed of three parts sharp, washed sand and one part cement mixed fairly dry with a little water-proofing agent added. Level the screed flush with the sur-rounding concrete and allow it to dry thoroughly before matching up the existing floor covering.

Timber floor

Remove all the rubble infill material below the old hearth to provide air space. Fix a new joist close to the wall and spanning the two sleeper walls on either side; cut back the existing floorboards to the nearest joist and fix new boards between this and the chimney-breast.

Finishing off

Fix a new skirting board in the gap and match up decorations on the wall, the skirting and floor covering if you are not redecorating the entire room.

To prevent rainwater entering the flue, but to provide adequate ventilation, insert a louvred spigot in the chimney pot or set a half tile in a mortar bed on top of the chimney stack.

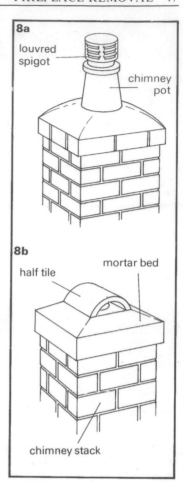

7 With a suspended timber floor, you will have to fix a new joist close to the old fire and extend the boards
8a Fit a louvred spigot to the chimney pot to provide ventilation but prevent rainwater penetrating
8b Alternatively bed a half tile in mortar on top of the chimney stack

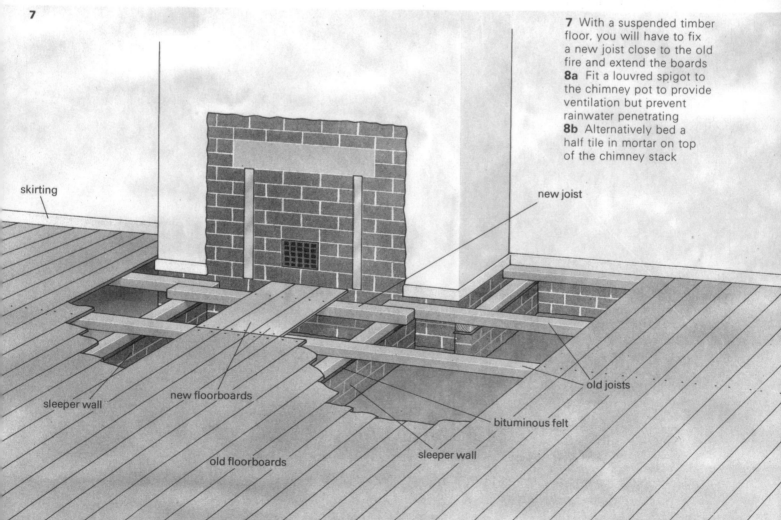

Plastering

Plastering a large area is a relatively skilled operation, but one which the DIY enthusiast can master with sufficient practice, following carefully the methods here. First decide whether the job is necessary at all: if you need to replaster over half of the wall surface because the plaster is loose or uneven, it will probably be easier and quicker to hack off the remaining solid plaster and resurface the entire wall. This could be done with sheets of plasterboard fixed to battens, which are secured to the wall at intervals; alternatively you could use plasterboard fixed directly to the wall with a gap-filling wall panel adhesive.

There may be situations where you decide to replaster a large area using conventional plastering techniques, for example where a doorway has been bricked up or a fireplace removed. In these cases, the job is made easier since you can use surrounding sound plaster as your guide and the new plaster is quite easily applied smooth and flat. If this is not the case, you can achieve a smooth finish by fixing temporary battens to the wall; these are used as a guide for a straight-edge drawn over the plaster.

Types of plaster

Traditional plasters were based on lime and were very slow in setting; they have now been replaced by gypsum plasters which are prepared from natural rock and harden much more quickly.

For DIY work Carlite plaster can be used in almost every case; it is ideal because it only requires the addition of clean water to make it ready for use. Because it is premixed, Carlite avoids the possibility of mistakes in proportioning which can affect the ultimate strength of the plaster; most other gypsum plasters require the addition of sand to the undercoat. Carlite is easy to mix indoors without mess and is lightweight; it contains perlite and/or exfoliated vermiculite as aggregates which make it about one-third the weight of sanded plasters and give it much better thermal insulation qualities.

Since Carlite is virtually lime-free, decorating can be started as soon as the plaster has dried; it has good fire resistance and provides greater resistance to shrinkage cracks if properly applied. There are four undercoat grades of Carlite plaster and one finishing grade; each sets in about an hour and a half.

Undercoat plaster

Undercoat plasters are available from builders' merchants in 50kg (110lb) sacks; Carlite bonding is also sold in DIY shops in 7½kg (16lb) bags. Always follow the recommended undercoat thicknesses (see application chart); if a heavy thickness of plaster is required, build it up in two layers, scratching the first coat to form a key. Make sure you use the same type of undercoat plaster throughout; in particular, never use Carlite browning over metal lathing, bonding coat or welterweight bonding coat. As a rough guide, 10kg (22lb) of Carlite browning 11mm ($\frac{7}{16}$in) thick will cover between 1.3 and 1.5sq m (1.5 and 1.8sq yd).

Carlite browning This type of undercoat plaster can be used in the majority of cases because it is suitable over bricks, blocks and most solid backgrounds.

The backgrounds should have normal suction, that is water should be absorbed at a normal rate. If suction is high and large quantities of water are absorbed into the background fairly quickly, you should use Carlite browning HSB plaster as an undercoat.

Carlite bonding coat Low suction backgrounds with a smooth surface, such as plasterboard, expanded polystyrene, normal ballast concrete, masonry and engineering bricks, require Carlite bonding coat. Certain surfaces need pretreating with a PVAC bonding agent to ensure the subsequent plasterwork adheres well; in these cases Carlite bonding should be used as an undercoat plaster.

Metal lathing This type of undercoat plaster, which contains a rust inhibitor, is mainly used over galvanized or bituminous-painted expanded metal lathing. Newtonite lath undercoat plaster can be used to waterproof damp walls.

Finishing plaster

This type of plaster is for the finishing coat. Carlite finish, which is premixed and contains exfoliated

A range of tools needed for plastering
1 Soft wide brush for dampening the surface
2 Hawk
3 Laying-on trowel
4 Wood float
5 Gauging trowel
6 Internal angle trowel
7 External angle trowel
8 Straight-edge

vermiculite, requires only clean water to make it ready for use; when dry, it forms a smooth matt finish. Carlite finish is sold in 50kg (110lb) sacks and 2½kg and 7½kg (5½ and 16lb) bags; at 2mm ($\frac{5}{64}$in) thick 10kg (22lb) will cover between 4.1 and 5sq m (4.8 and 5.9sq yd).

Thistle plaster The best alternative to the Carlite range for DIY use, Thistle plaster is available in four undercoat and two finishing grades. Thistle browning is a dense, heavy plaster because the undercoat requires the addition of clean, sharp sand (proportions as recommended in the application chart); this makes it less convenient to use. The finishing grade of Thistle plaster can be used as a skim coat finish without the addition of sand or lime on plasterboard; if you use taper edge plasterboard, you can achieve a flush finish without a skim coat since these boards will fit neatly together.

Care of plaster

Store all types of plaster in a dry place; plaster should not absorb moisture since this will shorten its setting time and reduce its strength. If you store the bags on a concrete floor, place them on a timber platform so they are clear of the ground. Once you open a bag of plaster, seal the remainder in a polythene bag until you come to use it. Ensure you use your plaster as soon as possible and only buy enough for the job in hand; if stored for more than two months, plaster may deteriorate.

Preparation

Surfaces to be covered should be dry and free from old plaster and other materials; use a hard brush to remove all dust, crystallized efflorescent salts and loose mortar from the wall. Cut any grooves necessary for cables, pipes and conduits using a club hammer and cold chisel; all pipes and metal objects should be protected by galvanizing, painting or applying a thick layer of lacquer. Sweep the floor before you begin to plaster.

Wood laths Don't attempt to plaster large areas of wood laths if they have become exposed. Cut back the existing plaster until the timber studding is exposed around the damage, cut away the laths and replace them with expanded metal mesh fixed firmly to the studding with galvanized clout nails. Alternatively you could fill the hole with sheets of plasterboard, fixed grey side outwards and held with galvanized clout nails. These backgrounds can be plastered as described below.

Using guides

If the area is between existing plaster, use this as a guide for the new plaster so it can be levelled with a straight-edge. If a large area of new plaster is

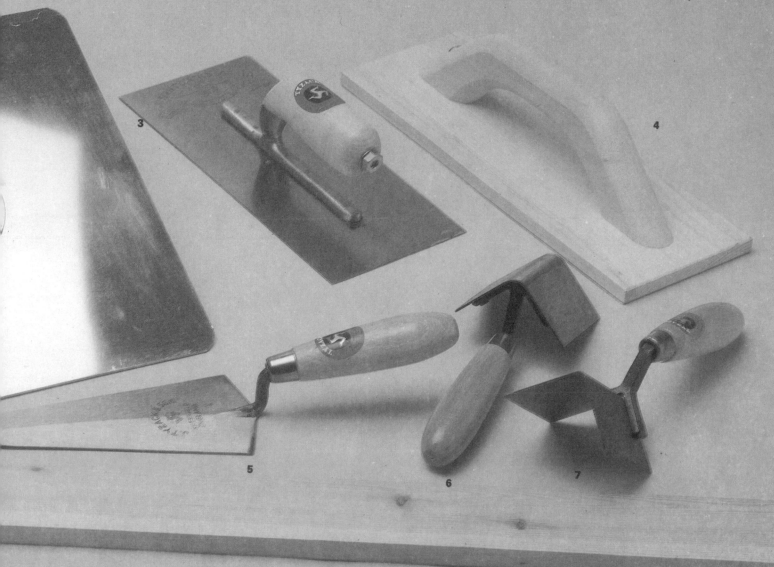

involved, you may need some other guide for the new plaster. Professional plasterers use screeds as guides for the new plaster; screeds are 300mm (or 12in) wide strips of undercoat plaster of the required thickness – usually 11mm ($\frac{7}{16}$in) – in horizontal bands near the ceiling and just above skirting level. Once the screeds have hardened, the area between is filled with the first layer of undercoat plaster, known as the floating coat; a straight-edge is drawn across the screeds to level the new plaster.

Unless you are familiar with plastering techniques, it can be difficult to place plaster screeds accurately; it is easier to fix timber battens to the wall. The battens must be the thickness of the undercoat you require, usually about 11mm ($\frac{7}{16}$in). Fix two with masonry nails to the wall in horizontal strips, one below the ceiling and one at skirting height. Ensure they are perfectly flat since the finished job will depend upon how accurately you place them. Battens thinner than the required undercoat thickness can be brought to the correct distance from the wall using timber offcuts as packing; bring hollows in the wall to the correct surface in the same way. Use a spirit level against a straight-edge to check the faces of the battens are vertical; this will ensure the plastered wall remains vertical. To plaster an external angle use battens vertically, working on one wall face at a time.

Dampening surface
Before applying plaster to the prepared wall, you will need to dampen the surface; most walls should be dampened until no more water is immediately absorbed. The exceptions are plasterboard, which should be plastered while perfectly dry, and walls plastered with Carlite browning HSB undercoat.

Mixing undercoat plaster
Cleanliness is of the utmost importance; keep everything clean and don't allow portions of old mix to come into contact with the new plaster, since this will affect both the setting time and strength of the new plaster. Keep a bucket of water at hand to clean your tools and change the water frequently; use only fresh, clean water to mix plaster – never the water used to clean tools.

To mix large amounts of plaster use either a timber platform or a clean firm base such as concrete. Small amounts can be mixed on a spot board;

Below Chart showing plasters suitable for DIY application on different backgrounds
9 Applying undercoat
10 Using straight-edge to level off undercoat
11 Applying finishing plaster
12a Using timber battens as guide when applying plaster on straight wall; place battens below ceiling and above floor and check vertical with spirit level
12b Using timber battens as guide when plastering external corners

Application guide for building plasters

Plaster	Carlite browning	Carlite browning HSB	Carlite metal lathing	Carlite bonding coat	Thistle browning	Carlite finish	Thistle finish	Sirapite finish	Thistle board finish
Approximate coverage (m²/10kg)	1.30-1.50	1.30-1.50	0.70-1.60*	1.10-1.70*	1.44-2.34*	4.10-5.00	3.90	2.50	1.65
Approximate setting time (hours)	1½	1½	1½	1½	2	1½	2	†	1-1½
Background	Undercoat plaster					Finishing plaster requiring an undercoat			Finishing plaster requiring an undercoat
Brick	11mm	11mm		11mm	11mm				
Blocks	11mm	11mm		11mm					
Stone				11mm	11mm				
Concrete	11mm	11mm		8mm	11mm				
Metal lath (from face of lath)			11mm						
Expanded polystyrene				8mm					
Gypsum plasterboard				8mm					5mm
Thistle/sand undercoats							2mm	3mm	
Carlite undercoats						2mm			
Cement/sand undercoats							2mm	3mm	
Backgrounds treated with proprietary bonding fluids				8mm					
Key	*Exact coverage depends on the background					†Early initial set and gradual continuous set			

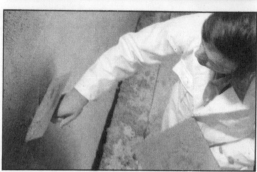

this is simply a flat piece of plywood or hardboard about 700mm (or 28in) square.

Using a spot board, spread the plaster in a ring and pour clean water into the centre in the same way as you would mix cement mortar. If you are using an undercoat plaster which requires the addition of sand, mix sand and plaster thoroughly in a dry state before you add the water. Draw plaster from the outside into the middle of the ring until all the water is absorbed; mix the heap with a hawk and trowel and gradually add more water until the plaster is well mixed.

The mix should not be too sloppy or too dry; the consistency of thick whipped cream is about right. It might take some trial and error until you achieve the right consistency which allows the plaster to be applied in the correct thickness without falling off. Mix only the amount of plaster you can apply comfortably in about three-quarters of an hour. Plaster starts to go off in about an hour; once this occurs, you cannot retemper it by adding more water.

Method of plastering

As already described, Carlite browning is used in most cases in a layer about 11mm ($\frac{7}{16}$in) thick. Don't attempt to apply the undercoat plaster to this thickness in one go. First apply a thin coat of plaster using firm pressure to force out air and create a good bond; apply a second layer before this has set to leave the surface slightly above the battens or screed. If you attempt to apply the thickness in one go, you will not achieve a good bond.

12a

ceiling

masonry nails

timber batten

75mm

straight-edge

spirit level

timber batten

75mm

masonry nails

floor

skirting

12b

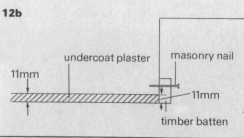

11mm

undercoat plaster

masonry nail

11mm

timber batten

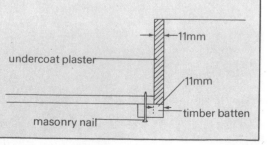

11mm

undercoat plaster

11mm

masonry nail

timber batten

and
tios

oportions of thistle browning/
nd mixes

½ Rendering

/2

Applying undercoat

The technique of applying plaster between battens or screeds will be gained with practice. First take up some of the mixed plaster on a hawk; this is a 200mm (8in) square plate screwed through its centre to a short handle and held in the left hand for right-handed people. Left-handed people should reverse the following instructions throughout. Hold the laying-on (or steel) trowel in your right hand and transfer some plaster from the hawk onto the flat side of the trowel. Start on the right-hand side of the wall at the bottom, move the trowel and angle the blade towards the wall so you can use firm upwards pressure to force plaster onto the surface. Work from right to left and from bottom to top until you have covered a good area of the wall; apply the second layer in a similar manner while the first is still wet. The surface of the plaster should be brought above the level of the battens, screed or surrounding plaster.

Draw a timber straight-edge in a sawing motion across the surface to leave a flat area of plaster; apply more plaster to any hollows and draw the straight-edge over the surface again. Using surrounding plaster or battens as a guide, you will need to scrape the floating coat away carefully to a depth of 2mm ($\frac{5}{64}$in) once it begins to set; this will leave enough room for the finishing coat. Don't use a steel trowel to polish the undercoat since its textured surface gives a good key for the finishing coat. You can increase this key by rubbing the surface with a timber float pierced with the points of two nails; alternatively use a wire scratcher; this can be made by driving a line of headless nails into a piece of scrap timber, ideally shaped as a paint brush handle so it looks like a comb.

Battens Once the area plastered between your battens or screeds has begun to set, you can fill the areas between the top batten and the ceiling and the bottom batten and the skirting. When these are also beginning to set, prise away the battens and fill the grooves which are left; finish these areas so they are level with the main body of plaster.

Metal laths If you are applying undercoat plaster over expanded metal laths, you will need two coats. The first coat, called the pricking-up coat, is applied lightly to avoid too much plaster being forced through the holes in the lath. Scratch this coat thoroughly to form a key and allow it to set before applying the next coat. This coat, called the floating coat, is built up to the required thickness; this is governed by battens or the level of surrounding plaster.

Setting time The undercoat will take between one and a half and two hours to set, after which time you can apply the finishing coat. If you leave the undercoat for a longer period, several days for example, you must dampen the surface with clean water before applying the final coat.

At this stage you should have a perfectly flat, scratched floating coat plaster wall surface ready for the final finishing coat, which will only be 2mm ($\frac{5}{64}$in) thick. If the final surface is to be smooth and level, it is vital you prepare the floating coat properly as already described.

Cleaning tools

Clean up all tools, the spot board and any buckets you have used to apply the undercoat; wash them in fresh water and wipe them with a dampened cloth to remove all traces of plaster. If you do not do this, the plaster will set on the equipment.

Mixing finishing plaster

Before you begin to mix the finishing plaster, fix new skirtings or door architraves over the floating coat if these fittings are required.

Quarter-fill a clean plastic bowl or bucket with clean water and gradually sprinkle finishing plaster into it until the water seems to be absorbed. Give the mixture a stir with a stick and leave it for a minute or two; add more plaster or water as necessary until the mixture has a soft plastic consistency. The finishing plaster is now ready for use.

Applying finishing coat

The best time to apply this coat is in the morning when the light is best; mixing should take place just before you require the plaster.

Transfer some of the finishing plaster to a hawk and load some plaster onto the laying-on trowel; working from left to right in this case, use firm pressure to apply plaster to the wall. It is best to apply the finishing coat in two very thin layers; apply the second when the first has stiffened under suction since some of the water will be drawn out of it and into the undercoat below. The aim should be to build up a finishing coat about 2mm ($\frac{5}{64}$in) thick. If there is existing plaster round your new work, use it as a guide to allow a straight-edge to be drawn across the finishing plaster to highlight low spots and remove high ones. The surface can then be smoothed with a laying-on trowel.

Laying-on When working on a new area you use only a trowel to produce a flat surface; it is, therefore, very important to have a flat undercoat surface. As suction begins to stiffen the finishing coat, work the trowel over the surface to smooth it; as the plaster begins to set, dampen the surface lightly with a wide, soft brush or a fine sprayer. Work the trowel over the plaster with lighter and lighter pressure until it becomes perfectly smooth, but not highly polished; the final strokes should be in an upwards direction. Stop trowelling before the plaster finally hardens and don't use too much water in the early stages since this could cause blisters.

Right Use our chart to determine the cause of and remedy common plastering problems. **13** Efflorescent salts on plaster surface. **14** Shrinkage cracks. **15** Mould growth. **16** Cracks caused by background movement

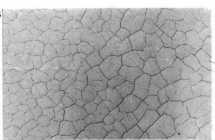

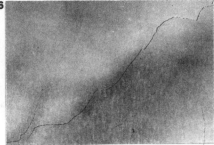

Plaster problems and how to tackle them

Problem	Cause	Comments
Large cracks	Differential movement of building components	Cracks with a definite line are caused by movement of the background; they generally appear above doors and windows and around window sills. Repair them by cutting out and filling with cellulose filler; since the cracks are liable to reappear, delay these repairs for as long as possible in the hope movement will cease.
Fine hair cracks	Shrinkage/movement of plaster	The result of using too much lime in a finishing coat. If cement rendering is used for the undercoat, the cause may be the application of a finishing coat before the undercoat has dried and completely shrunk. Walls with this fault should be decorated with wallpaper or a textured paint rather than ordinary paint.
Finishing coat falls away from undercoat	Loss of adhesion	The result of a weak undercoat containing an excessive amount of sand or a sand with too much loam. Loss of adhesion can also occur if gypsum finish plaster is applied to a cement or cement/lime-based undercoat which has set but is not dry. It can also occur if the undercoat is not properly scratched to provide a good key.
Skim coat falls away from plasterboard	Loss of adhesion	In one-coat work this is probably due to the addition of lime to the plaster.
Plaster sets too quickly	Lack of cleanliness, plaster too hot	Dirty mixing water and impurities in the mix will speed up the setting time. Very occasionally plaster comes very fresh from the manufacturer and still hot; this will also speed setting. Open the sack and allow the plaster to cool before using it.
Undercoat/plaster sets too slowly	Unsuitable sand	The use of unsuitable sand can effect the setting of undercoat plasters; use clean, washed sharp sand.
Plaster soft and powdery	Dry-out	If plaster dries out before it has set, it will fail to develop its maximum strength. Make sure the background is dampened where applicable (not plasterboard) and the correct thickness of plaster is applied. If dry-out occurs, strip off and replace with a fresh coat of plaster.
Uneven surface of finish plaster	Incorrect application	Failure to follow the instructions in this section can make it impossible to achieve a smooth plaster surface. If the surface is bumpy but firm, it is possible to level off high spots with a medium abrasive disc held in an electric drill. This is a very messy job, so wear a dust mask and old clothes. Hollows can be filled with cellulose filler.
White powder on surface	Efflorescence	White powdery crystals can appear on the surface of plaster, usually as a result of salts coming through from the background surface. These salts usually appear as the wall dries out; they can be brushed off. Increase heating and ventilation to speed drying out and temporarily decorate the wall with emulsion paint until drying out is finished, when the problem should cease.
Paint peels away from plaster surface	Sealed-in water	Gloss and other impermeable paints should not be applied until the plaster has thoroughly dried out, which may take up to two months, depending on the background.
Sooty black mould on plaster surface	Mould growth	This is a sign of damp conditions. Improve ventilation and heating and remove the source of dampness. When the wall is dry, scrape off the mould and treat with a fungicide.

RSJs and lintels

When an opening is made in a wall, the area above the opening has to be supported; this can be done either by building an arch over the opening or by spanning it with a lintel. Since load-bearing arches are difficult to build in existing walls, lintels are most often used.

Theoretically lintels only carry the weight of the wall contained in a triangle above the opening. If you look closely at the brickwork over an opening, you will see it forms a series of steps or corbels from each side of the opening until the steps meet in the centre a few courses higher up. This means small openings of not more than 450mm (or 18in) wide, such as for an extractor fan, can be cut in a sound brick wall without the need for a lintel; doorways can also be cut in sound brick walls without the door opening having to be supported while the lintel is being installed.

There are exceptions, however. For example parts of the building structure such as floor joists which are supported by the brickwork of the triangle have to be taken into account when assessing the load to be carried by the lintel. Also, if the triangle is not complete because of a window or other opening above the lintel, the lintel has to carry all the load imposed in the area vertically above the opening. The same applies if the lintel is positioned at the end of a wall so there is only the minimum abutment at one end of the lintel. A lintel has to rest on a minimum of 150mm (6in) of wall at each end; with large openings which have to support great weights, you will have to employ an architect to design a suitable support system.

Types of lintel

Lintels can be made from timber, steel or concrete. Galvanized steel lintels are usually light enough to be installed by one man and can be bought in a variety of shapes and sizes to suit most situations. Reinforced concrete, although heavier, has the advantage of being able to be cast on the spot.
Timber Timber lintels, although less common than concrete and steel, are suitable for openings such as serving hatches and doorways. One advantage is they are able to take fixtures for sliding doors.

Steel Galvanized steel lintels are lightweight and the smaller sizes can be handled by one person. They can be bought ready-made in a variety of shapes to suit most types of walls and situations and their size has been calculated not only to carry the required load, but also to fit in with the brickwork courses. Small steel lintels are suitable for the same openings as timber. Pressed steel lintels are also light, act as a damp proof course and are particularly suited to cavity walls. For a large opening you will probably require an RSJ (rolled steel joist), although you can obtain galvanized steel lintels for single brick or cavity walls which span openings of up to 4.2m (14ft) and which carry a uniformly distributed load of 3 tonnes.
Concrete Reinforced concrete is an excellent material for lintels, but it is heavy to handle. Small concrete lintels can be cast in timber moulds and lifted into place; larger ones need to be cast in position, however, and are therefore not a suitable proposition unless a new building is being erected.

There is no rule-of-thumb method of working out the correct size of the lintel for the span; for openings with a span of up to 1.2m (4ft) the depth can be two courses of bricks and for openings with a span of up to 1.8m (6ft) the depth should be three courses. Concrete lintels are reinforced with mild steel rods of 9mm ($\frac{3}{8}$in) diameter, hooked round at each end and placed about 38–50mm ($1\frac{1}{2}$–2in) from the bottom of the mould; the top of the lintel is marked to avoid putting it in position upside down. The concrete mix consists of one part cement, two parts sand and three parts coarse aggregate not larger than 19mm ($\frac{3}{4}$in) in diameter.

Lintel shapes

The type of opening, the wall thickness and the finished appearance required dictate the shape of the lintel. Concrete lintels have their surfaces roughened to provide a key for the plaster while steel lintels have an expanded metal mesh welded to them to provide the necessary key. This metal can be supplied on one or both sides and is needed only on one side when the lintel is used to support the inner leaf of a cavity wall.
Rectangular This is the most common shape and is

1 In theory a lintel supports only the wall contained within a triangle above the opening; but where parts of the building structure – such as ceiling joists – are supported by the brickwork of the triangle, the lintel must support these as well as the brickwork
2 A rectangular steel lintel used above a door opening in a single skin wall

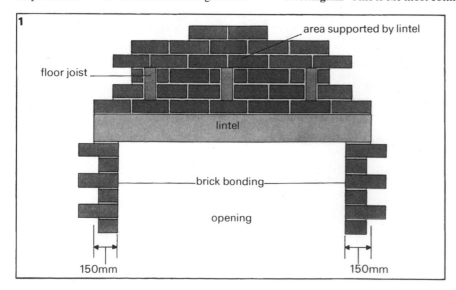

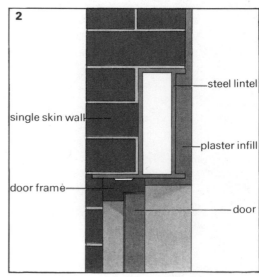

usually sufficient for an opening in an interior wall; each side of the lintel is plastered so it is hidden when the job is finished. A rectangular lintel is also used on the outer leaf of a cavity wall and will be hidden behind cladding material.

Boot These lintels, which as the name implies are shaped like a boot, are made of steel or concrete and are used in cavity walls with the rectangular, box-like section of the lintel resting on the inner leaf of the wall and the outer leaf of bricks laid on the projecting toe. Steel lintels are impervious to damp, but concrete lintels need a damp proof course which usually consists of felt laid over the top of the inner leaf section, down to the front of the lintel inside the cavity and over the projecting toe. The bricks are then laid on top of the dpc, preventing any water which might have penetrated the outer leaf of the wall or been condensed inside the cavity passing through the concrete or brick joints. It is a good idea to rake out one or two of the vertical mortar joints of the outer leaf of the cavity wall in the first course of bricks on top of the lintel to allow trapped water to escape.

Concrete boot lintels are difficult to cast because reinforcement is more complicated than with the simple rectangular lintel. Reinforcing rods are needed in the toe of the lintel and are strapped in place by stirrups made of lighter rods which pass around the rods of the main beam; these stirrups have the additional task of preventing the toe of the lintel breaking away from the main beam. It is usual to cast the boot lintel upside down so the toe of the mould can be filled properly and the reinforcement accurately positioned. Outer lintels and the toe of boot lintels need a drip groove or throat on the underside to make water run clear of the structure and not down the face of the wall. This is done on steel lintels by turning the outer edge of the toe slightly downwards.

L-shaped These are specially shaped steel lintels for supporting the brick exterior skin of timber-framed constructions. They have no rectangular section but have supporting fins and a high rear flange which is fixed to the inner timber frame using the special retaining clips provided.

Installing a lintel

Many of the alterations required round the house necessitate installing a lintel; although many people are deterred by the thought of knocking

down parts of their house, it need not pose any problems provided allowance is made for additional loads and care is taken in the work. House foundations are simple, unreinforced concrete strips intended to carry a uniformly distributed load. When an opening is made in a wall it relieves a section of the foundation of its load and the lintel above the opening transfers the weight to the foundation at each side of the opening. Usually this extra load does not matter since there is a sufficient margin of safety in the bearing strength of the existing foundation. The usual bearing for a lintel is not less than 150mm (6in); it can be increased where the remaining wall is not in good condition, although it is better to rebuild the sides of the opening with sound bricks. Where a very large opening is to be made, such as when a long section of the house wall has to be removed to provide access to an extension, the building control officer might insist on a square brick column being built on a deeper foundation to take the concentrated weight which will be imposed.

Warning It is important to remember door and window frames do not carry any load so they cannot be included when working out the size of lintel required. Nevertheless you cannot always rely on this; before taking out old door and window frames, remove some of the plaster to find out whether a lintel exists.

Padstones For large openings each end of the lintel must rest on a padstone which can be made of natural stone, concrete or engineering bricks. The padstones should be at least the thickness of one course of bricks and with very large openings carrying heavy loads they should be two courses thick. They should be 225mm (9in) long to bond in with the brickwork and so the bearing of the lintel can be increased to 225mm (9in).

Needles Whether the wall above the proposed opening is load-bearing or not, it will have to be propped up until the lintel is installed. This is done by putting temporary beams called needles through the wall above the level of the lintel. For light internal walls each needle could be 100 × 50mm (4 × 2in) and not more than 1.8m (6ft) long; but for load-bearing and exterior walls each needle will have to be 150 × 50mm (6 × 2in) and can be up to 2.7m (9ft) long. For normal domestic work these needles are placed so not more than 900mm (or 3ft) of wall is left unsupported.

The first step is to cut a series of holes slightly

3 A steel boot lintel used above a window opening in a cavity wall
Positioning concrete boot lintels and dpcs above door openings in cavity walls:
4a Where the door frame is in the inner leaf of the wall
4b Where the door frame is towards the front of the outer leaf
4c Where the door frame is central in the cavity wall

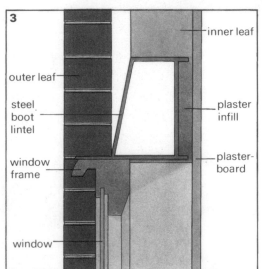

3
inner leaf
outer leaf
steel boot lintel
window frame
window
plaster infill
plaster-board

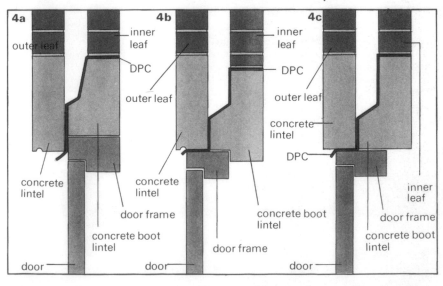

4a
outer leaf
inner leaf
DPC
outer leaf
concrete lintel
concrete lintel
door frame
concrete boot lintel
door

4b
inner leaf
DPC
outer leaf
concrete lintel
concrete boot lintel
door frame
door

4c
inner leaf
DPC
outer leaf
concrete lintel
DPC
inner leaf
door frame
concrete boot lintel
door

larger than the needles to be inserted. When in place, the needles are jacked up tightly against the top of the hole. This can be done either by inserting adjustable steel props under both ends of each needle or by fitting vertical timber props in place. Whatever their type, the props must stand on firm ground. If the floor is of timber, boards will have to be taken up and a short plank placed on the ground beneath the floor on which the foot of each prop can rest. Timber props are tightened by driving folding wedges under them; these wedges are made out of 50mm (2in) square timber and are about 225–300mm (9–12in) long. They are placed one on top of the other and the prop is set on top of them. The prop is held in position while the wedges are driven home; both wedges must be hit at the same time, using a hammer in each hand. Once the wall has been pinned up in this manner, the opening can be cut using a cold chisel and a club hammer. The slot for the lintel is cut first, at least 150mm (6in) wider than the proposed opening at each side. The rest of the opening can then be cut carefully; this is not only to save bricks, but also because the sides of the opening wall will have to be rebuilt if they become ragged and start crumbling.

Positioning the lintel

Once the sides of the opening have been made good by smoothing out the brickwork, you can position the lintel. If using padstones, bed them on mortar, cover them with another layer of mortar and place the lintel on top; if not, use mortar to lay the lintel directly onto the brickwork. Use a mortar mix of one part cement to three parts sand. When the lintel is secure, wedge shims of slate or asbestos sheet between the lintel and the brickwork and ram relatively dry mortar into the spaces between the lintel and the brickwork. To ensure the space is completely filled it is a good idea to fill from one side only, ramming the mortar in until it starts to come out the other side. When the whole of the joint has been filled, leave it for at least 48 hours to cure; don't work on the opening during this time to ensure you do not disturb any of the filling. After this remove the props and needles.

Lifting the lintel Galvanized steel lintels should be easy enough to lift, but with RSJs and precast concrete lintels you will need to put up secure scaffolding from which to work. You will also need scaffolding when working at a height, even if you are only using a lightweight steel lintel.

Lifting a heavy RSJ presents a number of problems. The best method of lifting a lintel 2–2.5m (or 7–8ft) up is to raise each end a little in turn with jacks, securing each end as you work with scaffolding. The lintel can be raised gradually to a level at which it can be levered from its supports into the prepared opening. Medium weight lintels can be lifted by hand with the help of two or three people raising alternate ends onto a pair of trestles. Whatever method you use, it is best to lift the lintel slowly and safely rather than risk it falling.

The job of getting a heavy RSJ up to a height must be undertaken with great care. The scaffolding must be strong enough to take the combined load of the lintel and those lifting it. It must also be firmly secured at the top otherwise the weight of the RSJ suspended on the outside of the scaffolding could pull it over. For lifting gear use two sets of chain blocks; these are hooks on chains which are raised and lowered by pulling on a continuous chain. The gear must be hooked over the scaffolding poles and

lashed in place with wire. You can use one lifting block, but it tends to allow the load to swing about during lifting. Once the load is lifted to the required height, scaffold poles can be slid over the guard rail, under the lintel and secured; this will enable you to ease the lintel onto the brickwork or padstones.

An alternative to lifting on the outside of the scaffolding is to raise the lintel up through the inside of the framework; this avoids overloading the scaffolding at one side.

Warning You will need a lot of help when moving RSJs and it is important your helpers are used to handling heavy loads. Don't take chances; when in doubt, use the services of a professional.

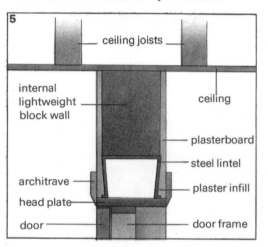

5 A small steel lintel used above a door opening in a single skin partition wall
6 If an unreinforced concrete lintel is used to span an opening, its top surface will be compressed and its bottom surface tensioned. Concrete is strong in resisting compression but weak in resisting tension and, if a heavy load is imposed, the lintel will break at its lower surface; for this reason steel reinforcing rods are cast into the bottom surface

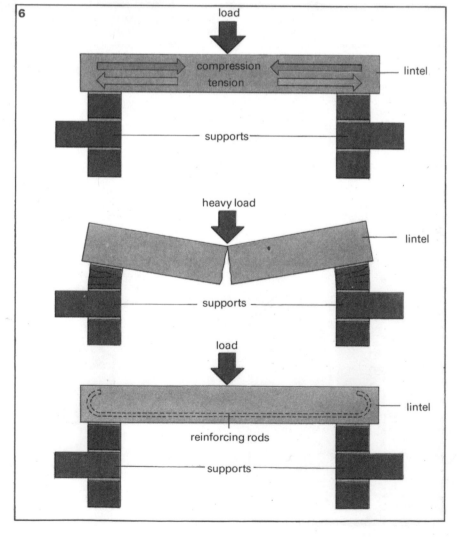

7 An L-shaped lintel used to support the brick exterior skin of a timber-framed construction; the lintel is fixed to the timber frame with special retaining clips which allow for the differential movement of the brickwork and the timber
8 A padstone used to support a lintel spanning a wide opening; where the support beneath the lintel has broken away, engineering bricks can be used
9 The position of the needle and lintel/RSJ when building a door opening in a single skin wall and in a cavity wall (**inset A**); when building an extension where the new joists run parallel with the cavity wall (**inset B**), where the new joists run at right-angles to the cavity wall (**inset C**) and where the extension ceiling is at a lower level (**inset D**)

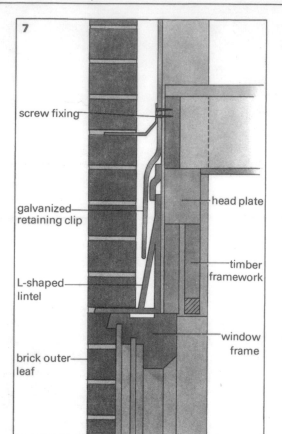

7
screw fixing
galvanized retaining clip
L-shaped lintel
brick outer leaf
head plate
timber framework
window frame

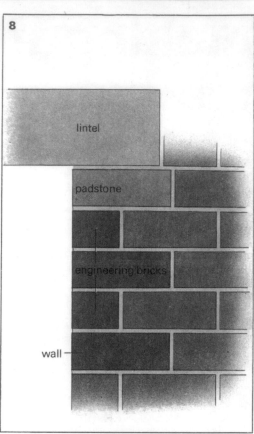

8
lintel
padstone
engineering bricks
wall

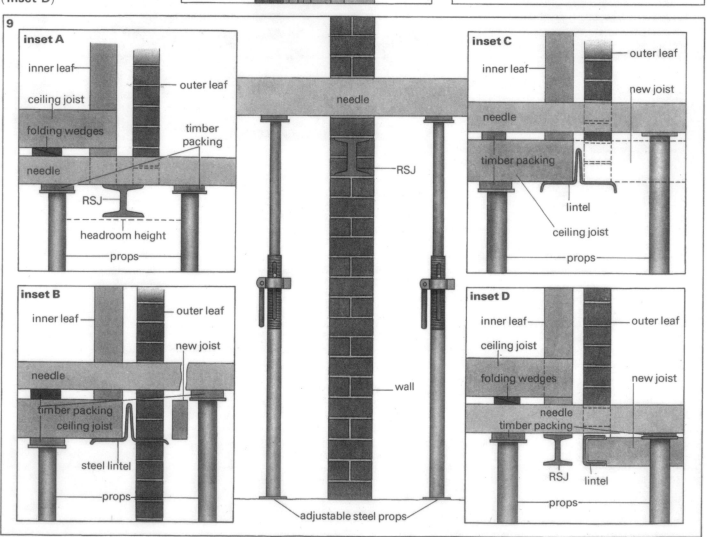

9

inset A
inner leaf
ceiling joist
folding wedges
needle
RSJ
headroom height
props
outer leaf
timber packing

inset B
inner leaf
needle
timber packing
ceiling joist
steel lintel
props
outer leaf
new joist

needle
RSJ
wall
adjustable steel props

inset C
inner leaf
needle
timber packing
lintel
ceiling joist
props
outer leaf
new joist

inset D
inner leaf
ceiling joist
folding wedges
needle
timber packing
RSJ
lintel
props
outer leaf
new joist

Making an internal arch

One way of overcoming the squareness of rooms in modern homes is to incorporate the flowing lines of arches into the interior design. In older houses, too, arches can provide an important link between rooms in keeping with the original decor. As well as being easy on the eye, arches create a feeling of space and light; obvious places for them are above alcoves, doorways and interconnecting walls of through rooms. In houses with central heating, it is often convenient to remove doors between certain rooms and an archway in the opening will do much to improve its appearance; and an arch over an alcove, for example, will turn it into an attractive bookshelf or display area.

Shapes of arch
Arches can take many forms; the most common shapes are semi-circular, elliptical, horseshoe and segmental.

Semi-circular This is the most common form of arch and probably the easiest to mark out. With this shape the depth of the arch at each side will be half its span. This is not a problem across a small opening such as a doorway, but an arch spanning a 4m (or 13ft) opening – such as may be found where a wall has been removed to make a through room – will have a depth of 2m (or 6ft 6in) at the sides; this will considerably reduce the headroom under the arch.

A modified type of circular arch has a raised point in the centre; this is often called a four-centre arch because it is constructed from segments of circles with four different centre points.

Elliptical For large, as well as small, spans an elliptical arch may be a better choice. In this case a 4m (or 13ft) span arch need be only about 760mm (or 30in) deep at each side, which gives more headroom at each end of the span and does not obstruct light passing from one end of the room to the other.

Horseshoe A horseshoe arch is really a semi-circular arch where the curve is continued below the imaginary line of the diameter. It is difficult to build into an existing doorway, but can be used as a decorative feature in an alcove or through room.

Segmental This is most suitable where a gently curving, shallow arch is required. It is useful over a wide opening because it does not restrict headroom to any great extent at each side.

Flat In bricklaying terms there is also a flat arch; this shape is sometimes seen over door and window openings in older houses. Flat arches can be used over short spans only and have been superseded by the ordinary lintel, although they can be used to make a decorative feature of exposed brickwork.

Types of arch
An internal arch is a decorative feature only; the support for the walls above is always provided by

a lintel. The arch consists of a simple framework which can be prefabricated or cut and shaped on site.

Prefabricated This consists of a lightweight galvanized steel frame covered with galvanized mesh; once the arch is fixed in place, it is simply plastered over – a job you can do yourself or leave to a plasterer.

Prefabricated arches are easy to fit and save time when building the arch. Because they are accurately made, they also eliminate some of the problems which can be encountered when building an arch on site. You can, for example, get flat spots on the curve, have one side of the arch slightly different in shape to the other and find the plaster cracks around the perimeter of the curve.

Home-made You can make the framework for an arch from chipboard and/or hardboard panels; but care should be taken when measuring and marking out the panels to ensure the arch is the correct size. Once in position, the framework is usually papered or plastered over. You can make the arch look like load-bearing brick or stone by covering the framework with brick or stone slips. These materials can be cut to shape with a masonry cutting disc held in a power saw; they are then stuck onto the framework with a special adhesive. A similar effect can be achieved using decorative wall materials, which are coverings available in kit form.

Above By installing an arch you can bring two rooms together, making them seem lighter and more spacious; the gentle curves of this elliptical arch provide relief from the solid square lines
Shapes of arch:
1a Semi-circular
1b Four-centre
1c Elliptical
1d Semi-circular superimposed on elliptical to show extra headroom at sides
1e Horseshoe
1f Segmental
1g Flat
2a The joint between the arch and the wall surface can be hidden with a timber batten and scotia moulding
2b Alternatively you can use quadrant moulding
3 Drawing an ellipse

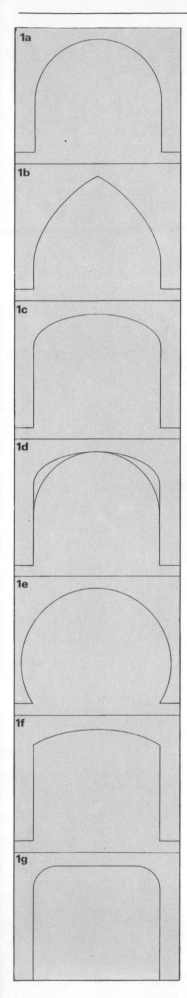

1a

1b

1c

1d

1e

1f

1g

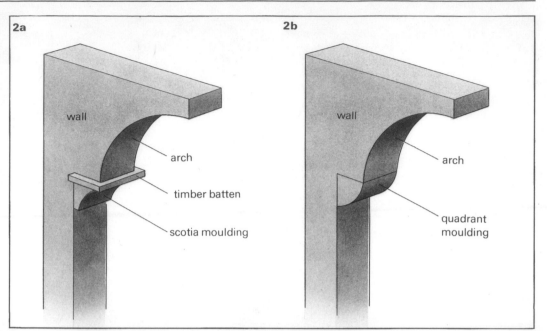

2a

wall

arch

timber batten

scotia moulding

2b

wall

arch

quadrant moulding

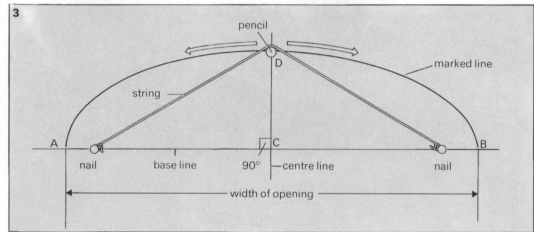

3

pencil

D

marked line

string

A   base line   90°   centre line   nail   B

nail

width of opening

Planning an arch

The size of the arch will be governed by its shape and the width of the opening it will span. It is important to keep the arch in proportion to the size of the room, but there are no hard and fast rules to help get this right. It is best to make a template of the proposed arch from brown or felt paper or even newspapers which can be stuck together with adhesive tape. Pin or glue the template across the opening to get an idea of the look of the arch.

Where space is at a premium in a through-room opening, you could use segmental arches each side of a flat arch. In an old house where there is plenty of room, the proportions and decoration of the room may permit the construction of a semi-circular arch supported on each side with glass fibre columns. At the planning stage think about accessories which could be used to give a neat finish to the arch. Georgian-type pilasters in fibrous plaster or timber can give style to an arched opening; fibrous plaster mouldings, available precast, are simply fixed to the wall with tile adhesive.

In most cases, both prefabricated and home-made arches can be installed in an existing door-way, alcove or other opening without alteration of the wall on each side. However, when a new open-ing is made or when an existing opening is ex-panded, it will be necessary to install a lintel across the opening before the framework for the arch is

fitted. In this case the work must comply with Building Regulations.

Over a wide span bear in mind the wall must be propped while the lintel is fitted and the lintel should be properly supported on at least 100mm (4in) of brickwork at each end. Once the opening is made fitting the arch is the same regardless of the width of the opening.

Building the arch

If the arch is to be positioned in a doorway, it will usually be necessary to remove the door frame. Take off the door and prise away the architraves and the frame with a club hammer and cold chisel. Remove the side frames first, prising them away from the wall at the bottom so they can be pulled free at the top. In some cases it is possible to retain the frame, such as when a cottage style door is to be fitted into an arched top.

There are two ways of dealing with the walls at the sides of the opening. You can remove the plaster so, after replastering, the arched opening has a smooth flowing line; or you can leave the plaster on the wall and simply plant the arch on the wall surface. The joint can be hidden with a decorative timber moulding. In the case of a planted arch, you need only remove the wallpaper or paint from the plaster surface before fixing the arch.

Home-made arch

The front and back panels of a made-up arch are best constructed from 12.7mm ($\frac{1}{2}$in) chipboard, although a lightweight arch with a span of up to 1m (3ft 3in) can be made from 3mm ($\frac{1}{8}$in) hardboard. Decide on the shape of the arch and the span required and mark out one panel accordingly. To draw a semi-circle, use a piece of string with a nail tied to one end and a pencil or felt tip pen tied to the other; or use a long batten with a nail through one end and a pencil through a hole drilled at the other.

To mark an ellipse, first draw a base line (AB) to the width of the opening; at the centre point draw a line (CD) at right-angles to the base line to the required height of the ellipse. Measure the length of AC and insert two nails on the base line at this distance from point D. Make a loop in a length of string which, when held taut, should go from point D round the two nails; by holding a pen or pencil in the loop, you can draw an ellipse. With one panel marked out as required, clamp or pin it on top of the panel for the face of the other side of the arch and cut out both panels together to ensure they are identical.

If using chipboard for the front and back panels, you need only screw mounting blocks to the inside of the opening to support the panels. If using hardboard, however, this must be supported along all edges. In the latter case screw 25 × 12mm (1 × $\frac{1}{2}$in) battens to the wall round the inside edge of the opening; fix the battens back from the faces of the wall so when the panels are fixed in place they will be flush with the wall surface on each side of the arch. Chipboard panels must be drilled so they can be fixed to the battens or mounting blocks with PVA adhesive and zinc-plated countersunk screws. Hardboard panels should be fixed with PVA adhesive and hardboard nails.

Underside The curved underside of the arch is best formed with hardboard. If possible, cut a strip of board long enough to go round the curve in one piece and make it slightly wider than the thickness of the arch; the board will be trimmed flush with the face later.

You may be able to bend the hardboard to the required shape in its dry state; if a very small radius curve is required, however, you will have to wet the board by soaking it in warm water for 30–60 minutes. If the panel is too long to soak like this, scrub the rough side with cold water and leave the board flat for 24 hours; cover it with a polythene sheet to prevent evaporation. Repeat the treatment and leave for a further 12 hours. To shape the board, bend it and tie a loop of string round the bend until the correct curve is achieved; alternatively bend the board round a suitably curved object which can act as a former. It is best to bend a slightly tighter curve than required to allow for slight spring-back when the tension is released as the board dries out.

If the front and back panels are made from chipboard, the curved panel can now be fixed in place, shiny side outwards, with PVA adhesive and hardboard nails inserted into the edges of the panels. If the front and back panels are made from hardboard, glue fixing blocks round the edge of the curve to support the curved panel; use small zinc-plated countersunk screws to hold the panel in place while the adhesive sets.

When the curved panel is firmly fixed, trim the edges flush with the front and back panel using a plane and glasspaper. If you are finishing the base of the arch with decorative timber mouldings at each side, glue and screw these in place.

The wall decorations may tend to crack where the arch is joined to the wall, but you should be able to overcome this problem by gluing scrim tape over the joints. Fill all holes and cracks with cellulose filler and, when dry, rub this down with glasspaper. Apply two coats of wall size before redecorating.

Alcove fitting If the arch is being fitted in an alcove, only one face panel will be required. The curved underside panel should be fixed to the front panel as already described, but on the alcove wall side it should be fixed to wood blocks glued directly to the wall plaster. Hold the face panel against the wall and mark round it to give the correct curve on which to mount the blocks.

If a cavity is required behind an alcove arch so concealed downlighters can be fitted, the building technique is the same as for an ordinary arch.

Prefabricated arch

Prefabricated arches are made in several standard sizes and it may be necessary to pack the opening or cut it back to get a standard arch to fit; if this is not possible, you can have an arch made-to-measure at

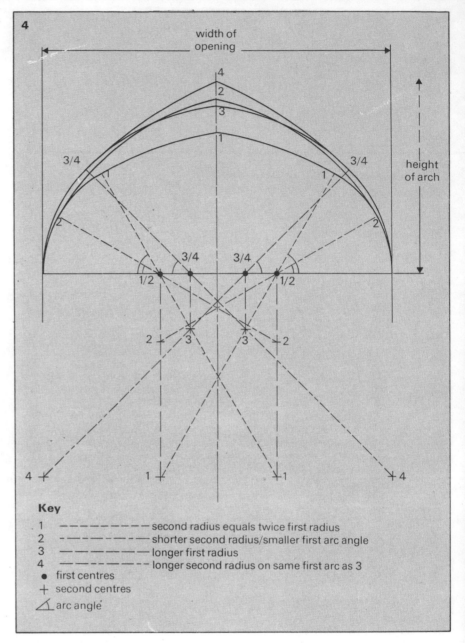

Key
1 – – – – – – – – – – second radius equals twice first radius
2 – · – · – · – · – · – shorter second radius/smaller first arc angle
3 – — – — – — – — longer first radius
4 · · · · · · · · · · · longer second radius on same first arc as 3
● first centres
+ second centres
△ arc angle

4 Drawing a four-centre arch; different shapes and heights can be obtained by altering the length of the first and second radii and the angle of the first arc
5 You can construct an arch with a span of up to 1m using hardboard; fix timber battens round the inside edge of the opening, so the hardboard is supported along all edges, and glue mounting blocks round the edge of the curve to support the curved panel
6 If the arch is to be fitted in an alcove, only one face panel will be needed; again you should fix mounting blocks to support the curved panel

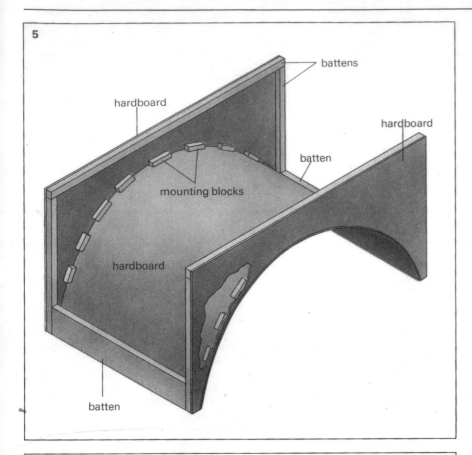

5

battens

hardboard

hardboard

batten

mounting blocks

hardboard

batten

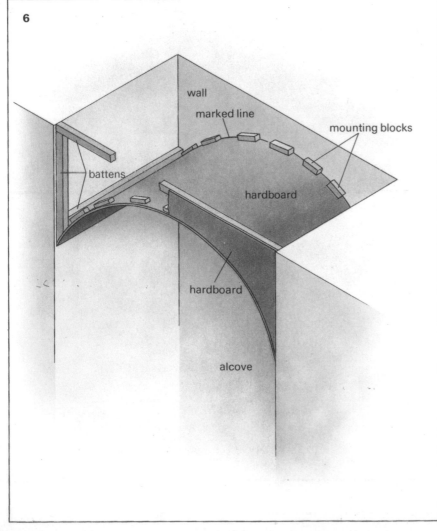

6

wall

marked line

mounting blocks

battens

hardboard

hardboard

alcove

extra cost. When measuring up for a prefabricated arch, bear in mind a clearance of 13mm ($\frac{1}{2}$in) should be added to the nominal size to allow for fitting. When the arch is supplied it will be about 75mm (3in) larger than the nominal measurement to allow surplus mesh for fixing.

Remove the door frame, if fitted, and measure the opening; select an arch nearest to the size of the opening. In most cases prefabricated arches are made so their thickness after plastering is about 130mm (or 5in); this will replace a standard door frame or 100mm (4in) of brickwork with a plaster finish on both sides. If the arch is wider than the existing opening, you must cut away the wall until the arch will fit. In this case, ensure the lintel has a minimum bearing of 100mm (4in) on each side of the opening; if necessary, a longer lintel must be fitted. If the arch is smaller than the existing opening, you will have to build out one or both sides of the opening; brickwork, building blocks or rough sawn timber can be used for this. Build out the opening to the nominal arch size plus about 13mm ($\frac{1}{2}$in) for clearance.

There will be extra mesh at each side of the arch to help in fixing; fold these pieces back so you can position the arch from one side. When it is in place, turn back the mesh and use zinc-plated screws or nails to fix round the edges of the mesh at approximately 150mm (6in) intervals. Fixing may be difficult if there is a reinforced concrete lintel above the arch unit; either make the fixing holes with a hammer action drill or make up some fixing hooks from heavy galvanized wire. Make a loop to fasten one end of the wire to the mesh and secure the other end to a screw fixed at a point just above the lintel.

To ensure the inside face of the arch and opening will be smooth after plastering, the sides of the opening must be built out to a depth of about 25mm (1in) and to a width of 100mm (4in). For this use two strips of 100 × 12.7mm (4 × $\frac{1}{2}$in) plasterboard, fixed grey side outwards, or a strip of 100 × 25mm (4 × 1in) rough sawn timber.

If the arch is to be fixed in an opening where the wall thickness is about 230 or 330mm (9 or 13in), the arch will look best if it is fixed in the middle of the wall. Surplus mesh can be turned back to allow fixing directly to the wall surface or the mesh can be nailed to a simple 100 × 38mm (4 × 1$\frac{1}{2}$in) timber framework fixed round the opening. In a tall opening this framework can be extended to bring the arch nearer the ground, although in this case the minimum headroom required is 2050mm (6ft 9in). A similar framework is used if you want to build an arch between two parallel walls – in a hallway or on a landing, for example. To avoid a great deal of replastering, the ends of the arch can be finished with a built-up timber moulding or a protruding brick or stone plinth.

If a full width arch across a wide opening is not required, you can extend the timber framework each side of the arch. For spans up to about 2m (6ft 6in), use 100 × 38mm (4 × 1$\frac{1}{2}$in) timber; for spans above this, use 100 × 50mm (4 × 2in) timber. Non-supporting, decorative columns can, if required, be fitted when the framework is complete. Use plasterboard to clad the framework or nail galvanized expanded metal to the frame and the arch so they can be plastered as one unit.

In new work a prefabricated arch can be fitted in position as the job proceeds or you can leave a hole and fit the arch later. In the latter case, the width of

7

lintel

width of opening

prefabricated arch

new brickwork

batten

the top part of the hole should be the nominal size of the arch plus 13mm (½in) for clearance. The depth of the top part should be the nominal depth of the arch as stated by the manufacturer. The width of the lower part of the opening should be the nominal width of the arch less 50mm (2in).

Plastering After the arch has been fitted, cut away any existing plaster to at least 150mm (6in) on each side to allow for the new plaster to blend in smoothly. Dampen the wall and edges of the existing plaster with water using an old brush or garden spray. Use Carlite Browning plaster for the undercoat and Carlite Finish for the top coat.

Mix the undercoat plaster with water until it forms a stiff paste. First apply the plaster to the underside of the arch, pressing it in place so it oozes up through the mesh and is level with the plaster guide lines. Use a short piece of timber to level off the plaster and apply the surplus to the sides of the arch. Complete the front and back of the arch, using a long straight piece of timber to level the plaster across the guide lines and the existing plaster. When the plaster is beginning to set, scrape off about 3mm (⅛in) where the new and existing plaster meet and scrape off about 1.5mm ($\frac{1}{16}$in) over the rest of the arch so a thin finishing coat can be applied level with the existing plaster.

Mix the finishing plaster to a creamy consistency and apply this over the hardened undercoat. Keep the trowel clean by occasionally washing it in a bucket of water and check the surface is level with a straight piece of timber. As the finish coat begins to set, smooth it with a clean wet trowel. Finish the back and front faces of the arch first, then tackle the underside.

8

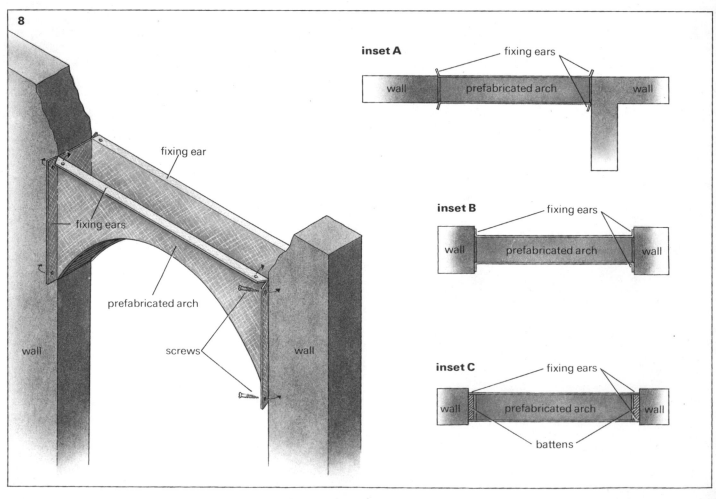

fixing ear

fixing ears

prefabricated arch

screws

wall

wall

inset A

fixing ears

wall · prefabricated arch · wall

inset B

fixing ears

wall · prefabricated arch · wall

inset C

fixing ears

wall · prefabricated arch · wall

battens

7 When fitting a prefabricated arch you may have to build out the opening; battens or bricks can be used for this

8 Fixing a prefabricated arch with the position of the fixing ears where there is an L-shaped wall (**inset A**); where the arch is narrower than the supporting walls the surplus mesh can be turned back and fixed to the wall surface (**inset B**) or it can be fixed to a simple batten framework (**inset C**)

9a The construction of the framework where a full width arch across a wide opening is not required

9b The construction of the framework to bring the arch nearer to the ground

10 The dimensions of the opening you should leave if building a wall and fitting the arch later

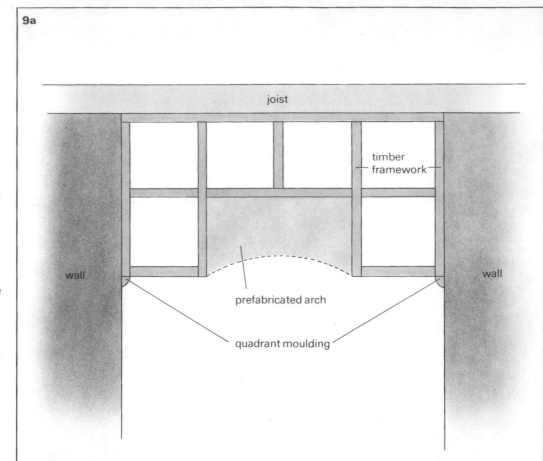

9a

joist

timber framework

wall

prefabricated arch

quadrant moulding

wall

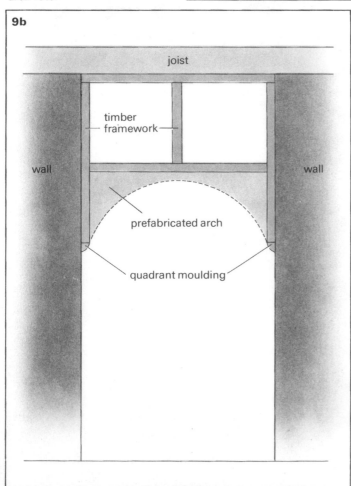

9b

joist

timber framework

wall

prefabricated arch

quadrant moulding

wall

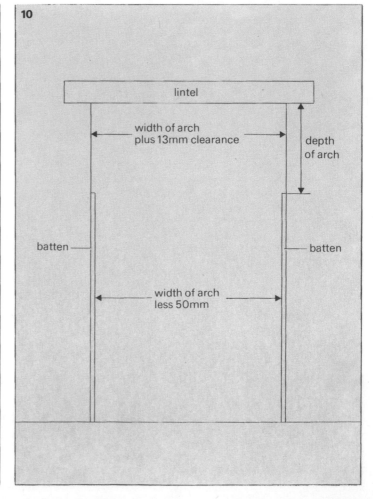

10

lintel

width of arch plus 13mm clearance

depth of arch

batten

width of arch less 50mm

batten

Making a wall opening

It is a quite straightforward job to make a small opening in a wall – for a serving hatch, extractor fan duct or a small window, for example. But bear in mind this work is classified as a structural alteration and the local authority should be consulted in case Building Regulations apply and approval is required.

In many cases a small opening in an internal wall will not require official approval; but an opening in an external wall, especially if the wall is close to the boundary of the property, may well require approval. Check with your local building control officer to see whether approval is required for the work you propose to do.

Before starting work on the opening, make sure the wall is sound and there are no cracks in the plaster or rendering. Even when the surface looks all right, there may be hidden problems. If when you remove the surface plaster you find the mortar between the bricks or blockwork is crumbling away, the wall may be unsafe and you should seek the advice of a builder or your local building control officer.

Try to ensure the opening is made as close to the centre of the wall as possible. As long as the opening is not more than 900mm (or 3ft) wide, you can safely make the opening without having to use shoring beams to support the wall while a lintel is inserted; this is a horizontal beam which spans the top of the opening and supports the bricks immediately above it. Simple shoring may, however, be required in an old wall made of stone; in this case you should seek professional advice.

Fixing supports

First cut a slot in the wall to take the lintel. It is quite likely at this stage some bricks or blocks will fall away from the area above the opening; this should not pose any serious problems as long as the mortar joints between the remaining blocks are sound. On openings up to 900mm (or 3ft) wide the wall will be self-supporting even without a lintel, since the stepped bricks act as corbels to support the wall above. In fact the lintel is required only to support the wall in the area of an imaginary equilateral triangle immediately above the lintel position.

When the opening is very small – up to 300mm (or 1ft) square – such as that required for an extractor fan duct, a lintel above the opening is not required. In this case all you need do is line the opening with the box supplied with the fan or with a made-up lining, as described below.

Making the opening

Start by marking the approximate position of the opening on the face of the wall. It is best to keep the position approximate at this stage since the exact location can be decided when the surface plaster or rendering is removed and the mortar joints of the bricks or blockwork are exposed. Position the opening so where possible complete bricks or blocks can be removed, rather than small sections.

Wearing protective spectacles chip away the plaster with a bolster chisel and hammer to expose

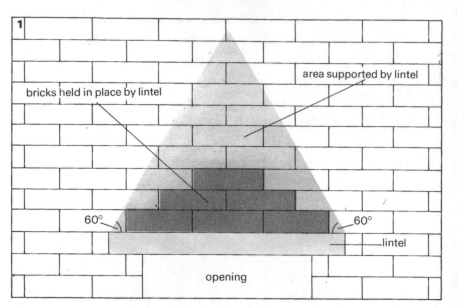

1 bricks held in place by lintel — area supported by lintel — 60° — 60° — lintel — opening

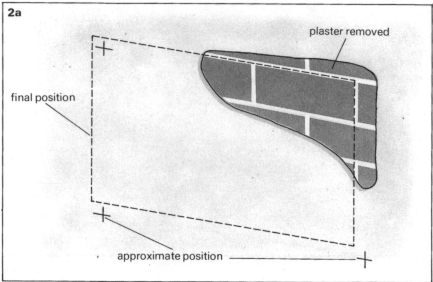

2a plaster removed — final position — approximate position

2b cold chisel — mortar — brickwork — club hammer — plaster

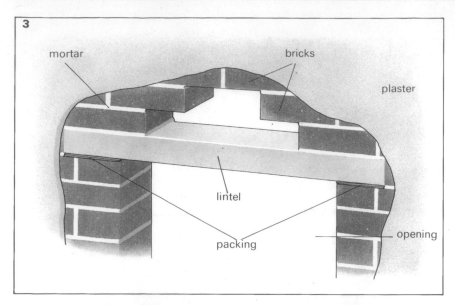

3

mortar

bricks

plaster

lintel

packing

opening

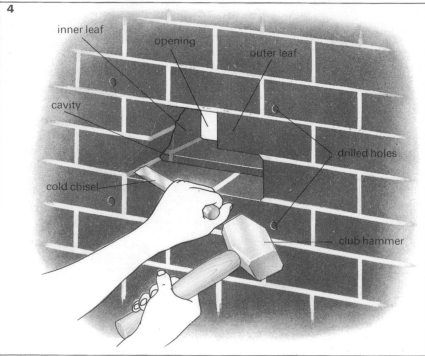

4

inner leaf

opening

outer leaf

cavity

drilled holes

cold chisel

club hammer

the brick or blockwork. If there is a cavity behind the plaster, you have a timber-framed stud wall; the techniques for this work are described below.

With the plaster removed, you can decide on the exact position of the opening. A convenient size for a serving hatch opening is 690 × 460mm (or 27 × 18in); this involves making an opening three bricks wide and six bricks deep. The finished hatch-way will be slightly smaller, due to the timber lining, so make the lowest part of the opening about 25mm (1in) below worktop level to allow for this.

By removing the plaster first you can check there are no water or gas pipes or electric cables hidden just below the surface.

Using the hammer and a cold chisel, now remove the two courses of bricks immediately above the intended opening. This will form a slot which will enable the lintel to be inserted before the bricks beneath it are removed. It does not matter if the bricks above the opening are removed to leave a triangular-shaped corbel. In fact if these bricks are even slightly loosened, they should be removed and reset firmly in new mortar.

Try not to hit directly into the face of the wall when removing bricks since this could loosen them over a wide area. Hold the chisel at an angle to the wall face and, starting at a mortar joint, remove the first brick piece by piece until a hole is made. Work away from this hole to enlarge the opening. Once the opening is a reasonable size, it may be possible to prise out whole bricks.

An alternative, easy way to make an opening in a wall is to cut it with a saw. Lightweight blocks are the easiest to work on since they can be cut with an old hand saw. You can cut any type of brick or block wall with a masonry cutting disc fitted in a power tool. A disc may be fitted in a portable circular power saw, but for a good depth of cut it is better to hire an angle grinding machine. Although they make neat holes, power grinders create a great deal of dust; it is therefore essential to wear a dust mask, as well as protective spectacles and thick leather gloves.

The slot for the lintel must be at least 200mm (or 8in) longer than the proposed opening since this will enable the lintel to rest on at least 100mm (or 4in) of brickwork at each side of the opening. The lintel can be made of reinforced, pre-stressed concrete, galvanized steel or from preservative-treated timber

1 Lintel holds in place bricks immediately above it; rest of bricks within triangle are self-supporting
2a Mark approximate position of opening; remove plaster and mark exact position to coincide with mortar joints
2b Chisel out bricks above top corners of proposed opening to form slot for lintel
3 Use mortar and slate or tile packing to hold lintel level
4 To make opening in cavity wall, remove bricks from each leaf carefully
5a Make fan duct lining using battens
5b Or using plastic angle strip

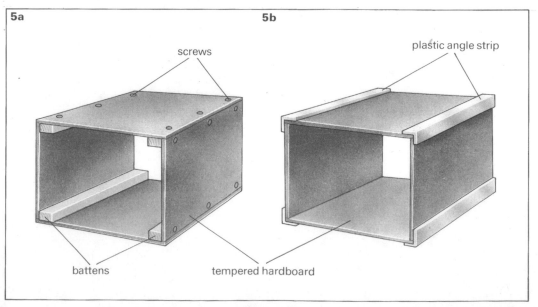

5a

screws

5b

plastic angle strip

battens

tempered hardboard

which is free from splits or large knots and will be as thick as the wall thickness. In most cases a serving hatch is made in a single brick wall, in which case the lintel will be 114mm (4½in) thick to match the thickness of the bricks. Two lintels can be used side by side for a double wall, regardless of whether it is a solid or cavity wall. The depth of the lintel should match the thickness of the bricks – that is 75mm (3in).

Fit the lintel into the slot which has been cut, checking the ends rest on sufficient brickwork at each side of the opening. Use pieces of tile or slate to pack under the lintel so it is level and wedged in place. Cement the lintel in place using a fairly stiff mortar mix of one part cement to three parts sand. Bricks or blocks above the opening can be refitted with a similar mix. With a block wall there is often a narrow gap above the lintel; this must be filled with bricks or cut blocks.

It is now quite safe to remove the bricks or blocks beneath the lintel and so form your opening.

Extractor fan opening
Most of the methods used to make an opening for a serving hatch also apply to an opening for an extractor fan; however the latter type of opening is smaller and invariably made in an outer, double-leaf wall. In modern houses the outer wall will be the cavity type, with two single block or brick leaves with a cavity between them. In older houses the wall will be of 230mm (or 9in) thick brickwork.
Warning When making an opening in a cavity wall it is important not to let debris fall into the cavity since this could bridge the cavity and allow moisture to penetrate to the inside wall.

Make the opening by working from each face of the wall in turn towards the centre; this way a neat part-opening will be made on the exposed face of each leaf of wall without any debris falling into the cavity, which could have resulted if the cold chisel broke through. When the opening has been made part-way through each leaf, use a long masonry drill bit to make a hole right through both leaves of the wall. You can use this hole as a reference point to ensure the openings align when continuing work from each side; chisel the remaining brick away carefully.

Stud partition wall opening
This type of wall consists of timber frames normally surfaced with plaster, which may be in the form of plasterboard sheets or the traditional lath and plaster. In both cases the opening must be made between the timber studs, which are the pieces of timber fixed vertically between the floor and ceiling.

The studs are fixed 400 or 600mm (or 16 or 24in) apart, according to the thickness of plasterboard or plaster between them; in most cases part of one stud will have to be removed so a sufficiently wide opening can be formed.

When you have decided on the approximate position of the opening, remove the plaster; use a hammer and bolster chisel in the case of a lath and plaster wall and a sharp trimming knife or pad saw in the case of plasterboard. It may be necessary to adjust the opening position so it falls somewhere between two studs. After trimming back, it is important to ensure any remaining plaster is still supported by these studs. If there are any noggings (horizontal timbers) across the opening position, you can remove them by knocking them out with a heavy hammer.

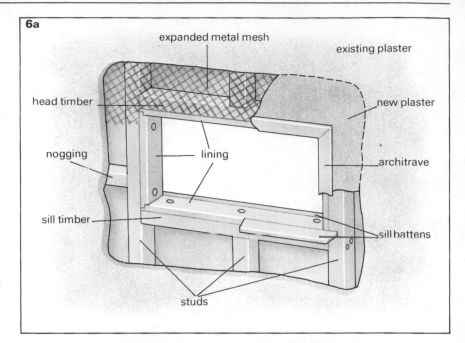

6a To form hatch in timber stud partition, make opening between studs and fit head and sill timbers; finish off surface with expanded metal mesh and plaster and line edges with timber architrave
6b To form smaller hatch in timber stud partition, use secondary stud between head and sill timbers
7 For brick wall opening make timber lining using rebate joints (**inset**); hold lining firmly in hole with folding wedges
8a Hinge doors, fitting stops round opening
8b Or fit doors on sliding tracks
9 Alternative method of finishing hatch in timber stud partition

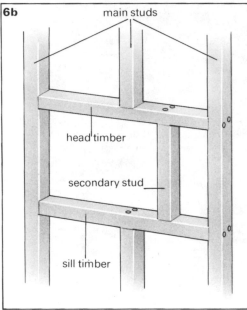

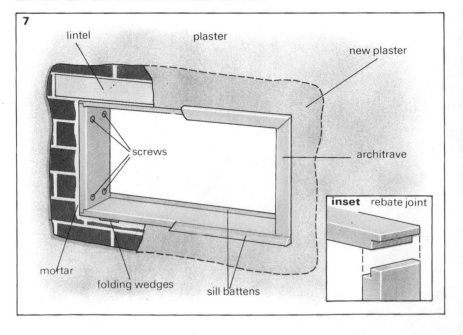

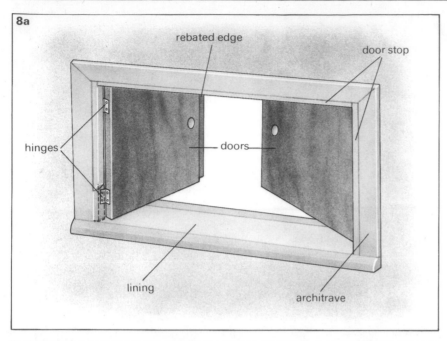

8a

hinges

rebated edge

door stop

doors

lining

architrave

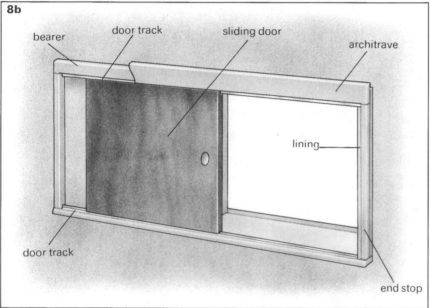

8b

bearer

door track

sliding door

architrave

lining

door track

end stop

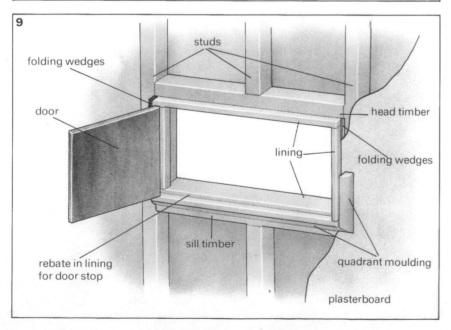

9

folding wedges

studs

door

head timber

lining

folding wedges

rebate in lining for door stop

sill timber

quadrant moulding

plasterboard

Where a stud falls across the opening, it must be sawn away at the top and bottom of the opening. The bead and sill timbers for the opening are nailed to the cut ends of the stud and to the outer studs to frame the opening. These pieces should be cut from 75×50mm (3×2in) timber or from a size to match the existing timbers in the framework. Check the head and sill timbers are level before fixing them.

If the size of the opening you want is not as wide as the space between the outer studs, you will have to fit a secondary vertical stud between the head and sill timbers.

Use plasterboard or plaster over expanded metal mesh to make good the wall surface around the opening you have created; you can then fit the lining timbers and finish the hatch, as described below.

Lining the opening

Missing or broken bricks at the sides of the opening should be replaced and the new ones fixed with mortar; you do not need to achieve a really smooth finish.

When a small window is being fitted, the frame itself forms the lining. With an opening for an extractor fan, the hole is lined with the duct supplied with the fan; alternatively a lining can be made with sheets of tempered hardboard or with sheets of a fire-retardant, moisture-resistant material composed of a lime cement mixture reinforced with asbestos fibres. The sheets are formed into a simple box, with timber battens or plastic angle strips used to join the edges.

Place the duct or made-up lining in the wall and pack the gap between the duct and the wall opening with mortar.

With a serving hatch, the door can be hinged to a timber lining and a seal formed by fitting battens to the sides and head. The lining timber should be 25mm (1in) thick and the same width as the wall, including the depth of the plaster on each side. Make up the lining timbers into a rectangular frame, using rebate joints.

The lining should be a tight fit in the hole; hold it firm using folding wedges. You must make sure the sill piece is level and the lining is square – by checking the diagonals are equal. Screw and plug the lining to the wall, pack the gaps around the lining with mortar and make good the surrounding plaster.

Nail a timber architrave around the opening to hide the joint between the lining and the wall. For a really neat finish tack battens to each side of the sill so it appears wider than the side pieces (jambs) and supports the architrave.

The serving hatch can be sealed with single or double doors. These can be hinged at each side, in which case a 25×12mm ($1 \times \frac{1}{2}$in) batten must be fitted around the opening to act as a door stop. Alternatively the door or doors can be hung on a sliding track.

Timber stud partitions

If you own an older property, it is quite possible some rooms may be too large for present day needs – and very expensive to heat. One answer is to install a simple timber stud partition, which consists of a sturdy timber framework covered on each side with wallboards. Tapered edge plasterboard is normally used to cover the frame, but other types of board may also be used; these will be covered later in the book. The vertical pieces of the frame are known as studs and the horizontal pieces between are noggings.

The timber stud partition, which stands between an existing floor and ceiling, usually divides a room and is known as a non-loadbearing partition. Although the structure is of lightweight timber, it will be necessary in some cases to submit plans of the proposed work to the local authority for approval under the Building Regulations; always check this before you start work.

A partition with one layer of 12.7mm ($\frac{1}{2}$in) thick plasterboard on both sides of the frame will give acceptable sound insulation each side for normal domestic purposes and has a fire resistance rating of 30 minutes. By adding to the density of the partition you can improve both sound insulation and fire resistance; two layers of plasterboard each side will reduce sound transmission considerably and increase fire resistance to 60 minutes. You can

achieve still further sound insulation by fixing 25mm (1in) glass fibre blanket inside the cavity of the framework.

For optimum sound insulation it is necessary to seal all cracks and air passages between rooms; pack large cavities such as the space behind skirtings with glass fibre blanket and seal gaps between plasterboards and between plasterboard and existing walls with a proprietary wall filler.

Designing a partition
A basic partition is taken straight across a room; usually a door is built at one end because this saves a lot of unnecessary alteration work – as long as you are prepared to have access to one room through another. However, it is not too difficult to design a partition which has two new doors and a small lobby; you lose a little floor space, but each room will have its own door. The lobby can be lit with a small fan light window above each of the doors or you can fit glazed doors with roller blinds for privacy. Another alternative is to build a plain partition and form a new doorway in an existing wall.

Sometimes you may find it is not necessary to take the partition right across the room; by building it only part of the way across, you can form an alcove – ideal for a baby's cot in the parent's bed-

1 By building a partition with a door at one end you can minimize alterations, but access to one room will be through the other
2 You can design the partition to give completely separate rooms by including two new doors and building a lobby
3 A bathroom can be divided to make a separate WC/shower room; if this means one section will be without a window, ventilation must be provided

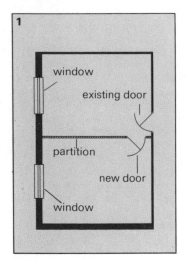
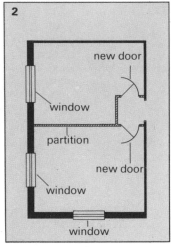
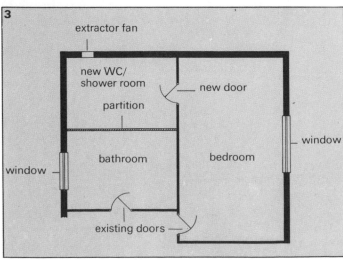
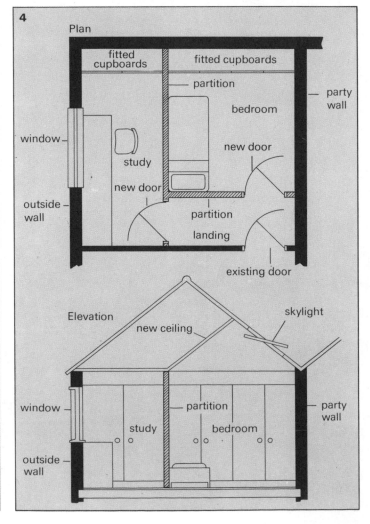

room, for a dining area or a shower cubicle. In this case you only fix one end stud to the existing wall; take extra care to ensure the head (ceiling) and sole (floor) plates of the frame are securely fixed.

Bedroom partition If a large room is to be divided to form two bedrooms, you must have a window in each room which opens direct to the outside air; you may need to form a new window in an external wall or to break into the loft space and fit a skylight which can be cord-operated for ventilation.

Bathroom partition Showers or bathrooms do not require external windows which open for venti-lation; you could have artificial lighting and mechanical ventilation, such as a wall-mounted or ducted extractor fan discharging directly to the outside. Bear in mind that plasterboard partitions used in shower cubicles must be tiled.

Borrowed lights These internal windows, which are fitted into the top of a partition, allow light to pass from a room with an external window to the other side of the partition. They are useful for shower partitions and are normally glazed with obscured glass; they can be double-glazed to increase sound insulation. It is usual to keep borrowed lights above head height, from about 2m (6ft 7in) up to the ceiling.

Serving hatch You can easily incorporate a serving hatch into a stud partition; it can be built anywhere in the frame and is lined with planed timber in the same way as a door or window opening. This has been covered earlier in the book.

Electrics Wall light points, light switches and socket outlets can be fitted into the frame before the plasterboard is fixed. You should ensure any holes drilled through studs for conduit or cable runs are placed dead centre so there is no danger of nails piercing the cable as the plasterboard is fitted. If switch or outlet points fall between the main studs and noggings, fit extra studs or noggings to support the fixings or buy self-supporting fixings.

Plumbing Pipework can also be concealed within the partition; you must fit the main pipe runs before the plasterboard is fixed. Fit extra noggings or studs to support heavy fittings such as wash-basin support brackets and make sure pipes are fitted on the centre lines of the studs.

Making the frame
Once you have decided upon the wall panelling to be used and taken delivery of it, you can take exact measurements directly from the panels so you can place studs and noggings accurately at the edges; this will ensure trimming of panels is kept to a minimum. It is usual to use 2400 × 1200mm (8 × 4ft) sheets of tapered edge plasterboard, which give a smooth and continuous wall finish suitable for any decoration once the joints have been filled. If the partition is to include a door, you should buy it before starting so the doorway will be made exactly to size.

Timber size If you are fitting plasterboard panels, use 75 × 50mm (3 × 2in) unplaned softwood for the frame if the floor-to-ceiling height is under 2.4m (or 8ft) and 100 × 50mm (4 × 2in) timber if the floor-to-ceiling height is between 2.4 and 3.7m (or 8–12ft). A ceiling above 3.7m (12ft) is rare;

4 Where a large bedroom is divided into two, there must be a window direct to the outside in each room; this can be provided by fitting a new sloping ceiling and inserting a skylight

5 The main components of a partition are the head plate, sole plate, main studs and end studs; additional support is provided by intermediate studs and noggings. Extra noggings can be used to support power points or light switches

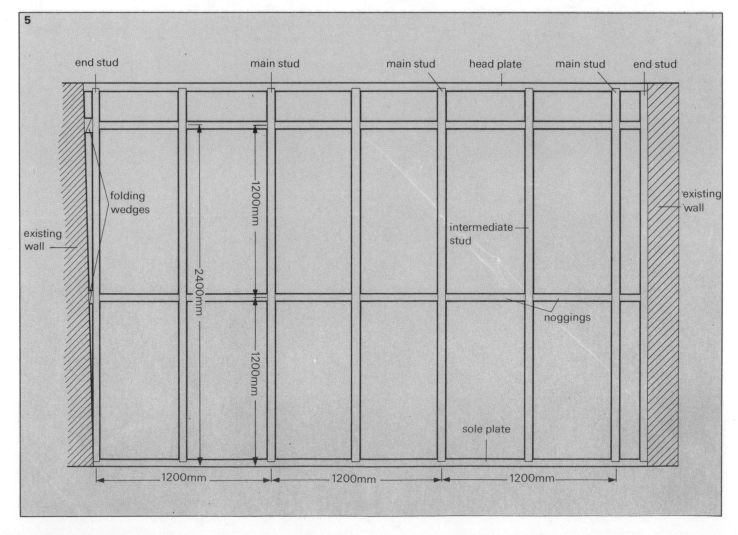

5
end stud   main stud   main stud   head plate   main stud end stud

folding wedges

existing wall

1200mm

2400mm

1200mm

1200mm

existing wall

intermediate stud

noggings

sole plate

1200mm   1200mm   1200mm

6

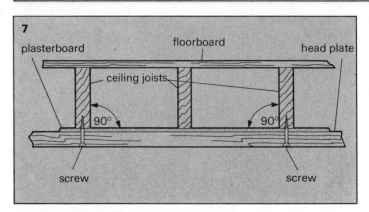

joists

75 x 50mm headplate

folding wedges

75 x 50mm door head

75 x 50mm door posts

75 x 50mm noggings

75 x 50mm studs

plasterboard

joists

75 x 19mm architrave

100 x 38mm door lining

75 x 50mm sole plate

if you have a room this high, consult a wall panelling manufacturer for suitable timber sizes.

Head plate Remove any ceiling cornice which will be in the way when you come to fit the head plate of the frame. To fix the head plate securely to the ceiling you will have to determine which way the ceiling joists run. If the line of the proposed partition runs across the joists, it can be fixed anywhere. If it runs parallel to the joists, you can move the partition to come under a joist or else fit 75 × 50mm (3 × 2in) mounting blocks between joists. Fix the blocks close to each end of the partition and at approximately 800mm (or 32in) intervals; they should be a snug fit between joists and in contact with the ceiling.

You may be able to see the joists by going into the loft space or, if there is a room above, by looking at the run of the floorboards (at right-angles to the joists). If you are not able to locate the joists from above, you will have to probe through the ceiling with a bradawl; once you have located one joist, bear in mind the usual spacing between joists is roughly 400–460mm (about 16–18in). Ideally the joists should run at right-angles to the head plate. Fix it to them by drilling and screwing through the plate into every other joist using 89 or 102mm (3½ or 4in) screws; do not use nails, because they will disturb the plaster.

If you have a lath and plaster ceiling, it is best to remove the portion of ceiling between joists where the head plate is to run and replace it with a strip of plasterboard. After the partition is finished you will have to replaster the portion of ceiling. Once you have located and prepared the joists for fixing, adding mounting blocks if required, cut the head plate to length and temporarily fix it in place with two or three screws.

Sole plate It is essential the partition is vertical, so use a chalked plumb line to mark vertical lines from

7

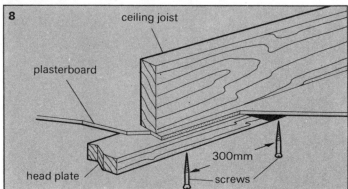

plasterboard

floorboard

head plate

ceiling joists

90°

90°

screw

screw

8

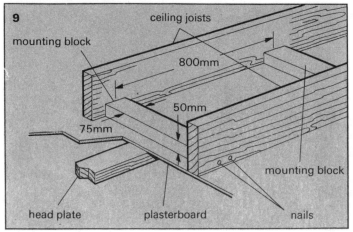

ceiling joist

plasterboard

head plate

300mm

screws

9

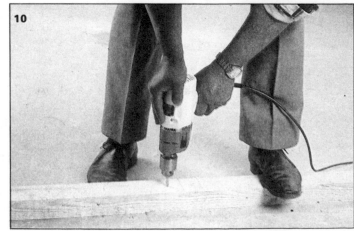

ceiling joists

mounting block

800mm

50mm

75mm

head plate

plasterboard

mounting block

nails

10

6 When building a doorway into a partition, the door head must fit into housings at each side of the opening; if both studs are truly vertical, you can fix the door lining directly to the framework. Cover the join between the plasterboard and the door with an architrave
7 Ideally the head plate should be fixed at right-angles to the ceiling joists
8 If this is not possible, fix the head plate so it runs along a joist
9 Where the head plate must run between joists, fix mounting blocks between the joists; the blocks should be a snug fit and in contact with the ceiling
10 When fixing the sole plate to a solid floor, drill the plate and the floor to take screws and plugs or expanding bolts
11 To measure the length of each stud, place two battens between the head and sole plates and mark where they overlap; you can then lay the battens onto the studding timber and accurately mark the ends for cutting
12 The position of studs at a corner
13 The position of studs at a 'T' junction

ceiling to floor on the walls at each end of the head plate. Chalk a line across the floor to line up with those on the walls; this is the position of the sole plate. This plate takes very little weight once the partition is finished, so there is no need to fix mounting blocks between floor joists if the sole plate position is mid-way between two floor joists. But the ideal position for a sole plate is at right-angles to or directly above a floor joist. Cut the plate to fit; if the partition is to include doorways, you can either cut them out of the plate now or saw the piece out later on. Temporarily fix the plate to the floor with nails. Cut a length of straight timber to fit between the ceiling and floor and use this with a spirit level against the sides of the head and sole plates to check once again they are correctly positioned to give a vertical wall.

End studs The studs at the ends of the frame must be located with a spirit level to ensure they are vertical; it is likely the side walls in an older house will be out of true. Mark the centre lines of the end studs onto the sole and head plates. If the end studs are not hard against the existing walls, you can trim the plasterboard later to fit (intermediate studs will be positioned to allow for this adjustment).

Main studs If you are using plasterboard, the vertical studs must be fixed at 600mm (or 24in) intervals if the board is 12.7mm ($\frac{1}{2}$in) thick and at 400mm (or 16in) intervals if the board is 9.5mm ($\frac{3}{8}$in) thick. Use the thicker board for a large partition because this will involve only a small increase in plasterboard costs and a considerable saving on timber costs. Assuming you are using 1200mm (47$\frac{1}{4}$in) wide sheets, mark onto the sole plate the centre line of a main stud 1155mm (44$\frac{1}{2}$in) along from the centre line of each stud. This will allow 45mm (1$\frac{3}{4}$in) to trim the sheet against an uneven wall. Mark the centre lines of subsequent studs at 1200mm (or 48in) intervals so the sheets

can be fixed without trimming and the studs will support their edges. Mark the main studs along the length of the partition; there will probably be a small gap to be filled with an offcut of board at the far end.

You can now mark in the centre lines of the intermediate studs – either 600mm (23$\frac{3}{4}$in) or 400mm (15$\frac{3}{4}$in) apart according to the thickness of the plasterboard you are using. Mark corresponding centre lines on the head plate and check again with a length of timber and a spirit level that each stud will be vertical. Studs at each side of a doorway must be sufficiently spaced to allow for the width of the door, the thickness of the door linings at each side and 4mm ($\frac{1}{16}$in) clearance.

Fixing studs You can butt-join the studs to the head and sole plate, but the partition will be stronger if you make simple housing joints for the studs. Remove the temporarily fixed head and sole plates and cut the housings across the full width of the plate to a depth of about 10mm ($\frac{3}{8}$in). The housings must be cut exactly over the centre lines you have already marked to enable the 50mm (2in) studding timber to fit smoothly into them. Screw the head plate permanently into place against the ceiling and fix the sole plate to the floor.

Use 69mm (2$\frac{3}{4}$in) screws if the sole plate is to be fixed to a timber floor (so there is no chance of damaging cables or pipes), inserting them at about 700mm (or 28in) intervals. For a solid floor, drill the sole plate and floor so the plate can be fixed with 89mm (3$\frac{1}{2}$in) screws and wall plugs or expanding bolts; insert the screws or bolts at about 800mm (or 32in) intervals. If the solid floor has only recently been laid, you should insert a strip of bitumen damp proof membrane under the sole plate to protect it as the concrete dries out.

Measure and cut each stud individually, because it is unlikely the floor and ceiling will be exactly

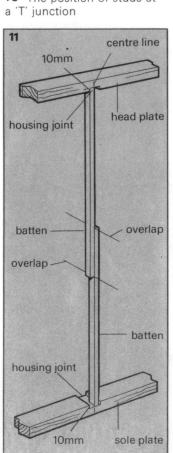

11
centre line
10mm
housing joint
head plate
batten
overlap
overlap
batten
housing joint
10mm
sole plate

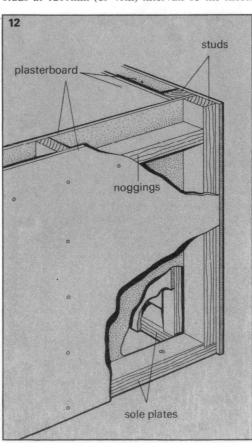

12
studs
plasterboard
noggings
sole plates

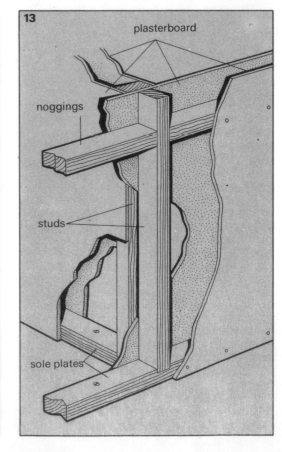

13
plasterboard
noggings
studs
sole plates

parallel. Use two battens to measure the length between the two housings and mark where they overlap so you can lay the battens onto the studding timber and accurately mark the ends for cutting. Cut the studs and coat their ends with adhesive before sliding them into place in the housings; you may need to use a mallet to ease them in. Skew-nail them to the head and sole plates; if there is a danger of dislodging ceiling plaster, you can use screws instead of nails.

Give additional support to the end studs by drilling and plugging the existing wall in two or three places so 89mm (3½in) screws can be fitted. If the wall bows away from the stud, hold the stud firm with folding wedges or packing pieces between the stud and wall.

Fixing noggings These are to stiffen the frame and to prevent the studs from bowing; they are glued and skew-nailed between studs. Make sure they are a tight fit and position them at 1200mm (or 48in) intervals if you are using 2400mm (94½in) high (or more) plasterboard. For 1800mm (70¾in) sheets, fix the noggings at 900mm (or 36in), 1800mm (or 72in) and at 2700mm (or 108in) from the floor if the partition is sufficiently high for this third set of noggings.

Doorways The head plate of a doorway must be securely fitted into a simple housing cut into the studs at each side of the opening. It must be fitted at door height plus the thickness of the door lining and a 4mm clearance; use a spirit level to make sure the head is exactly level. If both studs on either side of the doorway are vertical, you can fix the door linings directly to the framework. If the framework is out of true, you should pack the linings with wedges to bring them square; to check they are square measure the diagonals, which should be equal.

Make the door linings from 38mm (1½in) door moulding of sufficient width to cover the thickness of the framework, plus the thickness of plaster-board on each side. Later on you should cover the joint between the plasterboard and the door with an architrave. If the lining is not a moulding incorporating a door stop, make one from 25mm (1in) timber and glue and nail a 25 × 13mm (1 × ½in) strip to form the stop.

You can position borrowed lights either above the door openings as fanlights or along the upper part of the partition. They are made in the same way as doorways; but if you require larger windows than there is space for between the studs, you will have to alter the framework beforehand. Make the frame from 100 × 50mm (4 × 2in) timber regardless of ceiling height if you intend to include borrowed lights; this will ensure the frame is strong enough. To double-glaze borrowed lights you should fix two panes of glass either side of a 75mm (3in) parting bead.

The end of a plasterboard partition which runs only part of the way across a room can be finished off with a piece of lining timber and two architraves.

Fitting plasterboard

Plasterboard sheets should always be carried on edge between two people and stored flat in a dry place. Do not stack them more than 1m (or 3ft) high. Tapered edge plasterboard has an ivory coloured surface and tapered long edges which, when fixed and jointed, give a smooth, flat surface ready for decoration.

Start fitting boards at an end wall. If you need to trim boards to fit between floor and ceiling, cut them 25mm (1in) shorter than the floor to ceiling height. Cut through the ivory face with a trimming knife, snap the board over a timber batten to break the plaster core and cut through the grey paper face.

Cut a block of timber to a triangular shape and use this to position the boards. Press the top of the board against the ceiling (ivory face outwards) and fix with plasterboard nails driven into the studs at 150mm (6in) intervals. The edges of the boards should be exactly central on the studs and the nails should be no closer than 13mm (½in) from the edge; nail the boards to the noggings as well. Drive the nails in so they are below the plasterboard surface, but make sure they do not tear the paper.

Fix the end board temporarily over the second-to-last board and, with a pencil held against a 1200mm (47¼in) long batten, scribe a line onto the board following the wall line. As long as you keep the batten level so the board is cut to this line, it will fit exactly against the wall.

Cover all joints with filler and reinforcing tape, following the manufacturer's instructions. Using a special jointing applicator, apply a thin band of joint filler into the joints. Cut the required length of joint tape and press it into the filler using a filling knife; make sure the tape is firmly embedded and free from pockets of air. Apply a second coat of filler level with the surface of the boards. Moisten a fine-textured sponge and wipe off surplus material

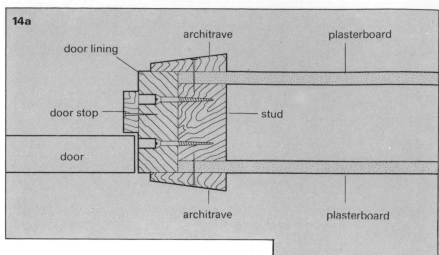

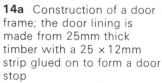

14a Construction of a door frame; the door lining is made from 25mm thick timber with a 25 ×12mm strip glued on to form a door stop
14b Alternatively you can make the lining from moulding incorporating a door stop
15a Detail of the door lining for a truly vertical frame
15b Detail of the door lining where the frame is out of true; use folding wedges to make the lining square

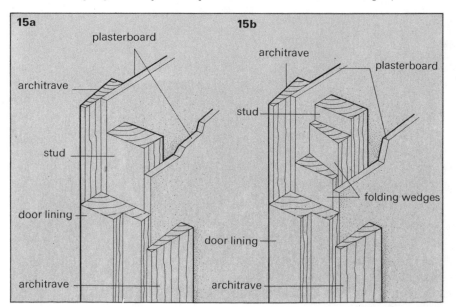

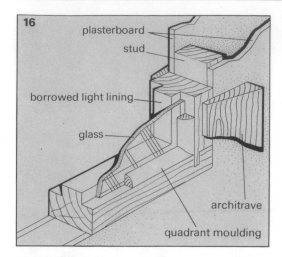

16 plasterboard
stud
borrowed light lining
glass
architrave
quadrant moulding

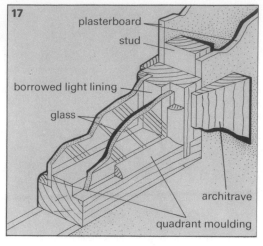

17 plasterboard
stud
borrowed light lining
glass
architrave
quadrant moulding

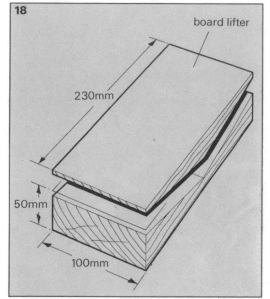

18 board lifter
230mm
50mm
100mm

16 You can build borrowed lights into a partition with the same method as for doorways
17 To double-glaze borrowed lights, fit one pane each side of a parting bead
18 Make a board lifter from a block of timber to help you position the sheets of plasterboard
19 To make sure the last board fits exactly to the wall, fix it temporarily over the last fixed board and, using a pencil and a batten cut to the width of a complete panel, trace the wall line onto the board; you can then cut the board to shape along the marked line
Filling joints between boards.
20 When all the boards are fixed, apply a band of joint filler to the taper between boards
21 Press lengths of joint tape firmly into the filler, then apply more filler on top
22 When filler sets, apply a thin layer of joint finish
23 Reinforce external angles with corner tape

from the edges of the joint; take care not to disturb the main filling. After about an hour the filler will have set, but not dried out; apply a thin layer of joint finish using the applicator supplied and feather out the edges with the dampened sponge. When the joint finish has set and dried hard, apply a second coat in a broad band.

After the joints have set and dried you can apply a thin slurry of joint finish over both board and joint with the sponge; this will even up any difference in surface texture. You can now fit skirtings and ceiling cove (as required) to match the existing room decorations.

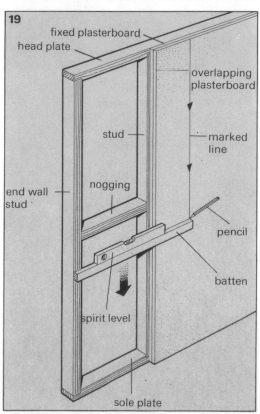

19 fixed plasterboard
head plate
overlapping plasterboard
stud
marked line
end wall stud
nogging
pencil
batten
spirit level
sole plate

20

21

22

23

Other methods

Although tapered edge plasterboard is normally used to cover the frame when putting up a timber stud partition, there are other materials that can be used to achieve a similar effect. There are other types of plasterboard available, as well as plywood, tongued and grooved panels, fibre building boards, chipboard and asbestos insulating boards. To reduce costs, or if you only want a temporary partition, it is worth considering fitting a single skin partition. Basically the savings are made in the quantity of timber battens or studs required for the job.

When planning a timber stud partition you should make sure the structure will comply with Building Regulations, particularly with regard to fire. If you are changing the use of a building (converting a house into flats for example), the regulations must be observed and great care should be taken to choose a suitable cladding material. Wood-based sheet materials can make a predictable contribution to the fire-resistance of a structure. As far as surface spread of flame characteristics are concerned, Building Regulations may require the use of boards treated with a flame-retardant or the application of a flame-retardant paint or coating. Further information can be obtained from the relevant advisory bodies or your local building control officer.

Alternative cladding

The timber stud partition previously described is clad with tapered-edge plasterboard; once the joints have been taped and filled, the result is a smooth, flat wall ready to be painted with a plasterboard primer and afterwards decorated with any type of wall covering or painted direct. The primer will seal the ivory surface of the plasterboard and allow greater coverage and a more uniform texture to be obtained from paint; it also allows wallpaper

Square-edge plasterboard You can use this type of plasterboard to cover a conventional timber stud partition. Fix the edges of the boards so you leave a 1.5mm (or $\frac{1}{16}$ in) gap between each one; the joints are finished off with strips of barbed T-section plastic extrusion. The extrusions, which are held in place with impact adhesive, are also available in F and L-section strips for external angles and smaller L-section strips for internal angles. The strips are finished in black, white or light grey and can be bought from plasterboard suppliers. When fitting boards, ensure fixing nails are within 6mm ($\frac{1}{4}$in) of the edge of the plasterboard so their heads will be covered by the extrusion. You can form an attractive panelled effect with square-edge plasterboard by gluing or pinning cover strips of wood, metal or plastic over the joints; the strips can be plain or patterned for extra effect.

Although not really intended for this purpose, you can use square-edge boards to produce a flush wall surface. Fit them so there is a gap of about 3mm ($\frac{1}{8}$in) between edges and rub down all cut edges with fine glasspaper to remove any paper burr; fill nail holes and the joints with wall filler. When the filler is dry, rub the plasterboard smooth with an abrasive block and add another coating to fill low spots on the surface. You can reinforce the joint, to prevent it cracking in the future, by covering it with plasterboard joint tape bedded into joint

Above By installing a timber stud partition you can make a hallway, divide one large room into two or simply form an alcove

finish compound; this should be feathered out in a band 150mm (6in) wide using a dampened sponge. When this has dried, apply a second coat of joint finish in a 200–250mm (or 8–10in) band, again feathering out the edges.

Bevelled-edge plasterboard This type of board can also be used to clad timber studs. V-joints, which are formed when the boards are fixed, are intended as decorative features. Finish the partition by simply filling nail holes and the base of the V-joint with joint filler, wiping off any excess with a dampened sponge.

Plywood This will give a partition strength and is easy to decorate; often the partition is double-faced with plywood and partially glazed to provide borrowed lights. Usually 6mm (or $\frac{1}{4}$in) thick plywood in 1200 × 2400mm (or 4 × 8ft) sheets is suitable. Studs should support sheet edges and intermediate studs should be fixed at 400mm (or 16in) intervals; one row of noggings between the floor and ceiling will be sufficient. Nail the sheets to the framework at 150mm (6in) intervals, keeping the nails at least 13mm ($\frac{1}{2}$in) from the edges of the sheets. Punch nail heads below the surface, fill all holes and rub down with an abrasive block before

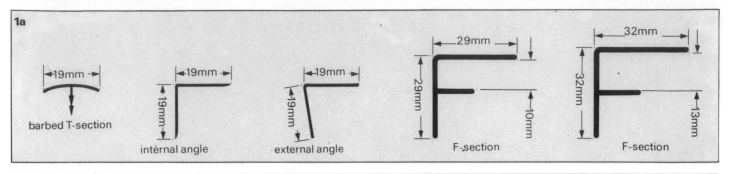

1a barbed T-section | internal angle | external angle | F-section | F-section

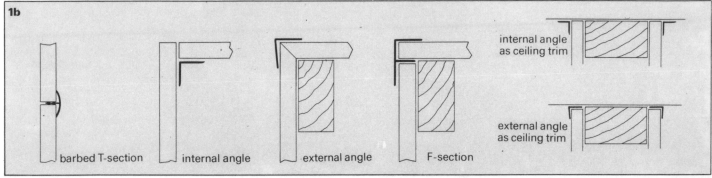

1b barbed T-section | internal angle | external angle | F-section | internal angle as ceiling trim | external angle as ceiling trim

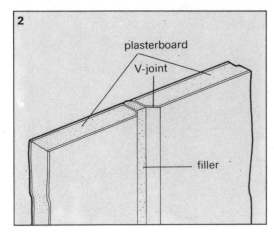

2 plasterboard / V-joint / filler

decorating. You can cover the joints with wood, plastic or metal strips or you can leave a 3–6mm ($\frac{1}{8}$–$\frac{1}{4}$in) gap between sheets; this will give a flat, panelled effect after the partition is painted. It is important in all cases to plan the work so you leave equal size panels at each end of the partition.

Tongued and grooved panels These plywood panels can be used in 1500mm (or 60in) lengths, 400, 500 and 600mm (or 16, 20 and 24in) widths and 12mm (or $\frac{1}{2}$in) thicknesses. You can fit them vertically or horizontally and make a feature of the V-joint between panels. With plywood of this thickness supports can be up to 600mm (or 24in) apart. To improve sound insulation through any double-skin plywood partition, fill the cavity with acoustic material such as mineral wool.

Fibre building boards Because they are dense, smooth and easily fitted, fibre building boards are ideal material for cladding a timber stud partition. Use standard and tempered hardboard or the thicker, high density (HM) medium boards. They give a good standard of sound insulation; remember, the thicker and denser the board, the better the sound insulation. A layer of mineral wool quilting in the cavity of a hollow partition will improve sound insulation still further. In most cases, hardboards and high density medium boards satisfy Building Regulations with regard to surface

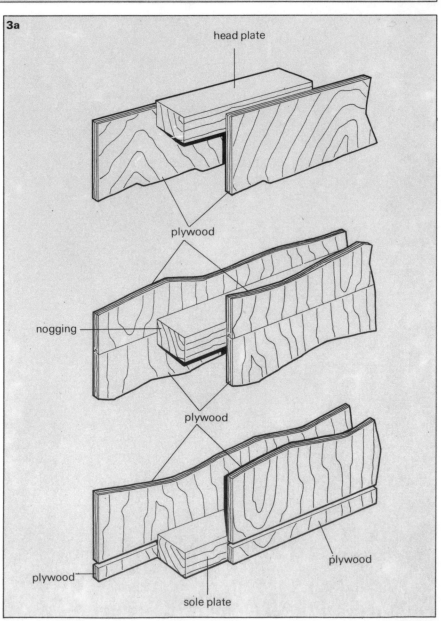

3a head plate / plywood / nogging / plywood / plywood / sole plate

Previous page
1a Different types of plastic extrusion for finishing joints in plasterboard cladding
1b Methods of applying different types of plastic extrusion
2 Forming V-joint in bevelled-edge plasterboard
3a Cutaway of double skin ply-faced partition, showing position of boards and framework

3b Cutaway of glazed partition, showing position and fitting of glass
4 Filling joint in hardboard cladding before wallpapering
5 Staggering joints when fitting chipboard cladding
6 Wood strip used to cover joints in asbestos cladding

spread of flame, but you can achieve an even higher level of resistance with flame-retardant boards or with flame-retardant paint. Your local building control officer will advise you.

Standard and tempered hardboard sheets are available in thicknesses of 3–6mm (or $\frac{1}{8}$–$\frac{1}{4}$in). HM medium board, also called panelboard, is available in thicknesses of 9–12mm (or $\frac{3}{8}$–$\frac{1}{2}$in). Most boards are supplied undecorated and have a hard, shiny brown surface on one or both sides; predecorated boards with a wide range of finishes are also available.

Before assembly, condition undecorated boards by standing them in the room where they are to be fitted; use blocks between them to let air circulate over all surfaces. The boards should be left at least two days before fixing; this enables them to achieve a moisture content in balance with that of the surrounding air and prevents them from bowing or buckling after they have been fixed.

The spacing of the studs will depend on the thickness and type of board you are using; for hardboard of 3, 4.8 and 6mm (or $\frac{1}{8}$, $\frac{3}{16}$ and $\frac{1}{4}$in) thickness, the maximum stud spacings are 406, 508 and 610mm (16, 20 and 24in) respectively. For medium board of 6mm (or $\frac{1}{4}$in) and 9mm (or $\frac{3}{8}$in) thickness, the

maximum stud spacing is 406mm (16in); for 12mm (or $\frac{1}{2}$in) and 18mm (or $\frac{3}{4}$in) board, the maximum spacing is 610mm (24in).

You can either nail the boards to the frame or fix them with impact adhesive; nails should be spaced at 100mm (4in) intervals approximately 13mm ($\frac{1}{2}$in) from the edges. Fix the boards to the intermediate studs at 150mm (6in) intervals. It is generally best to feature the joints between boards by fitting hardboard, timber, metal or plastic cover strips. Alternatively you can form a V-joint by bevelling the edges or make a feature of the joint by leaving a gap of about 13mm ($\frac{1}{2}$in) between the boards. Paint the background to match or contrast with the finished colour. Sand the edges of the boards so they taper to make a flush joint for wallpapering and fix the boards so there is a 3mm ($\frac{1}{8}$in) gap between each. Press cellulose filler into the joint, lay reinforcing scrim tape into place and smooth more filler over the top. When the joint has hardened you can sand it flat. Seal fibre building boards with hardboard primer before wallpapering to ensure the board is not damaged when you remove the wallpaper to redecorate.

Chipboard Chipboard is available in a wide variety of finishes. You can produce a textured surface

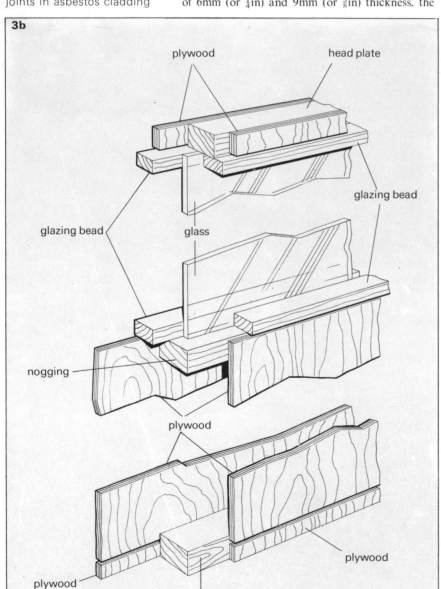

3b

plywood

head plate

glazing bead

glazing bead

glass

glazing bead

nogging

plywood

plywood

plywood

sole plate

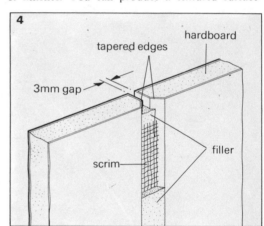

4

tapered edges

hardboard

3mm gap

scrim

filler

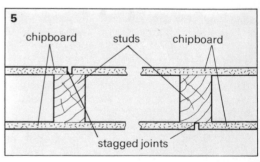

5

chipboard

studs

chipboard

stagged joints

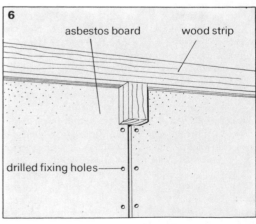

6

asbestos board

wood strip

drilled fixing holes

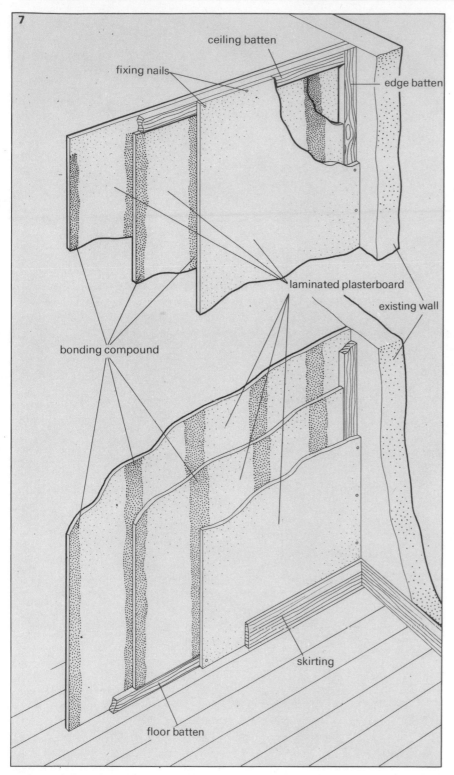

with standard chipboard, with medium to large particles on the surface, by applying emulsion paint which will swell the surface chips. Clear sealers will give a cork-like effect or you can prime and wallpaper the boards. You can also wallpaper chipboard which has a fine surface chip or finish it with matt or semi-gloss paint. Use melamine-faced chipboard if you require a hard-wearing, washable decorative surface and vinyl-faced chipboard for a medium wear, washable decorative surface. Chipboard is also available in natural wood veneer, textile-surfaced and painted finishes.

Chipboard is not generally as resistant to fire as plasterboard, although it does conform with the fire resistance requirements of the Building Regulations for domestic partitions. Apply fire-retardant paint to improve the surface spread of flame; your local building control officer will advise you.

For most purposes, 12–18mm (or $\frac{1}{2}$–$\frac{3}{4}$in) chipboard can be nailed, screwed or glued to a conventional 75 × 50mm (3 × 2in) timber stud frame; the perimeters of the boards must be supported by the frame, with additional intermediate studs. These studs should be placed at up to 610mm (24in) intervals if you are using boards up to 15mm (or $\frac{5}{8}$in) thick; place them at 750mm (or 30in) intervals if the boards are 18mm (or $\frac{3}{4}$in) and above.

Asbestos Asbestos insulating boards have good surface spread of flame characteristics, but you must be very careful not to inhale the dust when working with the boards. Seal them with emulsion paint or alkali-resistant primer after the partition is fixed. The sheets most widely available, 6mm (or $\frac{1}{4}$in) thick, are 2130 × 910mm (or 7 × 3ft) or 2440 × 1220 (or 8 × 4ft). Position studs at a maximum of 610mm (24in) intervals and drill holes for the fixing nails to prevent the sheets cracking. Use galvanized nails and place them no less than 13mm ($\frac{1}{2}$in) from the edges of the boards and spaced 300mm (12in) apart. Cover joints with 50mm (2in) wide timber, plastic or metal strips glued into place or screwed through to the timber framework.

7 Cutaway of single skin partition using laminated plasterboard. **8a** Plan of doorway using rebated frame to finish single skin partition. **8b** Plan of doorway using built-up frame to finish single skin partition.

Following page
9 Nailing first layer of laminated plasterboard to sole plate. **10** Skew-nailing adjoining laminated plasterboard to ensure first layer is aligned. **11** Pressing middle layer of board onto bonding compound. **12** Aligning outer layers of board. **13** Cutaway of single skin partition using box-section plasterboard

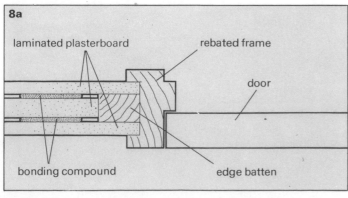
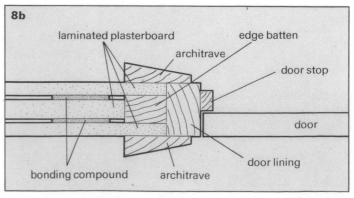

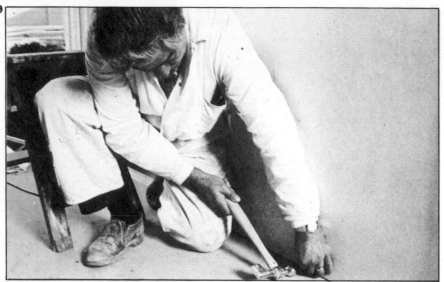

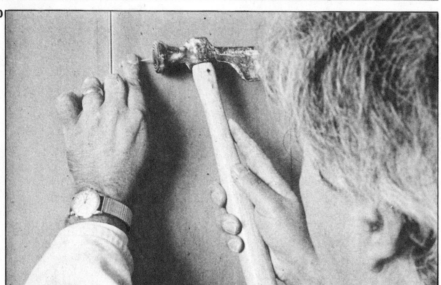

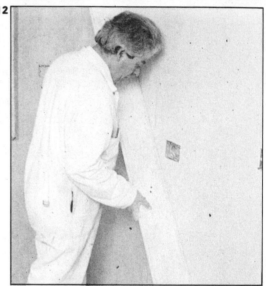

Single skin partitions

The timber framing is a considerable expense in the building of a stud partition; one way of reducing the cost is to erect a single skin partition which will require fewer timber battens or studs. This is also an advisable alternative if you require a temporary partition which can be fitted easily and quickly. It is well worth making comparative costings.

Laminated partition This type consists of three layers of plasterboard. Timber is only required round the perimeter of the partition and round doorways or other openings. If your ceiling is up to 2600mm (or 8ft 6in) high, a 50mm (2in) thick partition consisting of 13mm ($\frac{1}{2}$in) thick wallboards on each side of a 19mm (or $\frac{3}{4}$in) plasterboard plank will be suitable for most domestic purposes. For ceilings up to 3200mm (or 10ft 6in), the partition must be 65mm (or 2$\frac{1}{2}$in) thick and consist of three layers of 19mm (or $\frac{3}{4}$in) thick plasterboard plank. However, at this height and using this form of construction, the partition must not exceed 7300mm (or 24ft) in length – this is unlikely to affect the majority of domestic installations.

Edge the partition with 38 × 25mm (or 1$\frac{1}{2}$ × 1in) battens and fix a batten between the floor and ceiling on each side of a door opening, with a head

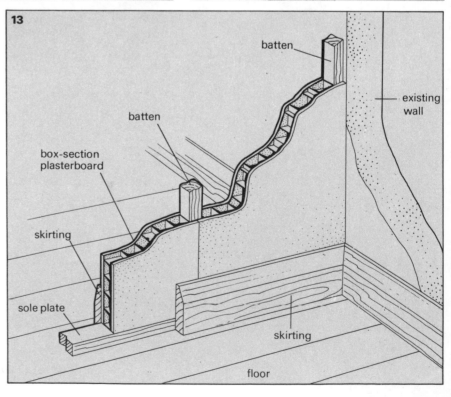

batten

existing wall

batten

box-section plasterboard

skirting

sole plate

skirting

floor

plate between. Finish doorways with a rebated door frame – or with frames built up from plain timber – and position pipe and cable runs, including socket and switch outlet boxes, along the centre line of the partition.

Fix the first layer of plaster wallboard or plank ivory face outwards to one side of the battens. Each 900mm (or 36in) wide wallboard is fixed with three 38mm (or 1½in) galvanized nails at the floor and ceiling; for 600mm (or 24in) wide plank, use two nails top and bottom. Apply plasterboard bonding compound to the grey surface of the first layer of board at 300mm (or 12in) intervals, in bands a minimum of 6mm (¼in) thick, with a nylon handbrush. The middle layer boards (square-edged with two grey faces) are now pressed into place; starting the middle section with a 150mm (or 6in) wide board will ensure joints between the boards are staggered. Apply more bands of bonding compound to the outer surface of this layer and press the second outer layer into place with the ivory face outwards. Nail these boards top and bottom, as for the first layer. Finally, fill nail holes and finish joints and angles as for tapered-edge plasterboard partitions.

Box-section (Paramount) panel This easily erected, lightweight partition consists of a cellular core of stiff paper with a layer of plasterboard sheet on each side. This forms a rigid panel unit which is fixed to a simple timber frame to form the partition. The panels are available in thicknesses of 50mm, 57 and 63mm (or 2in, 2¼ and 2½in). Use the 50mm (or 2in) panel for ceiling heights up to 2350mm (or 7ft 9in) and the 57mm (or 2¼in) panel for heights up to 2700mm (or 9ft). These partitions offer fire resistance for half-an-hour; the 63mm (or 2½in) panel should be used for partitions up to 3600mm (or 12ft) high.

To fix the 50mm (or 2in) partition, fit 30 × 19mm (or 1¼ × ¾in) timber battens to the ceiling and walls where the partition is to run and fit a sole plate of 50 × 19mm (or 2 × ¾in) minimum section to the floor. Place the first panel around the ceiling batten so it rests on the sole plate and push it along so one edge engages with the wall batten; use a fine-tooth saw to cut the panel to fit against a wall which is not true. Nail a batten to the sole plate to bridge the joints between panels. Break away the core on the exposed edge of the first panel with a claw hammer and fit a 30 × 37mm (or 1¼ × 1½in) joint batten halfway across the joint; this batten is held with nails at 230mm (or 9in) intervals through each side of the panels. Break away the core of the next panel and fit it into place over the other half of the joint batten. Repeat this procedure until the partition is complete.

To fix 57 and 63mm (or 2¼ and 2½in) partitions, use 37 × 19mm (or 1½ × ¾in) wall and ceiling battens with 37 × 37mm (or 1½ × 1½in) joint battens. Sole plates should be 57 or 63 × 19mm.

Provide a fixing for a door frame by fitting a joint batten flush with the panel edges. Fix a 19mm (or ¾in) batten at the top at each side to a spandrel panel, which fills the gap between the top of the door and the ceiling. Cable runs can be incorporated by using a hollow rod or length of conduit to pierce the core of each panel before installation. Make cut-outs for switch boxes and insert timber plugs on each side of the hole so the box can be secured with screws. Battens can be driven into the core if you need heavy fixings; for light loads use the normal cavity fixings.

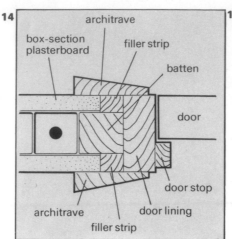

14

architrave

box-section plasterboard

filler strip

batten

door

door stop

architrave

door lining

filler strip

15

16

17

18

19

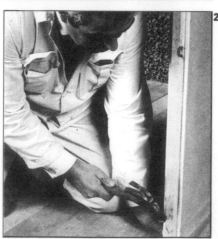

20

21

22a **22b** **22c**

head plate

blockboard

sole plate

ceiling

softwood channel

floor

head plate

blockboard

sole plate

aluminium angle

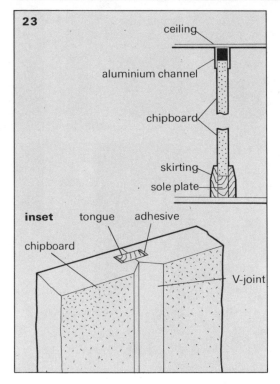

23

ceiling

aluminium channel

chipboard

skirting

sole plate

inset tongue adhesive

chipboard

V-joint

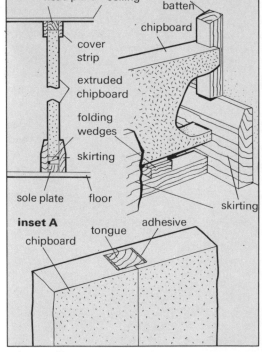

24 head plate ceiling wall batten **inset B**

chipboard

cover strip

extruded chipboard

folding wedges

skirting

sole plate floor

skirting

inset A

chipboard tongue adhesive

Previous page
14 Plan of doorway using built-up frame to finish box-section plasterboard partition
15 Joint batten fixed for spandrel panel
16 Fixing spandrel panel
17 Fixing first panel to sole plate and wall batten
18 Inserting base fixing plug into first panel
19 Inserting joint batten into first panel
20 Skew-nailing joint batten to base fixing plug
21 Installing second panel

22a Section through simple blockboard partition
22b Section through blockboard partition in softwood frame; space above top of board in head plate groove must be at least as deep as sole plate groove
22c Section through blockboard partition with aluminium angle; fix head and sole plate angles on one side of board, then fit board and other two angles
23 Section through chipboard partition, held at ceiling with aluminium U-section channel and at floor with timber sole plate; joints can be strengthened by inserting tongues at edges (**inset**)
24 Section through extruded chipboard partition; tongues are inserted for tight joints (**inset A**) and board is fixed to battens at walls (**inset B**)

Square-edge panels can be butt-joined and finished with plastic, metal or timber joint trims; with tapered-edge panels, make flush joints.

Blockboard You can easily make lightweight single skin partitions from blockboard and only minimal timber framing is required. It is best to seal vertical joints between boards with timber, plastic or metal strips – or groove the boards along the edges so a plywood or timber tongue can be inserted.

Chipboard You can make a more temporary partition, if sound insulation is not a problem, with chipboard panels at least 22mm (or ⅞in) thick. The panels can be held at the walls and ceiling with an aluminium U-section channel; a timber sole plate is fixed to the floor and the joint is covered with timber skirtings on both sides. Joints between boards are covered with finishing strips – or you

can groove the edges to take plywood or asbestos tongues, which are glued into place.

For a more solid single skin partition, extruded boards are available with either solid or, more commonly, hollow cores. These boards are often supplied faced or veneered in a variety of finishes; their long edges are usually grooved to enable easy fixing.

To fix an extruded chipboard partition, fix timber head and sole plates and battens onto adjacent walls. Position the first board against a wall batten and push it tightly against the head plate by inserting folding wedges onto the sole plate. Fit subsequent panels in the same way and insert softwood tongues along the long edges to ensure tight joints. Fit timber cover strips over the ceiling and floor joints to provide a neat finish.

Exterior work

When the weather is fine, there are plenty of tasks outside the home which will add to the facilities and enhance the overall appearance. These range from building your own porch, garage or carport to laying patios and terraces. And to gain access from a ground floor room, you can fit your own patio doors. If you have a garden, there is much that can be done to improve and organise it. Learn how to lay paths and drives, build steps and walls and put up fences, gates and posts. Think of the satisfaction of looking out on to your new garden, particularly when you have probably increased the value of your property.

Building fences

You can build any type of fencing on flat ground or ground which has only a slight gradient; on steeper ground you should build a fence which uses horizontal boards. There are two ways of coping with the problem of sloping ground. The first way is usually ruled out because of the extra work; it involves shaping boards, posts and panels so each bay of the fence will be horizontal. The second method is more practical; you step each fence bay an equal amount throughout the run of the fence to give it a uniform appearance.

On a slight slope you should be able to lay several bays to one level before forming a step and fixing the remaining bays at another. On a steep slope you will need longer posts because every bay may need to be stepped. Make sure you maintain uniform steps; to do this you may need to dig out some areas so the panels are clear of the ground as they are fitted to the posts. Conversely, if the gap between the bottom and the ground is too large, you may need to build up the ground.

If the ground level in your neighbour's garden is higher than that in your own, one side of the fence will be in contact with the ground. Even if you apply preservative, rotting is inevitable; if you leave a bank between the soil and the fence, the soil will probably subside. The answer is to build a retaining wall with the timber fence placed on top; bed in 50mm (2in) thick paving slabs so they stand vertically for a bank of 450mm (18in) of soil or less. For higher banks, build a small brick wall and leave a gap for drainage and for the posts, which should be inserted on concrete spurs.

Fitting timber posts

If you intend building a new timber fence on the site of an old one, the greatest problem is in removing the old fence posts which may have become stumps in the ground. The old posts could well have been set into concrete and rubble and you will have to excavate around them to break up the buried material before removing them. Individual posts may not prove to be too much trouble; if you have a series of old damaged posts, it is probably worth considering an alternative posting arrangement.

Short panel If the new posts have to be placed near or at the position of the old ones, which is quite likely since the standard panel width is 1.8m (6ft), you may find it impossible to dig through the old hardcore to make the new post holes. Consider fitting a shorter panel at the start of the fence; this will ensure the other posts fall midway between the old posts and so avoid the hardcore. Many fence panel manufacturers will supply shorter panels.

When building fence on slope, always take horizontal measurements between posts
1a For steep slope, raise each bay above previous one
1b For shallow slope, form step with several bays
1c Alternatively landscape ground to form stepped levels and build retaining walls

When ground is higher on one side of fence, build wall to support bank
2a If difference in levels is no more than 450mm, use paving slabs set in concrete
2b If difference is more than 450mm, build brick wall; leave out half brick for drainage

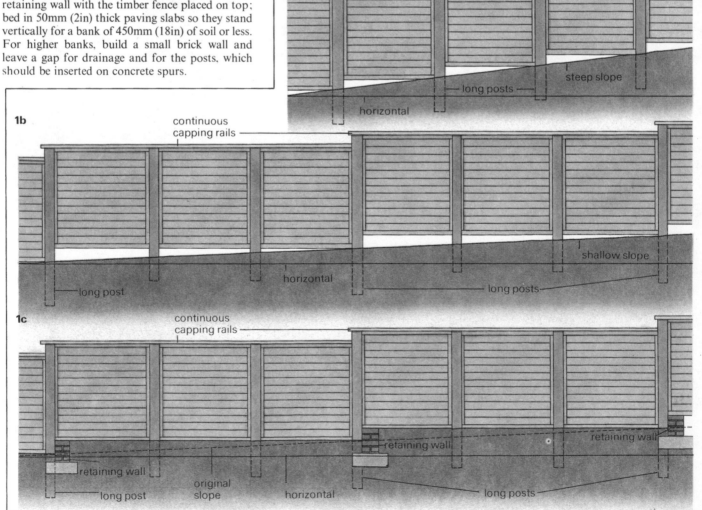

1a

long posts
steep slope
horizontal

1b
continuous capping rails
long post
horizontal
long posts
shallow slope

1c
continuous capping rails
retaining wall
retaining wall
long post
original slope
horizontal
long posts
retaining wall

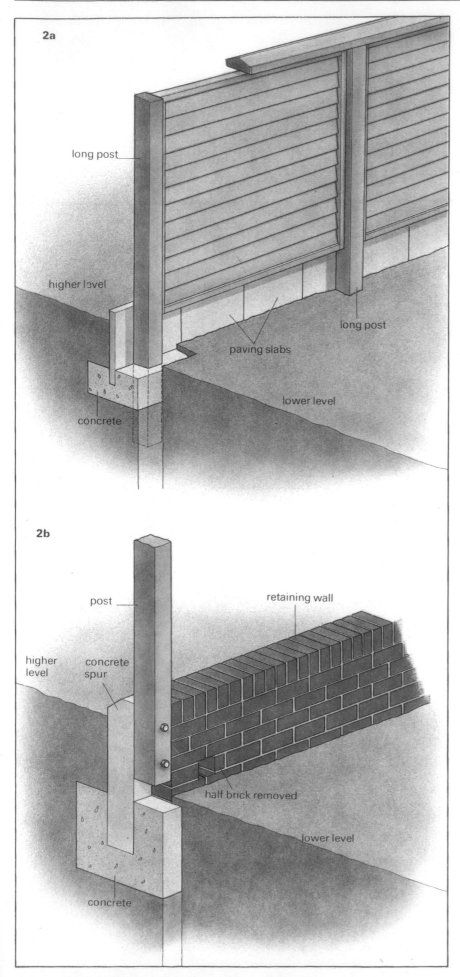

2a

long post

higher level

paving slabs

long post

concrete

lower level

2b

post

retaining wall

higher level

concrete spur

half brick removed

lower level

concrete

Paving slabs Another problem you may encounter is if you have to set a post into the base of a long patio, especially if the neighbouring house has one as well. If it is made of paving slabs laid on a base of sand, it may be a simple matter of lifting the appropriate slabs and digging down. But if the patio is made of concrete, you will have to hire a rotary action demolition hammer to break it up.

Tree roots These can also pose problems and a shorter fence panel may be the answer. Make sure you excavate all the post positions before ordering your fence to see if an odd size panel could help avoid the roots.

Concrete If you are faced with a layer of thick concrete across the proposed fence post position, you may be able to excavate about 450mm (18in) and strengthen the post by drilling through it and bolting it to the adjacent concrete; the technique is similar to bolting a post to a wall, as described below. Once concrete and rubble have been placed around the post and the concrete repaired, you should have a solid fixing. To ensure a post clears the edge of a concrete base or patio, you can screw a piece of timber to the previous post; the timber must be thick enough so the next panel ends clear of the concrete. The next post can then be fitted away from the concrete.

Preventing rotting and sagging

You can protect timber posts from rotting or sagging by fixing each one to a concrete spur buried in the ground and set in concrete. Bury the spur and push a nail through the holes to mark their positions on the post; drill right through the posts and secure them to the spurs with galvanized steel bolts. Make sure the bolts are long enough to pass through both spur and post for a secure fixing.

Putting in metposts

A metpost is essentially a 900mm (36in) long steel spike with a steel cup; it will save you digging post holes because the spike is simply driven into the ground. Bury about 750mm (30in) of the spike and leave 150mm (6in) of square steel cup projecting; tap the post onto the cup – a 1mm (or $\frac{1}{24}$ in) gap is allowable – and secure it with screws inserted through the predrilled holes in the cup. Problems of rotting are minimized because the post itself is not in contact with the ground; any rainwater will eventually drain out through a hole in the base of the spike. Manufacturers claim the metpost will not move once driven firmly into the ground, even in areas with high winds. When fitting posts near to obstructions, you only need to dig a small hole. One company will supply these posts in a package with their panel fences; the cup will only accept 75×62mm ($3 \times 2\frac{1}{2}$in) posts, but you can obtain 75mm (3in) square cups from builders' merchants. Larger posts can only be used if you taper the lower portions to fit the standard size cups.

When calculating costs, remember to offset the cost of metposts against the lower cost of shorter posts; you do not need to bury 450–750mm (18–30in) of post into the ground. They require no concreting, maintenance costs are less, labour is less and the cost of hiring or buying a post hole boring tool is eliminated.

Fitting post to wall

The key to a stable fence is well-anchored posts – and one of the best ways to fix a post soundly is to secure it to a house wall; if your screw fixings are

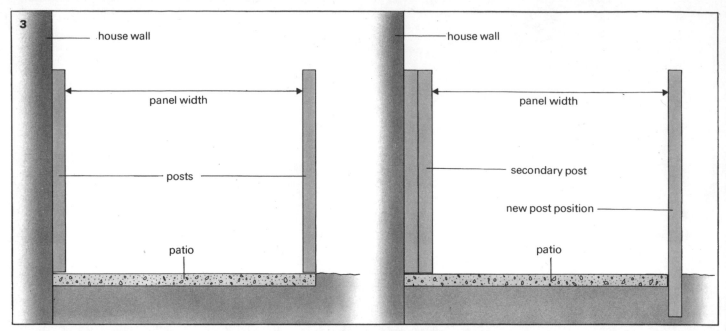

3 house wall · panel width · posts · patio

house wall · panel width · secondary post · new post position · patio

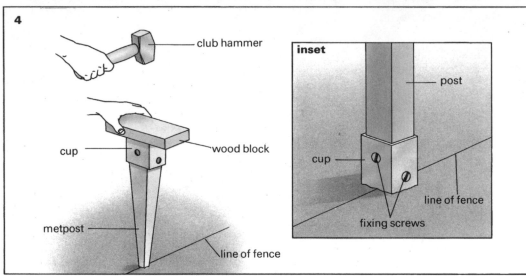

4 club hammer · cup · wood block · metpost · line of fence

inset post · cup · line of fence · fixing screws

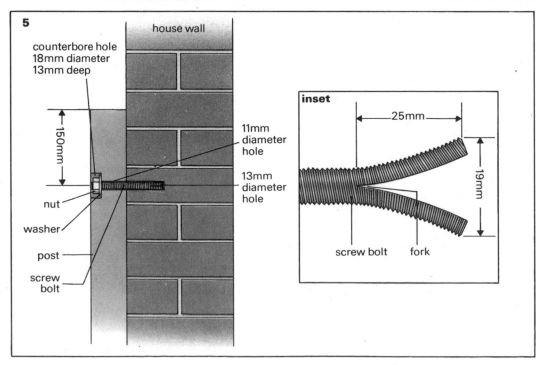

5 house wall · counterbore hole 18mm diameter 13mm deep · 150mm · nut · washer · post · screw bolt · 11mm diameter hole · 13mm diameter hole

inset 25mm · 19mm · screw bolt · fork

3 If post position coincides with edge of concrete patio, screw secondary timber post to first post to take fence panel clear of obstruction
4 Metpost is driven into ground with club hammer and block; secure base of post to metpost with fixing screws (**inset**)
5 Post can be securely fixed to wall with screw bolts; for extra strength cut fork in end of screw bolt before cementing into wall (**inset**)
6a Fit temporary struts to post until concrete has set; use nails driven into post to support strut
6b For extra support in exposed areas, fit permanent struts; bed in concrete and form rebate in post to accept. strut

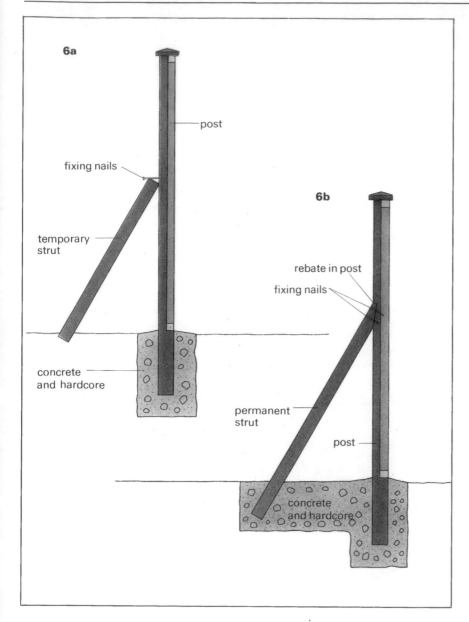

6a

post

fixing nails

temporary
strut

concrete
and hardcore

6b

rebate in post

fixing nails

permanent
strut

post

concrete
and hardcore

with a nail onto the wall. Remove the post and use a 13mm ($\frac{1}{2}$in) masonry bit to drill 75mm (3in) holes into the wall. Fit the bolts, forked end first, into the wall by squeezing the fork together and tapping with a mallet protected by a wood block; fill with a cement mix or wall filler. Locate the post over the bolts once the filler has set hard, making sure the bolts are level so the post holes fit over them squarely. Put the washers and nuts onto the bolts and tighten with a ring spanner. Because the end of the bolt is split inside the wall, the fixing creates extra anchorage to restrict post movement.

Fixing posts in ground

You can either fix each post as you build the fence or fix them all beforehand, in which case make sure your measurements are precise and use a spacer batten to ensure the posts are the correct distance apart. Once you have dug out each hole, fit the post and fill with alternate layers of hardcore and concrete. Use a weak concrete mix (one part cement, three parts coarse sand and six parts stone or broken brick); if the posts do rot, you will find it easier to remove them. Finish with a collar of concrete, about 25mm (1in) higher than ground level, and round it off away from the post to ensure rainwater flows away from the base of the post. You can also place a half brick in the bottom of the post hole before you fit the post to prevent the end grain coming into contact with the ground. Fix struts by driving two nails through them into the post, making sure the post is vertical first. Allow about a week for the concrete to harden before removing the struts.

Shrinkage The concrete may shrink slightly as it dries, resulting in a small gap between the post and concrete through which water could enter and rot the post. Regular treatment with preservative could help counter this problem.

Fitting permanent struts

In weak ground you really have no alternative to bedding posts in concrete, except if you are able to use a metpost. In strong ground, hardcore plus a mix of soil and gravel can be adequate for certain types of fence, such as a low boundary fence in a sheltered position. If you fix a high close-boarded fence in an exposed position where it will be buffeted by wind, you will probably need extra support in the form of permanent struts.

It is best to nail the struts to the posts and concrete both into the ground; this means you will have to dig a short trench from the post to the base of the strut. Remember to treat the struts with preservative before fixing them; they should also be treated regularly afterwards. Always support end posts with struts, except if you are able to bolt them to walls. Support of the intermediate posts depends on the height and length of your fence. Generally, if the fence is 1500mm (60in) tall, you should support every third post; but fences of 1200mm (48in) or under will require support at every fourth post. The supporting struts are not attractive, but they are insurance against future fence failure.

Capping

You will need to protect the tops of timber posts from rainwater which soaks into the end grain. Some manufacturers provide timber caps which you nail into place or you can saw off the tops to a bevel or add a capping piece.

weak, wind pressure could rock the post loose until the fence is separated from the wall. You could use expansion bolts to give a secure fixing, but screw bolts with nuts and washers (available in various lengths and diameters) are more economical. For a 75mm (3in) square post you will need three bolts about 137mm (5$\frac{1}{2}$in) long; if the post is less than 1200mm (48in) high, you will need only two. If you have 100×75mm (4×3in) posts, with the 75mm (3in) face fixed to the wall, use 160mm (6$\frac{1}{2}$in) bolts. Bury about 75mm (3in) of the bolt into the wall after 'forking' the end; hold it between padding in a vice, saw down about 25mm (1in) with a hacksaw and bend the fork open to about 19mm ($\frac{3}{4}$in). You may find it economical to buy a long length of narrow screw bolt and saw lengths off as you require them; usually about 9mm ($\frac{3}{8}$in) will be sufficient.

The wall post will usually be shorter than the others which stand in the ground. Drill three 11mm ($\frac{7}{16}$in) holes through the post – about 150mm (6in) from each end and one in the middle. Use an 18mm ($\frac{3}{4}$in) bit to counterbore these holes by 13–19mm ($\frac{1}{2}$–$\frac{3}{4}$in) on one face of the post. Hold the post in position and check it is vertical with a spirit level or plumb line and bob; mark the drilling positions

Erecting a panel fence

You will need someone to help you if you want to build a tall fence; low panel fences, however, can be easily built by one person. First stretch a string line at ground level between two stakes to mark the position of the proposed fence. Cut a timber batten to the length of the panels you are using and mark off the positions of the posts with pieces of brick; it is important to make these measurements correctly to avoid problems of joining the panels later. Dig out the holes to the required depth; you could use a spade or buy or hire a post-boring tool, which works like a large corkscrew.

Fixing posts

Once the holes have been bored you can fit the posts. To prevent the base of the post rotting from the end grain, place a half brick in the hole before fitting the post. Check the post is upright with a spirit level and stabilize it as you pack rubble round its base; wedge two struts of timber under nails temporarily driven into the post.

Fixing panels

Hold the panel against the post and leave a 75–100mm (3–4in) gap between its base and the ground by supporting both ends of the panel on bricks. Use aluminium alloy or galvanized nails about 62mm (2½in) long to secure the panel to the post; fix three nails on both sides of the panel (six per panel end in total). The relatively thin timber at the end of the panel may split as you drive in the nails; if this happens, drill pilot holes through the

panels or blunt the end of the nails with pincers before using them.

You can eliminate the need to level each panel (or post) as it is built by fitting a string line at the height of the fence; stretch the line between two posts driven firmly into the ground at each end of the proposed fence. This may not be possible on sloping ground where you will need to have one or more steps in the fence. Nail the free end of the panel to the second post as before, checking the panel is horizontal. The post can now be supported with temporary struts and you can pack the hole with concrete and hardcore as already described. Fix the remaining posts and panels in the same way.

Fixing capping rail

Fence panels are normally fixed so 50 or 75mm (2 or 3in) of post projects above the panels; this should improve the appearance of the fence as well as enable the post tops to be capped or bevelled. A useful way of protecting and strengthening a panel fence is to run a continuous capping rail across the posts and panels. Cut the posts or build them so they are flush with the panels; if the panels have fitted capping rails, you can prise them off and remove them. Make sure the panels are in line before you nail the capping strips back so each one spans a post top and most of the adjoining panel. You will need an extra length of capping rail, shaped to match, to make up the difference lost by covering the posts. If the strip is not wide enough to cover the posts completely, first fix a metal capping to the posts or shape to a bevel the portion of the post top which will be exposed.

Using concrete posts

For fence panels, the assembly methods are basically similar whether you use timber or concrete posts; the difference is each panel is fitted to the concrete post according to the manufacturer's instructions. The most common concrete posts have slots running down their sides to accept the edges of the panels. Hold the post upright and push the panel firmly into the slot; the panel is held by its own weight. Another system uses galvanized plates and screws; this allows you to remove each panel easily for repairs or for access through the fence – if you want to site a caravan for example.

7a With slotted concrete fence posts, panels simply slide in
7b With recessed type of concrete post, straight, end and corner brackets hold panels

Building timber panel fence using slotted concrete posts:
8 Digging post hole
9 Checking post is vertical with spirit level
10 Using straight-edge and spirit level to check posts are set at same height
11 Placing temporary struts to hold fence while concrete sets
12 Concreting post into ground
13 Fitting panel into slot in post

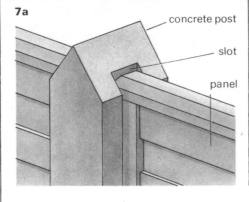

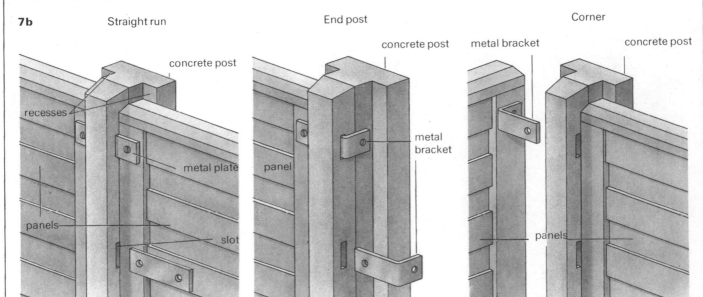

8

9

10

11

12

13

Other fencing

Apart from the timber panel type of fencing already described, there are other types of fencing you can easily put up yourself. These include the arris rail fence, chain link fence, decorative wire fence, wire netting, plastic fence, cleft chestnut paling fence, post and rail fence and concrete fence. Remember, however, to check on whether – and how much – the ground slopes and the exact positioning of your posts. The details on how to cope with slight and steep gradients have already been discussed in connection with timber panel fencing and the same principles apply, whatever type of fencing you decide to put up.

Arris rail fence

This fence can be built using the same basic methods as for a timber panel fence; two or three arris rails can be put up, depending on the height you require. If you buy prefabricated timber posts for the job, they will have preformed mortises to accept the arris rails; other types of post will have to be shaped on site. If you use concrete posts, their mortises may be wedge-shaped; you will have to cut the rails to a matching shape. This also applies to any rails which have square sawn ends.

Concrete posts   These will often have preformed grooves to accept gravel boards; if they do not, and you require gravel boards, you will have to set vertical battens into the ground alongside the posts and concrete them in with the posts. Make sure you treat the battens with preservative before fixing them. Concrete posts are heavy – a 2m (or 7ft) post weighs about 45kg (or 100lb) – and therefore not easy to handle; but they are long-lasting.

Putting up posts

Fit the first post and check it is vertical; make sure you keep it supported as you fit the rails. Normally the tenon is inserted half-way into the post so there is an equal amount of mortise available for the next rail's tenon. This distance is not important for the first and last posts; with these you can allow for the full width of the post as long as you allow for the extra rail length when ordering or cutting them.

Make sure someone holds the second post steady as you insert the opposite ends of the rails. Use a hammer or mallet to tap the second post firmly so the rails engage half-way into this post. You can now secure the rails in the previous post (by nailing if you are using timber posts). Check the second post is vertical and wedge it into place. Fit subsequent posts and rails in the same manner.

Fitting gravel boards

If you require them, gravel boards may be located in the preformed slots in the posts, if available; in this case they should be fitted at the same time as the arris rails. If you use timber posts without slots, use the technique of fitting battens alongside or nail them to the posts.

Fitting arris rail fence and concrete posts:
1 Tap second post onto rails. **2a & 2b** Alternative gravel board fixings. **3a** Nail through thicker edge of board into arris rail. **3b** Check vertical. **3c** Use filler piece as final board. **3d** Alternatively reverse board to finish bay

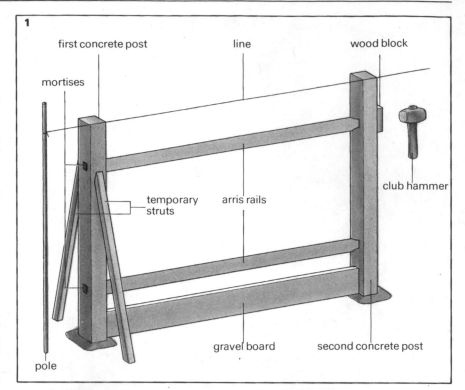

1 first concrete post · line · wood block · mortises · club hammer · temporary struts · arris rails · pole · gravel board · second concrete post

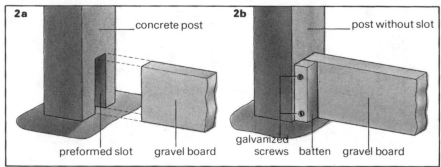

2a concrete post · preformed slot · gravel board
2b post without slot · galvanized screws · batten · gravel board

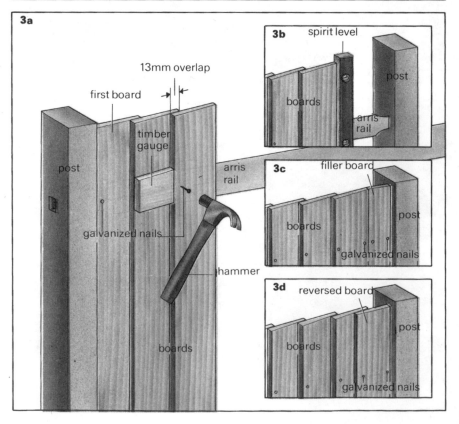

3a first board · 13mm overlap · post · timber gauge · galvanized nails · arris rail · hammer · boards
3b spirit level · post · boards · arris rail
3c filler board · boards · post · galvanized nails
3d reversed board · post · boards · galvanized nails

Fitting vertical boards

Finally fit the vertical boards with the thicker edge nearest to the first post; make sure you check they are vertical. Drive a nail through the thicker edge and into the centre of each rail; insert the nails at a slight angle so they will not pull straight out if the fence is subjected to pressure. Ensure the thicker edge of the next board overlaps the thin edge of the first one by about 13mm (½in).

Use a piece of timber cut to the size of this overlap to provide a uniform gap all the way down the board. Hold it in position at the top before nailing its overlapping neighbour through its thick edge, through the thin edge of the board below and finally into the rail; insert these nails at an angle. Use the gauge at the bottom before nailing through and finally nail the board to the centre rail – if you are using one. After you have fitted every fourth or fifth board, check the overlap of the board you have just nailed to make sure all the boards remain in line. If you wish to fit a gravel board afterwards, remember to leave a 150mm (6in) gap below each board.

Final boards The overlap of the last two or three boards will have to be increased or decreased slightly to ensure the final board meets the end post. Alternatively you could continue with uniform overlaps and cut a filler board to finish off or reverse the last board so its thicker edge is against the post. Fit a capping piece to all boards since the end grain is subject to early rotting and splitting; skew-nail the capping piece to the posts.

Chain link fence

You can fix chain link fencing to timber, concrete or angle iron posts. It is very important to fix the posts solidly and brace the end posts because of the force exerted as you strain the fence during building.

Putting up timber posts

If you use timber posts, bolt timber struts to them within the top third of the post and concrete the struts into the ground to a depth of 450mm (18in). Space intermediate posts about 2.8m (or 9ft) apart and bury them to a depth of 450mm (18in); for long runs you will need an intermediate straining post at 69m (226ft) intervals.

Straining posts are also required at corners, changes in direction and where there is a substantial difference in the level of the ground. Line wires are strained between the posts to support the fence. The number of wires depends upon the height of the fence; use two if it is under 1.2m (4ft) and three if under 2.25m (7ft 6in). On long runs you can join up to three lengths of 25m (82ft) rolls and strain them quite safely.

Fitting chain link

Allow the concrete to set in the post holes. Use a brace and bit to drill a 10mm (⅜in) diameter hole through the posts at the required wire height. Insert an eye bolt through each post so there is at least 50mm (2in) of thread projecting. Fix the washer and nut to the bolt, thread the end of the wire through the loop and twist it several times with pliers. Unroll the wire and pass it through staples driven into the intermediate posts.

Fix the wire to the other end post with an eye bolt as before; use a spanner on the nut of the eye bolt to turn it to draw the wire tight – the eye bolt will stretch the wire by about 75mm (3in). On long

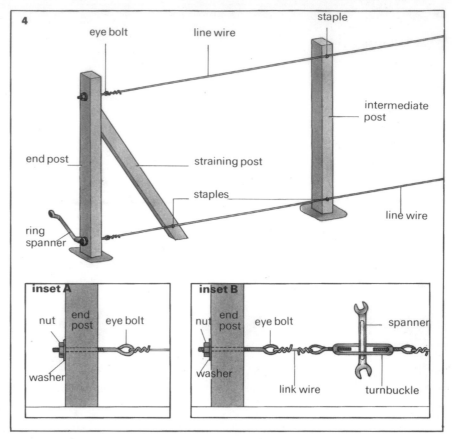

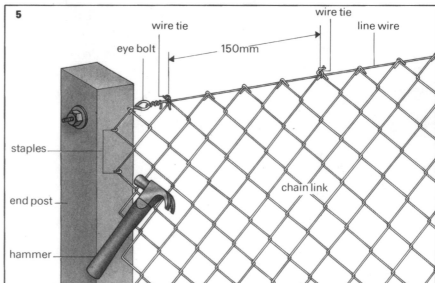

runs you will need to stretch the wire with a turnbuckle; cut the wire and twist its ends through the loops of the turnbuckle. Insert a spanner through its centre and turn it enough to tighten the wire; repeat this process for each wire.

Loosen the first end of the fencing and stand it alongside the post to fit it. Staple every loop of the mesh to the first post to prevent it sagging. You could use a stretcher bar instead of staples, as described below.

Unroll the fence, pull it taut by hand and fix it at 150mm (6in) intervals to the line wires at the top; fix it every 450mm (18in) to the other wires. To fix the fence, use tightly twisted fine galvanized wire; at corners or changes of direction, unravel a spiral and staple through each loop. Finally staple the free end to the last post.

4 Fitting chain link fencing to timber posts; line wire fitted to end post using eye bolt (**inset A**) and turnbuckle fitted to stretch long runs of wire (**inset B**)

5 Stapling chain link fencing to timber end post; use wire ties to secure chain link to line wire

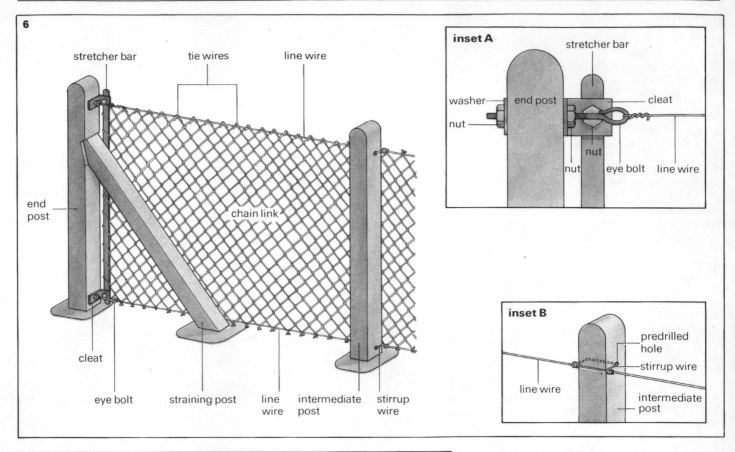

6

stretcher bar   tie wires   line wire

end
post

cleat

eye bolt   straining post   line
wire   intermediate
post   stirrup
wire

chain link

inset A   stretcher bar

washer   end post   cleat

nut

nut   eye bolt   line wire

inset B

predrilled
hole

stirrup wire

line wire

intermediate
post

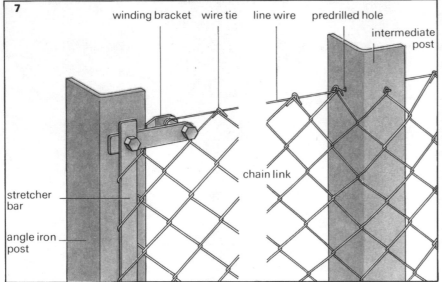

7

winding bracket   wire tie   line wire   predrilled hole

intermediate
post

chain link

stretcher
bar

angle iron
post

6 Fitting chain link fencing to concrete posts; stretcher bar fitted to end post using cleat and eye bolt (**inset A**) and stirrup wire used to fix line wire to intermediate post (**inset B**)

7 Fitting chain link fencing to angle iron posts; winding bracket secures stretcher bar

Putting up concrete posts
You can use concrete posts in a similar way, with eye bolts to strain the wire and angled cleats to secure the stretcher bars, which are passed through the last rows of meshes on the chain link; the posts are predrilled to accept the eye bolts. Tension the wire with the eyebolts before tightening the securing nuts onto the cleats. Secure the line wire at intermediate posts by threading a stirrup wire through the predrilled holes and twisting its ends over the line wire. Concrete posts are supplied specially notched to accept the supporting struts.

Putting up angle iron posts
The difference here is merely the type of fixings used for the straining posts; special winding brackets are required to secure the stretcher bars and wires to the iron posts. The line wire passes through predrilled holes in the intermediate posts.

Joining rolls
To join rolls of chain link fencing, release the knuckles at the top and bottom of the first spiral on the roll to be joined, then detach the spiral from the roll by unscrewing it anti-clockwise. Join the ends of the rolls by twisting the loose spiral clockwise through the links of the next roll. When you have threaded it to the top, bend over the knuckles at the top and bottom.

Decorative wire fence
You can build this type using timber posts or angle iron stakes set at 1.5m (5ft) intervals. Fences 600 and 900mm (24 and 36in) high require posts fixed between 450 and 600mm (18 and 24in) below ground according to whether you have firm or weak soil. Use supporting struts for the end posts, which should be set into concrete.

Fixing wire fencing
Unravel the end of the fencing and fit it centrally to timber posts with 20mm ($\frac{3}{4}$in) 20 gauge staples at roughly 75mm (3in) intervals. It is always best to hammer home staples at a slight angle rather than straight to the grain where they might pull out. With angle iron posts, use plastic-coated wire as a fastener, twisted round to secure the fencing.

Fences 250 and 400mm (10 and 16in) high will be self-supporting; but you should drive in small stakes at 1.8m (6ft) intervals to ensure the fencing remains in place. Unravel the fence to the first post, pull it taut and fix it again; repeat along the roll.

On undulating sites it is worth providing additional support centrally between the posts by driving a 25mm (1in) square stake into the ground and stapling the bottom of the fence to it. Any gaps in the bottom of the fence, through which children or animals could crawl, will need to be filled in; you can do this by making up the ground, building a low wall or burying the bottom portion of the fence. You should remember, however, this type of fencing is purely decorative and the above precautions will probably indicate a stronger fence is required.

Wire netting

Use timber, angle iron or special wire netting stakes at 1.8–2.4m (6–8ft) intervals; each post should be buried for about one third of its height. The wire netting must not be over-tensioned since the mesh will distort and cause the fence to balloon out. Because this fence is often used to retain small animals such as rabbits, it is best to bury the bottom 150mm (6in) in the ground to prevent burrowing.

Line wires Although you can fix the fence directly to the posts, it will be stronger if you use line wires. Use 3mm (⅛in) galvanized wire; two lines for a fence under 1.2m (4ft) high and three for higher fences. Space the line wires evenly down the posts and secure with netting fasteners or tie wires.

Posts Manufacturers advise holes for posts up to about 1400mm (56in) should be 450mm (18in) square and 750mm (30in) deep; set the posts in concrete. If you are using line wire, unroll it and strain it between the posts. Fix the edge of the netting to the first post using 15mm (⅝in) 16 gauge staples (timber posts) or tie wire (angle iron).

Netting stakes To fix these, hook the top edge over the top hook and the lower edge over the bottom one; gradually unroll the fence, pulling it taut and securing it to the line wires and posts with tie wire.

Plastic fence

There are various types of proprietary plastic fence; manufacturers supply detailed fitting instructions which differ slightly from type to type.

One system uses posts slotted to accept 100mm (4in) planks; you can buy posts capable of accepting two or three planks, at heights of 1000 and 1300mm (40 and 52in) respectively. You must carefully align the posts at 1.5m (5ft) intervals so they will accept the planks. With 1000mm (40in) posts, 300mm (12in) should be below ground; with 1300mm (52in) posts, 400mm (16in) should be below ground.

Putting up plastic fencing

The fence is built in a similar manner to a timber fence; fit the post, check it is vertical, insert the planks and fit a second post to accept the ends of the planks. As with arris rails, insert planks half-way into a post where they butt the next plank. Planks are 1.5 and 3m (5 and 10ft) long; use long and short planks alternately so where two planks butt at a post, the ones above and below run straight through and are joined at the posts on each side. The planks are retained in the posts by plastic nibs which project at the ends from the upper edge.

If you have to cut planks to suit your layout, for example if you need a short length to finish off, form new nibs by cutting a shallow groove across the top of a plank and prising up a nib with pincers. Support the posts as work proceeds and finally infill their holes with concrete; fit plank end caps and post top caps with the recommended adhesive (usually a solvent cement).

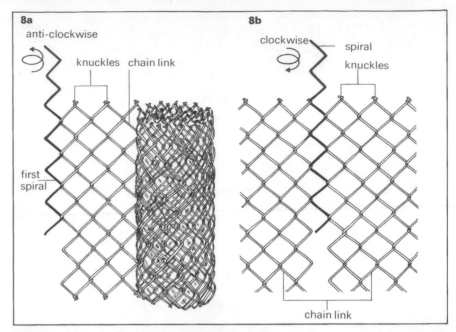

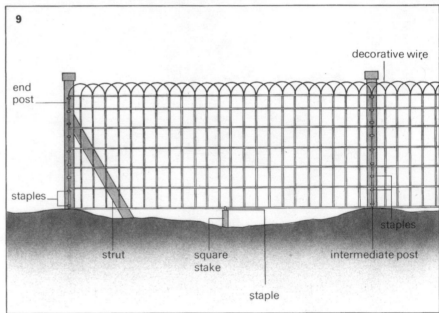

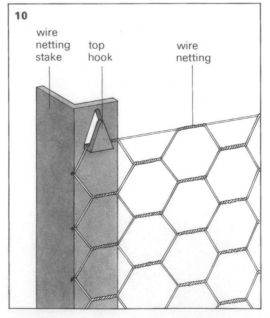

8a When joining rolls of chain link fencing, unscrew first spiral anti-clockwise
8b Thread spiral down by twisting it clockwise
9 Fitting decorative wire fence using timber posts; where ground undulates, staple bottom of fencing to timber stake
10 Fitting wire netting to special stake

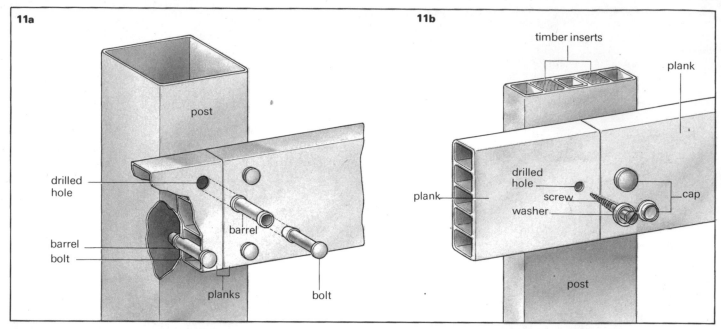

11a

11b

timber inserts

plank

post

drilled
hole

barrel

barrel
bolt

planks

bolt

plank

drilled
hole

screw

washer

cap

post

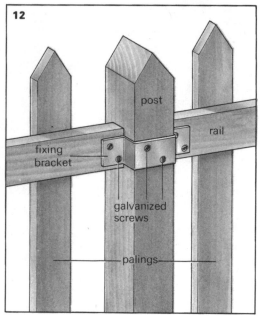

12

post

rail

fixing
bracket

galvanized
screws

palings

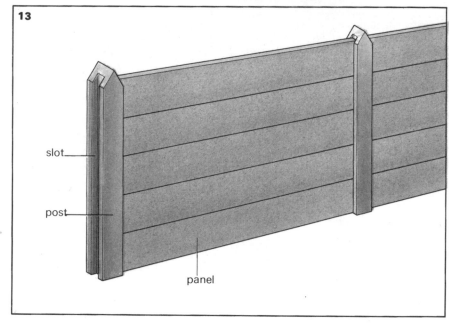

13

slot

post

panel

11a When building snap-in plastic fence, bolt planks to post through drilled holes
11b When building screw-in plastic fence, screw planks to timber inserts in post
12 Building paling fence using brackets to fit arris rails to post
13 When building concrete fence, drop panels into slots in posts

Alternative methods You could set all the posts into the ground and fit the bottom plank to ensure the correct spacings. After the infill concrete has set, insert further planks by springing in their ends.

Another common plastic fencing system has special plastic barrels and bolts which are snapped into place to hold the planks onto the faces of the posts. Drill the holes on site, through both posts and planks; it is best if you build the fence in small sections – three posts with planks fixed – by laying the components flat on the ground. The whole assembly is then joined up as the sections are positioned in the post holes. It is important to carry out this assembly on a perfectly flat surface so the planks are fitted square to the posts.

One manufacturer supplies a special jig which ensures the holes are accurately drilled. Lay the planks in their correct positions and spacings on the posts; place the jig on the face of the planks and drill the holes. Plastic barrels and bolts are snapped into place to lock the planks into position.

A further plastic fence system uses screws inserted through planks and posts and driven into

timber inserts inside the posts. Again, the planks butt on the faces of the posts. You can use plastic, timber or concrete posts for this system.

Cleft chestnut paling fence

Use end posts 100mm (4in) square with 75mm (3in) square struts; set intermediate posts the same size as the struts at 2.7m (9ft) intervals. Staple the top and bottom wire to the posts, retain the tension while stapling and pull the fence taut as work proceeds.

Post and rail fence

Sawn posts should be 75mm (3in) square and fixed at 1.8m (6ft) intervals; rails should be 37×87mm ($1\frac{1}{2} \times 3\frac{1}{2}$in) minimum, nailed to your side of the fence and butted up at the post centres. Stagger the joints in the rails so where the rails butt at a post, those above and below butt at the posts on each side. Allow 300mm (12in) spaces between the rails and allow 260mm ($10\frac{1}{2}$in) between the bottom rail

Building snap-in plastic fence system:
14 Saw posts to length
15 Use jig to drill holes through planks and post
16 With fence laid on flat surface insert barrels and bolts
17 Check each section is vertical using spirit level
18 Fix subsequent sections in same way
19 Completed fence

and the ground. Use galvanized or aluminium alloy nails.

Fitting palings
Post and rail fences with palings should have 75mm (3in) square end posts set at 1.8m (6ft) intervals. For fences up to 1050mm (42in) you will need two rails; fences over this height should have three. Space palings with 50mm (2in) gaps and nail them to all the rails. Proprietary fences supplied with ready made panels (cross rails with pales already fitted) are joined to the posts with special brackets.

Concrete fence

Set the posts in concrete at exact intervals to receive the particular width of panel you have ordered. The slots in the sides of the posts accept the panels which are simply dropped into place.

Fitting gates and posts

Regardless of the type of gate you choose (and there is a wide selection available), it is essential the posts are substantial and well-fixed. These can be of timber, steel or reinforced concrete and piers of brick, stone or concrete blocks can also be used. Alternatively you can fix a gate to brick, stone or concrete block walls, provided they are at least 230mm (or 9in) thick.

Timber posts Oak is the best timber for gate posts. It should be at least 100mm (4in) square and 125mm (5in) square if your gate is more than 1.8m (6ft) high and 1m (or 3ft) wide. Larch is suitable if you cannot obtain oak. For all five-bar gates, strong oak posts are very important. For gates of 1.2–2.1m (4–7ft) wide, 150mm (6in) square posts should be used; they should be 2.1m (7ft) long. This length allows 0.9m (3ft) to be buried; 1.2m (4ft) should be buried for gates of 2.4–3.6m (8–12ft) wide and the posts should be 2.4m (8ft) long and 175mm (7in) square. To save expense, the post on the catch side can be 2.1m (7ft) long and 150mm (6in) square.

Metal posts Metal posts are available for metal gates. They are tubular, square or rectangular welded box section; hinge pins, catch and slam bars are usually welded in place. The ready-made posts should be carefully painted with a thick coat of rust-resistant primer; dip the portion to go below ground in black bitumen paint to give it additional protection.

Concrete posts You may be able to buy purpose-made concrete posts but it is usual to adapt standard concrete fence posts to hang a gate. The main problem is to fix the hinges and the catch. The posts may be predrilled so these fittings can be bolted through the holes, although more usually the hinges and catch have to be screwed to lengths of timber which are bolted through the post holes.

Masonry piers Piers must be substantial; the minimum size for a brick pier is a brick-and-a-half square – or 337mm (13in) square. Use strong bricks or stones and strong mortar – one part Portland cement to three or four parts clean sand. Hinge and catch fittings are usually designed for building into the mortar joints as you construct the piers. This is quite a skilled job.

Obviously the gate must be purchased before you begin so you can position the fittings accurately. It is easier to use fittings which you plug and screw to the completed pier, as supplied with gates you intend to fit to existing piers, although these fittings are not as strong as the built-in type. Fit protecting coping stones to the tops of piers to throw rainwater clear of them.

Fitting gate posts
If the manufacturer does not specify the correct distance apart to set the gate posts, you will have to lay the gate on the ground and position the hinges, hinge post, gate catch and catch post. Measure the distance between the posts and allow a slight clearance to ensure the gate will swing freely when hung; check the distance is the same top and bottom. Cut a timber batten to this length and use it as a gauge to set the posts the correct distance apart. If you are fitting a pair of gates, you can use the above method to determine the correct distance; but you must place a 6mm (¼in) thick batten as a spacer between

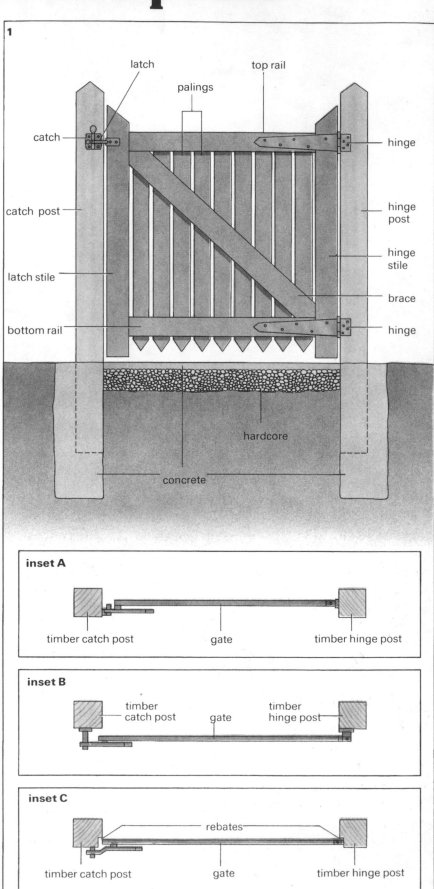

1

latch

palings

top rail

catch

hinge

catch post

hinge post

latch stile

hinge stile

brace

bottom rail

hinge

hardcore

concrete

inset A

timber catch post — gate — timber hinge post

inset B

timber catch post — gate — timber hinge post

inset C

rebates

timber catch post — gate — timber hinge post

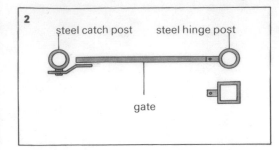

2 steel catch post   steel hinge post

gate

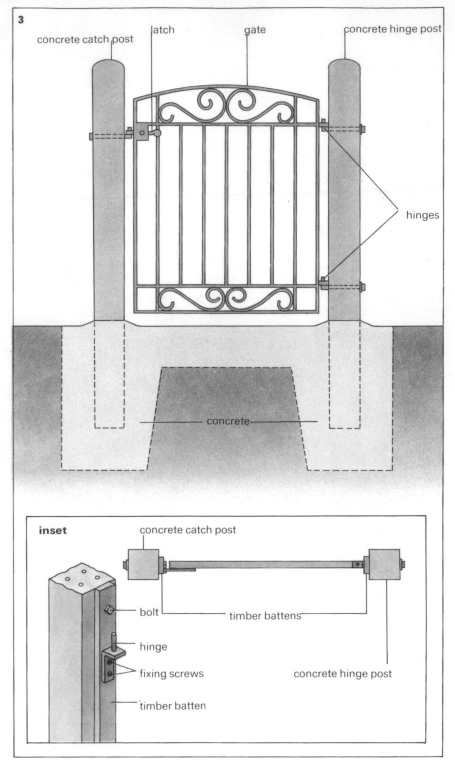

3 concrete catch post   latch   gate   concrete hinge post

hinges

concrete

inset   concrete catch post

bolt   timber battens

hinge

fixing screws   concrete hinge post

timber batten

---

the joining stiles of the gates to ensure they will open and close freely.

Post holes You can now begin to excavate the post holes as described earlier in the book. If your posts were supplied with the gate, make the depth of the holes sufficient to give a clearance of at least 50mm (2in) under the gate. If the ground rises behind the gate, you may have to set the posts higher so the gate can be opened fully without scraping on the ground. If you are buying posts separately, make sure they are sufficiently long to allow 450mm (18in) to be set in the ground if the gate is up to 1m (or 3ft) high and 1m (or 3ft) wide; if the gate is wider than this, 600mm (or 24in) should be set into the ground. You will almost definitely need a post hole borer to dig holes to the depth required for farm-style gates.

In soft ground you should dig a 150mm (6in) deep trench between the post holes to form a concrete bridge between the posts in the gateway opening; this is to counter the considerable strain exerted on the hinge post. Place about 100mm (4in) of concrete in the bottom of each post hole and position the posts; check they are lined up with the other posts in a fence run and are vertical on all faces. Use temporary struts of scrap timber to hold the posts steady and check the tops of the posts are level with a spirit level and straight-edge; alternatively you can saw timber posts off level afterwards. Use the timber batten to check your posts are the correct distance apart top and bottom and pack round the posts with concrete – or concrete and hardcore – as described earlier in the book. If you prefer, you can set one post accurately and line up the other to it; this has also been described earlier in the book.

Metal gate posts often have welded-on metal projections near their bases; these must be set into concrete for a secure fixing. Allow about seven days for the concrete to harden before hanging any gates.

Post fittings Metal posts often have hinges and catches already fitted and hanging becomes a simple matter of placing the gate on the hinge pins and checking it swings freely and the catch operates. To prevent vandals removing a metal gate you can drill the hinge pins to take split pins; slip a washer over the hinge pin before fitting the split pin. If the gate fittings (hinges and catch) have to be screwed to the posts, place the gate in position and hold it clear of the ground on suitably sized blocks; check the gate is upright. In the case of a metal gate, hold the hinge pin in position on the gate and mark the fixing holes onto the post. For a timber gate, first check the gate is the right way round; the diagonal brace should have its lower end on the hinge side.

Fixing gate hinges

In the majority of cases, timber garden gates are hung using T-hinges. These are available in various sizes in either painted steel or a galvanized finish, the latter being preferable. For an 'old world' look of wrought iron, rust-resistant malleable iron hinges are available. This type of hinge looks most effective if it is matched on the gate with a sturdy ring latch set.

Garden gates Heavy garden gates need substantial hinges and it is best to use a cranked single strap and plate hinge (also called a hook and band hinge); alternatively you could use a heavy reversible cup hinge. With all the hinges, you screw the pin plate flap to the face of the post and the long strap portion to the gate itself; the latter should correspond with the horizontal rails on the gate. These heavy hinges

1 Components of a typical timber gate and plans of hanging between posts (**inset A**), to the rear of posts (**inset B**) and on rebated posts (**inset C**)
2 Hanging a gate using either round or square steel posts
3 Hanging a metal gate between concrete posts; use predrilled concrete posts or screw a timber batten to the posts (**inset**)

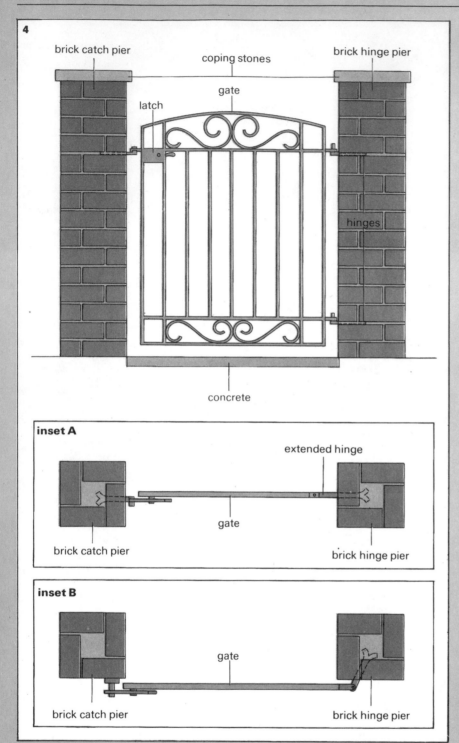

4

brick catch pier

coping stones

brick hinge pier

gate

latch

hinges

concrete

inset A

extended hinge

gate

brick catch pier

brick hinge pier

inset B

gate

brick catch pier

brick hinge pier

have a square hole punched through them to take the collar of a coach bolt, which you pass through the hinge and bolt right through the gate, holding it in place with a nut; this gives additional security around the area of the hinge pin.

Farm gates These types of gate require heavy-duty fittings; use double strap and hook hinges. Most of the weight of the gate is taken by the top hinge, which should be larger than the bottom one. The top ride, as it is often called, extends some way along the top rail to which it is bolted. It hinges on the top hook, which is driven through the gate post and held in place with a nut and washer; this counteracts any tendency the gate has to pull the top hinge from the post. At the bottom, the gate will tend to swing towards the post; the bottom hook is spiked so you can drive it into the post. Both these hooks are wedge-shaped for a secure fixing in the post; the bottom ride is smaller than the top and it simply bolts through the hanging stile. In some cases, the bottom ride is adjustable, which makes it easier to adjust the gate so the latch stile is well clear of the ground.

Fitting gate catches
A common type of catch for farm-style five-bar gates is the spring catch; sometimes an auto-catch is chosen because this type is drilled to take a padlock. Both catches will only work from one direction and the posts must be set so the gate closes onto them. If there is a clearance between the latch stile and the post, you could fit a Chelsea catch which allows the gate to open inwards or outwards.

Loop-over catch Where two farm-style gates meet, they are usually held closed with a simple loop-over catch. One gate is held closed with a heavy-duty drop bolt which fixes into a socket concreted into the ground.

Conventional catch Standard garden gates can be fitted with their catch once they have been hung and are swinging freely. Carefully align the fittings so the latch bar (the moving part) strikes the catch (which is fixed to the post) at around its mid-point. The latch bar should then drop easily into the catch rebate and be securely held in place. When a gate is slammed, the latch takes a good deal of strain; make sure it is securely fitted with large screws.

Thumb latch Also called a Suffolk, a thumb latch can be fitted to a gate by cutting a slot in the gate to allow the latch lifter to pass through. Fit the handle plate and lifter to the front side of the gate; position the latch bar on the reverse side so the lifter will raise the latch bar to its full extent. Finally fit the catch plate.

Automatic catch This is a common latch for low

5

7

6

4 Hanging a gate between brick piers and plans of using extended hinges where the existing opening is too wide (**inset A**) and hanging the gate to the rear of the piers where the existing opening is too narrow (**inset B**)

5 Farm-style bottom ride and hook

6 Top ride and hook

7 Farm-style loop-over catch

8 Cranked single strap hinge

9 Chelsea catch set

10 Ring latch set

11 Automatic catch set

12 Drop bolt and socket

13 Fitting a split pin to prevent the gate being removed; drill through the the hinge pin, insert the split pin and bend it round the hinge pin

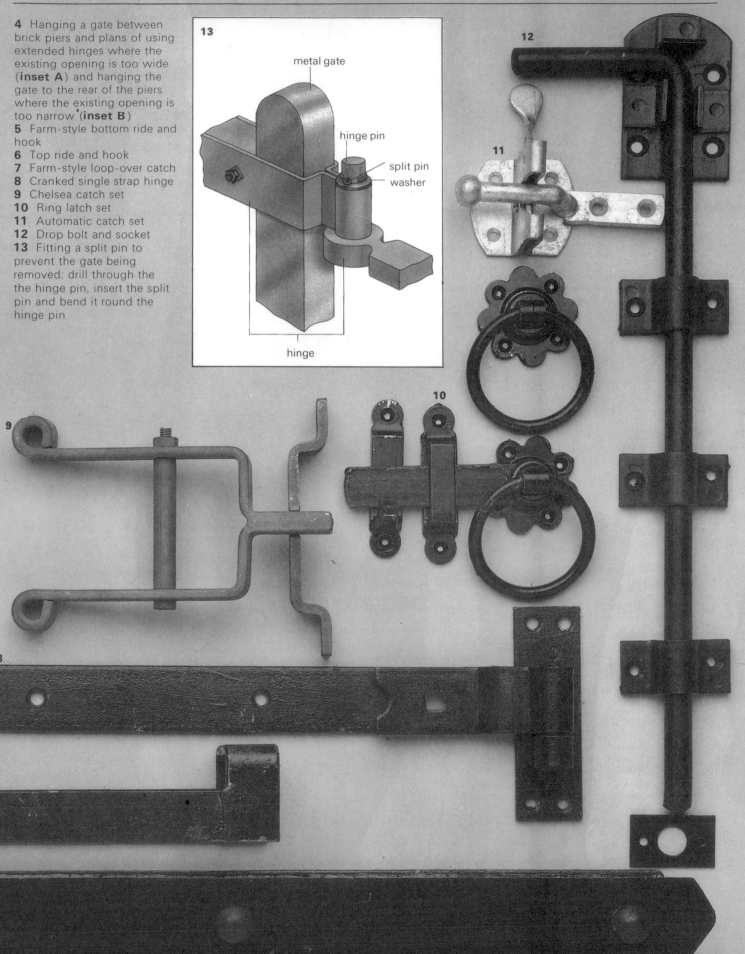

13

metal gate

hinge pin

split pin

washer

hinge

gates; if used on a close-boarded side gate, you can drill the post and fit a release cord which you then fix to the release lever. On some types of catch, you can drill the release lever so a small padlock can be fitted to hold the gate closed. For extra security, you may require a padlock hasp; fit the securing plates with large, long screws so when the hasp plate is in position it covers the screw heads. You could also fit a bolt, low enough to be out of reach from the face side of the gate (if the gate is close-boarded). If it is possible to reach this bolt from the front of the gate, fit a padlock bolt.

Drop bolt If you are fitting double gates, you will require a drop bolt fitted to one gate to hold it closed; concrete a socket or flat plate into the ground to accept the drop bolt barrel. If you are fitting the gates over existing concrete, use a large masonry drill bit in a hammer drill to make the socket.

Gate closers You may also require a gate closer, of which there are several types. The most common is a gate spring, which consists of an adjustable tension coil spring; one end is screwed to the hinge post and the other to the hinge stile of the gate. This is done in such a way as to compress the spring as the gate is opened.

Fitting gate to piers

You should excavate the foundation for each pier to a depth of at least 450mm (18in) and 150mm (6in) wider all round than the pier; in clay soil the pier should be fitted into a 600mm (24in) deep hole. Place a 150mm (6in) depth of concrete into each foundation hole; if the ground is subject to movement, link the foundations to form a strip between the piers.

Piers These must be built up carefully to ensure each is vertical without any twists; the courses of bricks must line up. Use a batten gauge which allows for the hinge and latch projection to ensure the piers are built the correct distance apart. Insert vertical battens on each side of the opening just clear of one outer corner of each pier; these will ensure the piers are built accurately. Make sure the battens are correctly aligned and check they are vertical with a spirit level. To ensure they do not move, join their tops with a crosspiece and secure the vertical battens with temporary struts. Mark each brick course on the battens, checking with a spirit level and straight-edge each course is level, and stretch a line between the marks as a guide to your bricklaying. Remember to build the hinge pins into the mortar joints as your work proceeds if you are using this type of fitting.

Fitting gates between existing piers

If you buy gates of the correct size, you can fit them between existing posts or piers as described above. If the gates are too wide for your opening, you will have to reposition one of the posts or piers.

Gaps If the opening is too wide for your new gates, the biggest problem is to fill the gap. The best solution is to remount the hinges or the latch catch on a strip of timber, which is then bolted to one or both of the existing posts to fill the gap. The timber can be up to 75mm (3in) thick, so you could fill a gap of about 150mm (6in) using this method. Fix the strip or strips of timber with coach bolts, which should pass right through the posts; in the case of a brick pier, fix them using projecting-type expansion bolts. Once the opening has been reduced to the correct width, you can hang the gate.

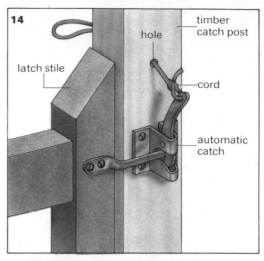

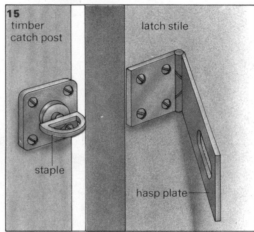

14 Fitting an automatic catch to a timber post; a release cord is fed through a hole drilled in the post
15 Fitting a padlock hasp for extra security; when the hasp plate is in position it conceals the fixing screws
16 Linking the foundations to form a strip between the piers if the ground is liable to movement; the hinge pins are set into the mortar joints as the hinge pier is built

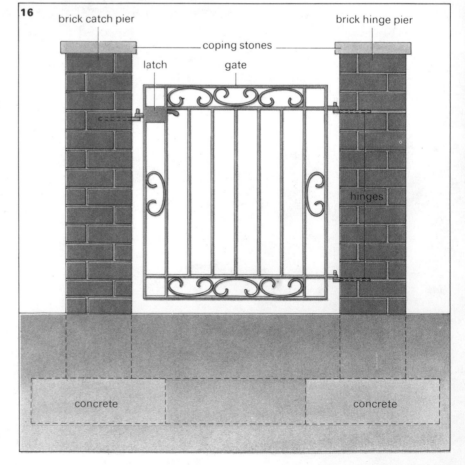

Laying patios and terraces

A patio or terrace should last indefinitely if it is properly laid. It is an expensive item, probably the most costly single item in the whole garden (unless you have a swimming pool) and it is therefore worth aiming for as high a standard of work as possible.

Planning the patio

Before you start laying any material you will have to design the patio, working out its size and make-up in relation to the house and adjoining garden. To do this effectively, make a survey of all the areas involved and transfer the information to a scale drawing.

There are various factors which will particularly influence the layout and construction of the patio and these you should check on when making your survey. Use a long tape to check the dimensions of the house, the position of doors and windows and any changes in level. If there are any trees in the immediate area, measure the distance of these from the house and fences – and indicate the angle of the fences to the building. Once the measurements are down on paper you should double check them since a mistake at this stage would influence the quantities of materials you order.

When you are making a scale drawing you can use a relatively large scale of, for example, 1 to 50 or 5 to 250mm (or ¼ to 12in) since the patio or terrace will probably not measure more than 9 × 9m (or 30 × 30ft). You can make the drawing on a sheet of tracing paper laid over a suitably scaled piece of graph paper; the advantage of using tracing paper is you can easily alter pencilled details as well as obtain unlimited dye-line prints once the design is finalized.

Ordering materials

Your scale drawing should indicate to you the quantity of material you will need to order. Paving slabs which have been drawn to scale are easily counted up; the same applies to bricks and granite setts. Smaller modules such as cobbles can be simply calculated by area; you should work out the amount required for one panel and multiply this by the number of panels there will be in the patio. The amount of sand, ballast, hardcore and cement required is calculated by volume; you should be able to make a rough estimate from your drawing, bearing in mind the thickness of hardcore and concrete areas. Sand and ballast are supplied by the cubic metre or yard and cement in 50kg (or 1cwt) bags; as a rough guide you will need six bags to mix a cubic metre of ballast for foundation concrete work and 12 bags to mix a cubic metre of sand for a mortar mix.

If you are ordering timber decking, choose exterior grade timber which is knot-free to avoid the problem of knots shrinking and dropping out to leave unsightly holes in the patio surface. Hardwood such as oak, ash or mahogany and some soft-woods such as cedar are suitable types of timber. It is worth buying long lengths to avoid joining timbers since movement resulting from the timber being exposed to fluctuating weather conditions will tend to cause joints to buckle or pull apart. Since the decking will be bearing considerable weight you should order timber which is 25–32mm

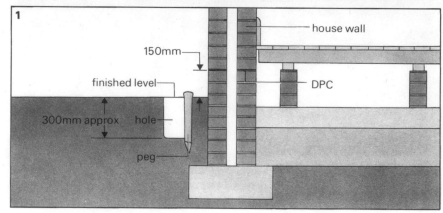

1

150mm

finished level

300mm approx   hole

peg

house wall

DPC

(or 1–1¼in) thick. The timbers which support the decking should be 75 × 50mm (or 3 × 2in) or 75 × 75mm (or 3 × 3in).

Remember normally the more you order, within reason, the cheaper it will be; so it is worth looking round for a supplier who stocks all the materials you need and obtaining them all in one delivery.

Making the patio

Once all the materials have been delivered and are neatly stacked on site, work can begin. One factor you will have to take into account is that a patio or terrace set against a house should be at least 150mm (or 6in) below the damp-proof course (dpc) to prevent rain splashing from the patio surface onto the wall above the dpc or causing the sill of French windows to rot. You should obtain a finished level which will be related to all the other paving on the patio; this must be as close to the house as possible. Dig a hole to a depth of about 300mm (or 12in) and drive in a peg so the top of the

Top Whatever material you choose for your patio, the foundations must be even and well packed; for the best results go over the surface thoroughly with a roller
1 Determining the finished level for the patio surface by driving in a peg so the top is 150mm below the dpc in the house wall

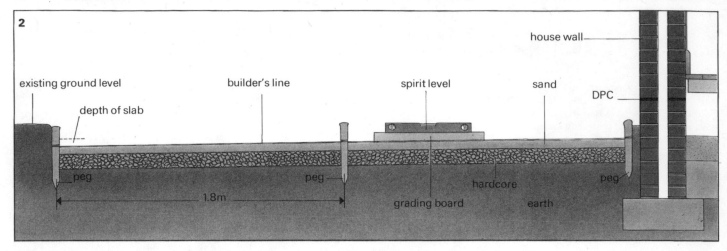

2

existing ground level

depth of slab

peg

1.8m

builder's line

peg

spirit level

grading board

sand

hardcore

earth

house wall

DPC

peg

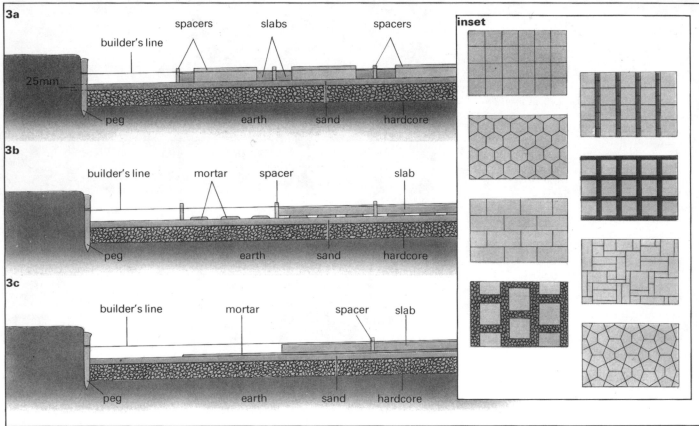

3a

builder's line

spacers   slabs   spacers

25mm

peg   earth   sand   hardcore

inset

3b

builder's line   mortar   spacer   slab

peg   earth   sand   hardcore

3c

builder's line   mortar   spacer   slab

peg   earth   sand   hardcore

peg is 150mm (or 6in) below the house wall dpc.

The type and consistency of the soil and the slope of the existing land will influence the construction of the terrace or patio. Soft ground will require a greater depth of excavation than hard ground to obtain a satisfactory foundation. The fall or slope of the ground may need to be rationalized since the finished paving should throw water away from the house. The finished slope should never be less than 1 in 72, which works out at 25mm in 1.8m (or 1in in 6ft); a slope which is steeper than this will drain more quickly and dry out faster after rain. Make sure the slope is as constant as possible without undulations or dips where puddles can form.

Preparing the foundation
Using lines and pegs, mark out the area to be excavated. The foundations will vary to suit the particular site conditions; with normal soils a base of hardcore 75mm (or 3in) thick will be adequate.

You can determine the depth of soil to be dug by making a calculation based on the thickness of the covering material, the bed on which it is laid and the hardcore. Remember to include the fall away from the house when you are making your calculation.

If you are using more than one material in the terrace, remember they may be of different thicknesses; for example, the difference between a 50mm (or 2in) precast slab and a brick laid on edge would be 63mm (or 2½in). This must be taken into account when you are preparing the foundation and is a good reason for keeping the design simple.

The soil excavated will probably be fertile top soil which can support plant growth and this should not be discarded. Stack it for use elsewhere in the garden or use it to fill any raised beds which form part of the finished scheme.

Once the excavation work is finished make sure the exposed ground is firm by thoroughly treading or rolling it; drive in pegs at 1.8m (or 6ft) intervals

2 Laying the foundations; use a grading board to obtain the correct fall
3a You can lay stones and concrete slabs on a bed of sand
3b Alternatively use blobs of mortar
3c Or lay the material on a continuous bed of mortar
3 inset Designs for laying slabs: (from top) regular pattern of squares, square slabs separated by bricks or granite setts, hexagonal slabs, square slabs infilled with tarmac, regular pattern of rectangles, random pattern, regular slabs set in cobbles and pentagonal slabs

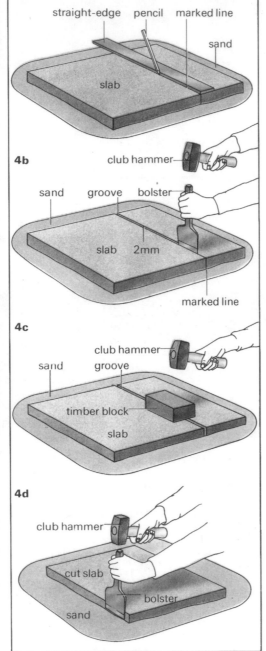

4a

straight-edge   pencil   marked line

sand

slab

4b

club hammer

sand   groove   bolster

slab   2mm

marked line

4c

club hammer

sand   groove

timber block

slab

4d

club hammer

cut slab

bolster

sand

Above Laying concrete slabs: (from top) apply blobs of mortar to the prepared surface and place the slab in position; alternatively spread the mortar over the surface and position the slab
4a To cut a slab to size first mark the cutting line using a pencil and straight-edge
4b Cut a groove along the marked line using a bolster and club hammer
4c Break the slab by placing a wood block over the groove and hitting it with the club hammer
4d Clean up any rough edges on the slab with the hammer and bolster

so 75mm (or 3in) of the pegs – the depth of the foundation – is left showing above the ground. The foundation material can vary from area to area (crushed stone from a local quarry can be ideal), but probably you will be using hardcore. This should consist of broken bricks or stone which is free from dust and old mortar and sufficiently broken down so it consolidates easily and so the gaps can be subsequently filled or blinded with sand. Clinker is sometimes used and suggested for this type of work, but it is best avoided since certain types contain soluble salts which can attack the brickwork in the walls of the house.

Laying stone and slabs
Once the foundation is in place you can begin laying the paving material. Precast concrete slabs or natural stone form the bulk of most terraces and one of three methods can be used to lay them. The most traditional method, which is still used to lay

virtually all public pavements, is to set the slabs on a 25mm (or 1in) bed of sand. This can be quite satisfactory, but bear in mind sand can be washed out of unpointed joints or undermined along an exposed edge; once rain gets in under the surface the slabs may move and start to wobble. The effectiveness of this method depends to a large degree on the weight of the slabs being used; a heavy piece of York stone will be slow to dislodge whereas a thin precast slab could be quite quickly undermined.

For a more durable method you can use five spots of mortar, one at each corner of the slab and one in the middle. The mortar should be a stiff mix of three parts sand to one part cement. The slabs are easy to lift again should this be necessary and the distribution of the mortar spots allows you to level the surface easily. For the third method a continuous bed of mortar of the same or a slightly weaker 5:1 mix is used. This will give an extremely durable result, but slabs bedded in this way are difficult to lift and could therefore pose a problem if laid over drains or services.

Start laying the slabs by the house and mark out the edge of the first row with a string line set at the correct level in relation to the dpc. Lay the slabs using one of the methods described above and allow 9mm (or ⅜in) between the slabs for pointing. To ensure the joints are even, insert pieces of plywood to act as spacers. Tap each slab with a club hammer, using a 75 × 50mm (or 3 × 2in) wood block to soften the blow, to bring it into line with the surrounding slabs. To ensure the correct fallaway from the house use a spirit level placed on a grading board – a timber batten which has one side planed to the angle of the fall. Once the spirit level is placed on the grading board it should indicate the usual horizontal reading, saving time and taking any guesswork out of the operation. Always work backwards from the first course of slabs, avoid stepping on them and check the line of the joints.

If you have used mortar to lay the slabs, leave the pointing operation for about a week until the mortar has set completely. For pointing use a 3:1 mortar mix and work this into the joints with a pointing trowel. Messy pointing can ruin the appearance of the paving and you should rub a rounded piece of wood along each joint so there is a slight depression between the slabs; this will emphasize the crisp nature of the modules.

Cutting slabs It is almost inevitable sooner or later you will have to cut a paving slab. If there is much cutting to be done, it would be worth your while to hire an electric stone saw. If there are only a few slabs involved, this would be uneconomic and you can cut the slabs using a bolster, a club hammer and a 229mm (or 9in) length of 75 × 50mm (or 3 × 2in) timber. Using a straight-edge and a pencil, mark out the slab to be cut on both faces and edges. Place the slab on a bed of sand so it will not rock or move and cut a groove approximately 2mm (or $\frac{1}{16}$in) deep with the bolster along all the marked lines. Position the length of timber at one end of the groove and hit it with the club hammer; repeat this along the length and the slab should break easily. Clean off any irregularities using the hammer and bolster.

Laying brick paving
One of the great advantages of brick is the variety of patterns in which it can be laid to give different design lines and emphasis. As with virtually all other paving surfaces the basic technique of preparing foundations and laying the material, using a

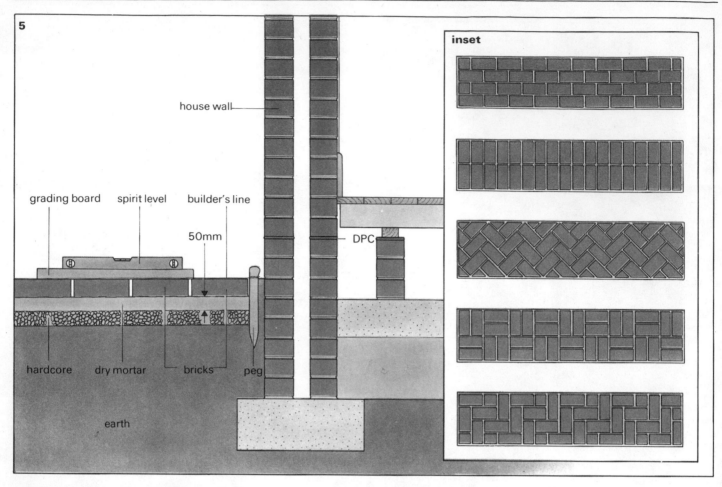

line and following the correct falls as described above, is utilized; but the exact method varies slightly. The types of paving bond are covered later in the book when dealing with laying paths, but laying brick patios and paths is similar.

After the foundation has been formed, bricks can be laid on a 50mm (or 2in) dry bed of five parts sand to one part cement; this can be easily raked to the correct fall and the bricks positioned with 9mm (or $\frac{3}{8}$in) gaps for pointing. Leave any cut bricks until last; use them where necessary to fill in any gaps, leaving a similar 9mm (or $\frac{3}{8}$in) joint. Brush more of the dry mortar into the gaps and carefully spray it with water from a can fitted with a rose. Where you have used a strongly coloured brick such as some of the engineering types, you may choose to use a coloured mortar. There is a range of pigments available and for dark blue bricks the traditional method for darkening the mortar is to use lamp black. As with all paving it is essential to keep the finished surface clean.

Laying granite setts
This extremely durable and attractive surface was traditionally laid with staggered joints 9mm (or $\frac{3}{8}$in) wide on a 25mm (or 1in) bed of sand to take up the inherent irregularities in the setts. The setts were well rammed down and the joints wedged with chippings prior to grouting.

Using modern methods, the setts are laid in the same way as bricks; to ensure the surface is as level as possible use a long straight-edge.

Laying cobbles
Cobbles provide an uneven surface and are best laid on a 50mm (or 2in) thick layer of sand over a suitably prepared foundation. Spread a 50mm (or 2in) layer of 5:1 mortar over the sand and press the cobbles in by hand, making sure there is no mortar between the stones and they are packed as tightly as possible. Alternatively you can lay the cobbles on a dry bed of mortar and add water from a watering can in the last stage of the work. Using a third method, the cobbles can be laid loose, tumbled one on top of the other. In this case there is no need to work to an exact level and you may find a foundation is unnecessary.

Laying timber decking
Before laying any timbers you should treat them with creosote or wood preservative to ensure their durability in such an exposed position. A 50mm (or 2in) layer of concrete over 75–100mm (or 3–4in) of well-rammed hardcore will provide a suitable base for a timber-surfaced patio; the base should be laid at a fall away from the house. The supporting timbers should be spaced about 400mm (or 16in) apart and laid on a single course brick sleeper wall with a bitumen felt dpc between the brick and the timber; the decking is laid at right-angles to the supporting timbers and secured with galvanized or rustproof nails or countersunk screws. Leave a 9mm (or $\frac{3}{8}$in) gap between the decking and any surrounding brickwork and a similar gap between adjacent boards to allow for rainwater drainage.

Build a single skin brick retaining wall round all unenclosed edges of the patio, using a concrete foundation; leave out an occasional half-brick in the first course to allow rainwater to drain off the base. For a natural finish you could use three coats of teak oil or a clear wood preservative on top of the timber decking.

5 Laying brick paving; use a grading board to obtain the correct fall
5 inset Designs for laying bricks: (from top) stretcher bond paving, soldier courses, herringbone, basket weave and herringbone set at right-angles
6a You can lay cobbles on a bed of wet mortar
6b Or set them in mortar and sprinkle with water
6c Or you can lay the cobbles loose, one on top of another
6 inset Designs for laying cobbles: (from top) coursed cobbles, random cobbles and flat cobbles laid parallel
7 For timber decking you will need a concrete base and support timbers laid on a brick sleeper wall with a dpc between the brick and the timber; the decking should be laid at right-angles to the support timbers
8 Building a retaining wall to overcome a steep change in level between the patio and the rest of the garden; dig a trench between the wall and the edge of the paving surface and fill it with gravel to form a soakaway

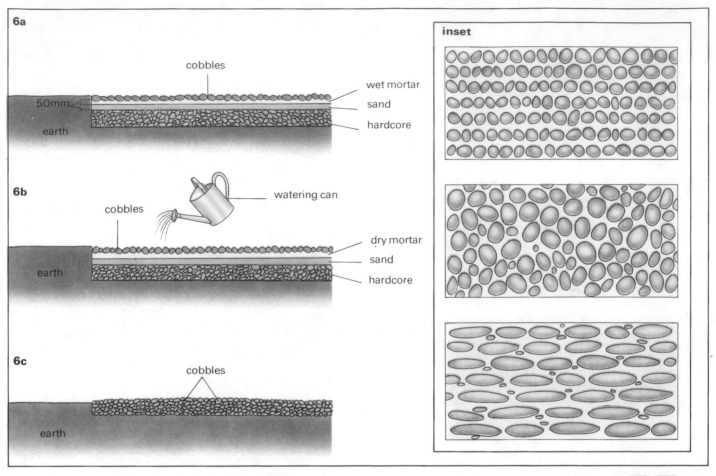

6a

cobbles

wet mortar

50mm

sand

earth

hardcore

inset

6b

cobbles

watering can

dry mortar

earth

sand

hardcore

6c

cobbles

earth

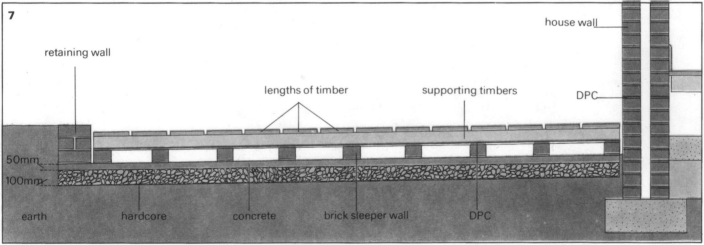

7

house wall

retaining wall

lengths of timber

supporting timbers

DPC

50mm

100mm

earth

hardcore

concrete

brick sleeper wall

DPC

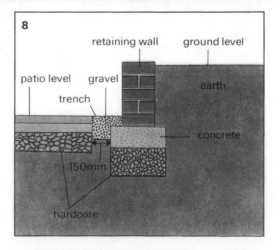

8

retaining wall

ground level

patio level

gravel

earth

trench

concrete

150mm

hardcore

Building a retaining wall

If there is a steep change in level where the patio meets the rest of the garden site, you can build a retaining wall to cope with the change in level. Leave a gap of about 150mm (or 6in) between the wall and the edge of the paving surface and dig a trench in the gap. You can then fill the trench with gravel to form a soakaway; in case this floods you should leave a few open vertical joints in the wall to serve as drainage holes.

Installing patio doors

Patio doors will make a room brighter and give an impression of spaciousness; they will also provide an almost uninterrupted view of the garden, which will then seem to become part of the house and the patio an extension of the room. The doors are available either single or double-glazed; the latter have the advantage of providing excellent insulation. The doors require minimum maintenance since the frames are made of aluminium which will not rust or warp and need never be painted.

Planning doors

Doors are available in standard sizes or can be supplied made-to-measure. Some manufacturers supply only made-to-measure doors and in these cases they will call on you, measure up and install the doors. This is expensive and you can save yourself money by ordering made-to-measure doors which you can install yourself. The cheapest method, however, is to buy and install standard size doors. Standard sizes vary from manufacturer to manufacturer; by studying their catalogues you should find doors to suit your needs.

Ventilation This is a factor you must consider when ordering doors; if you install floor-to-ceiling doors, you will have to leave one door slightly open to get ventilation. You can overcome the problem of security by fitting a proprietary security device which allows a door to be locked either fully closed or in a slightly open position; but the inevitable draught created might not be acceptable on a cold day. A night vent will give some ventilation; but this may not be sufficient and it is therefore worth considering a fanlight (see below).

Measuring up the opening

To find out the size of the opening you should ignore any existing timber frames and measure the size of the opening between walls. Measure outside the house so internal plasterwork or decorations do not interfere and take several measurements of the height and width in case the opening is out of square. Make sure you measure in the units in which the doors you want are available; most manufacturers work only in metric, although some still refer to Imperial sizes. Don't measure in metric units and then convert to Imperial, or vice versa, since critical errors may occur.

Reducing the opening

If the doors you want are a little smaller than the size of the opening, you can use a slightly thicker timber surround, to which the aluminium frame is fitted. If the doors are lower than the opening, you can install a night vent above the doors; this sliding ventilator is fitted above the aluminium head member to provide ventilation without causing excessive draughts or a security risk. Where there is no height difference and you wish to install a night vent, remember to reduce the height of the doors accordingly when you are ordering.

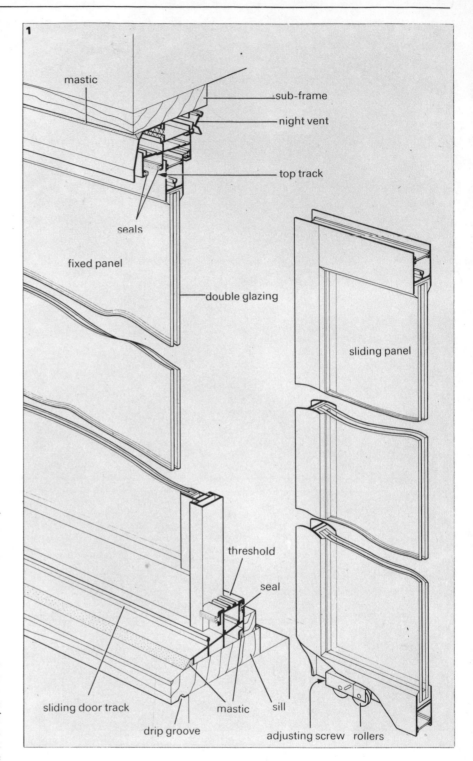

You can make up a height difference of about 300mm (or 12in) by fitting a fanlight unit above the door. You will probably need two or more units depending on the widths available. When ordering, list the door and fanlight units individually and as a combined figure.

Enlarging the opening

If you have existing French windows with wing-lights over side walls, it will not be too difficult to knock out these windows and the wall below to make room for patio doors which are too large for the opening. You will have to make sure you leave a clean brick edge against which the new timber surround can be fixed; you might be able to achieve this using a chisel and club hammer or you could

1 Section showing the typical installation of patio doors in a timber sub-frame; the doors consist of one fixed and one sliding panel, both of which are double glazed, and a night vent is fitted above the aluminium head member to allow ventilation without causing excessive draughts or presenting a security risk

also depend on the way you intend the doors to be used. If you want to provide the maximum traffic area, all panels must be movable. Most installations comprise two doors – with one fixed and one sliding panel.

Choosing glass
Most manufacturers normally supply 4–6mm (or $\frac{5}{32}-\frac{1}{4}$in) thick float glass which is very tough and quite adequate under normal circumstances; however, it can break if subjected to violent impact. Toughened or tempered glass is much stronger; if it does break under impact, it will shatter into very small pieces – like a car windscreen – so there is less likelihood of serious injury. Laminated glass is another safety type, which consists of a sheet of resilient plastic sandwiched between ordinary sheets of glass; if the glass breaks, the plastic interlayer will keep the glass panel basically intact.

Eliminating problems
You will not have to draught or weatherproof the doors after installation since these facilities are built into the design; normally a polypropylene strip is incorporated in the aluminium frame. After assembly you should run a bead of mastic round the joint between the frame and the timber surround as described below.

Condensation Condensation on the aluminium frames is a problem in some installations because water tends to condense on metal; but you are unlikely to encounter more than a minimal problem on the glass itself if it is double-glazed. One manufacturer supplies a system designed to eliminate condensation; it incorporates a thermal barrier between the inner and outer frame. However, the doors do cost more as a result.

Security Most systems incorporate a security device to reduce the possibility of an intruder gaining entry through the doors. The locks are usually built into the frames so they cannot be interfered with from outside. Many manufacturers will fit extra locks which can be key-operated from outside or inside and you can fit extra devices yourself.

Fitting doors
Manufacturers of DIY systems provide full fixing instructions for their products; these will differ in specific details, but the procedure given below is typical of most designs.

Preparing the opening
After you have removed the existing windows and surround and, where necessary, enlarged the opening, you should check there is a neat edge to the brickwork. Make sure the opening is squared up; although any slight discrepancies should be compensated for by the timber surround, the doors will not operate properly if the opening is badly out of square. It may seem obvious, but check again the opening is the correct size for the timber surround and doors which are being installed.

Installing the timber surround
The manufacturer will specify the minimum thickness and width of timber to be used for the surround. To make up this sub-frame, you should use hardwood; softwood is more likely to deteriorate and, if so, you will have to remove the doors and track to insert new timber later on. Before you fit the sub-frame, spread a band of mastic around the opening.

Installing aluminium-framed patio doors; the kit shown here can be cut down to fit
2 Assembling the aluminium frame
3 Positioning the aluminium frame in the timber sub-frame
4 Screwing the frames firmly together
5 Fitting the glazing seal

hire an industrial saw to do the job quickly.

If you want to increase the width of the opening further than the existing windows, a lot more work is involved. For example, the lintel above the existing window will have to be increased in length since it has to support the bricks in the wall above the glazed area.

Choosing panels
Depending on the width of the opening you will have to decide on the number of door panels needed; bear in mind the more panels there are, the more expensive it will be. You should also decide how many movable panels you want, since these are more costly than fixed ones.

Besides cost, the arrangement you choose will

Make up the complete frame and position it in the opening, using packing pieces where required at the sides, top and under the sill. Use a steel rule, plumb line and spirit level to check the frame; the internal dimensions must be correct, the sub-frame square, the uprights vertical, the top and bottom members perfectly flat and the diagonals equal.

The frame is screwed to the surrounding masonry. Drill countersunk holes in the frame and use these as a guide to make holes in the brickwork using a long shank masonry drill; insert wall plugs and drive the fixing screws home. The manufacturer will state the size of screws to be used and the intervals at which they should be fixed. After you have inserted the screws, check the frame again to make sure it is square and level.

Treatment The sub-frame will remain sound and stable for years provided it is treated during installation – and then at least every other year – with varnish or preservative. Alternatively you could paint the frame; apply a coat of aluminium primer followed by two undercoats and a gloss coat. Repeat as necessary to maintain the woodwork.

Installing the aluminium frame

Make up the aluminium frame on a flat surface since any unevenness in the work surface can result in a distorted framework. Follow the manufacturer's instructions closely. The screws used to hold the frame together might be a tight fit for the pre-drilled holes; if so, you should not try to force them in or distortions may occur. Apply a little soap or beeswax to the threads to ease them home, but don't overtighten them or some damage may be caused. Anodized aluminium can be damaged by abrasive materials so make sure the ground beneath the framework is smooth and the frame protected during assembly.

The aluminium frame is bedded onto the hardwood frame with at least one band of mastic set into the frame rebate to make a watertight seal between the aluminium and hardwood frames. In some cases a second band of mastic around the front edges of the frame is specified. Position the aluminium frame and lay its base on the sill. Swivel the frame to align it correctly, then raise it into position and press it firmly against the frame and mastic bed; check the frame for squareness. Drill appropriate size pilot holes into the timber sub-frame through the pre-drilled holes in the aluminium frame then drive aluminium or alloy screws of the length and gauge specified through the aluminium and into the hardwood frame. Again check the frame for squareness.

Installing the panels

Fixed panels should be inserted first; for this you will need someone else to help you. Place thick polythene sheeting on the sill to prevent it being scratched, lift the panel up into the top track and ease the bottom into the bottom track. Slide the panel into the side jamb and secure it to the frame with cleats or brackets at the top and bottom; use a hand drill to make pilot holes for the fixing screws since an electric drill could damage the aluminium.

To protect the rollers, a sliding panel should always be stored upside down prior to installation. Before it is lifted in, stand it the right way up on one or two 50 × 50mm (2 × 2in) wood blocks so the wheels are clear of the wood. With someone else to help you, raise the panel top into the frame and ease the bottom gently into place. Check the panel slides easily and, if necessary, raise or lower the panel

height by adjusting the rollers. Before carrying out adjustment, take the weight of the panel off the sliding rail to prevent damage to the screw threads. To raise or lower the panel, turn the adjusting screw on the roller mechanism clockwise or anti-clockwise as appropriate.

The locks can be adjusted by turning a screw in the appropriate direction; complete the installation by fixing the handles and door stops and any threshold strips and top vents. Any cement or plaster which is smeared on the anodized aluminium framework should be washed off immediately to ensure you get a watertight seal around the frame.

6 Assembling the door frame round the glass
7 Lifting an assembled panel into the aluminium frame
8 Adjusting the roller mechanism; take the weight of the door off the rollers when making the adjustment
9 Sealing around the aluminium frame with mastic

Garden walls

The kind of garden wall and its size will depend on the type and size of the area involved. The wall can be high or low, solid or partially open, and it can be constructed from a variety of materials.

Brick walls

The material most commonly used for constructing garden walls is brick. This is particularly suitable for climbing plants, but you should avoid adorning this type of wall with too many hanging plants or a forest of suspended plant troughs since they will spoil the inherent simplicity of the feature.

For any wall over 1.4m (4½ft) high, 229mm (9in) thick brickwork will usually be required, though 114mm (4½in) thick brickwork can occasionally be used; this will, however, need buttressing at frequent intervals. For walls over 2m (6½ft) high, 343mm (13½in) brickwork will be most suitable. If a wall adjoins a house which has brick walls, it is worth trying to match the bricks used in the garden wall with those used in the house; if your house is a listed building or you live in a conservation area, there may be a legal requirement to use sympathetic materials. In any event a garden wall more than 2m (6½ft) high usually requires planning permission and it is worth checking this out with your local authority before you begin work.

If you are unable to obtain bricks which match exactly the bricks in the house walls, the weather will often rapidly mellow the new wall. To accelerate this process you can paint on a solution of liquid fertilizer to encourage the growth of mosses and lichens.

One way of providing a link between the house and the garden is to match the colour of the garden wall with a colour scheme used inside the house. For example, where a room with sliding doors or French windows adjoins the garden wall you can paint or render the wall white or ivory if these colours are used for the walls of the room. Where the wall is to be rendered, you will not need to use expensive facing bricks since common flettons are quite suitable.

Coping For the coping or finish along the top of the wall it is usually best to keep to a straightforward design; bricks on edge placed side by side in a continuous line are most suitable for a 229mm (9in) thick wall. To make certain of weather protection you can use a 'creasing' course of staggered tiles below the bricks·laid on edge. The simple line of a 114mm (4½in) thick wall can be spoilt by an unsympathetic coping – and you should not stand bricks on end as a coping since this only emphasizes the flimsy structure of the wall. It is also worth avoiding patterns of bricks laid at 45 degrees or right-angles to one another since these tend to give a fussy effect. A suitable finish for a 114mm (4½in) thick wall is either to omit a coping altogether – and use a top course of a harder engineering brick instead – or to use cut headers; these are bricks cut in half to measure 114mm (4½in) and laid on edge to form the coping.

Brick patterns You can use brick in complicated patterns and designs, but on the whole these tend to detract from the beauty of the material. A possible exception is a simple honeycomb wall which is 114mm (4½in) thick and uses a simple stretcher bond with a gap left between each brick to produce a lattice effect. This gives a partial view and incomplete shelter from wind, but it can form an attractive screen within a garden by defining an individual area without cutting it off completely.

Concrete walls

Walls can be built from concrete blocks which are available in a wide range of sizes and textures. Walls using 229 × 229 × 457mm (9 × 9 × 18in) blocks are capable of carrying substantial loads and therefore make ideal bases for pergolas, barbecues and built-in seating. Bricks on edge are commonly used for coping on walls of this type, but simply detailed aluminium or other types of metal coping can also look most effective. You could make maximum use of a concrete block wall by using it to enclose a sitting area on one side and put up a lean-to greenhouse or a carport on the other side. Concrete blocks do not require rendering since they are quite weatherproof when coped; a simple application of a stone paint can make them very attractive in appearance. When you are pointing, make sure the joints are neatly ironed back to emphasize the crisp shape of each module.

Decorative walling Concrete blocks are commonly used in a wide range of decorative walling. Screen blocks are a familiar sight in many gardens, but be careful if you intend using these since they have an

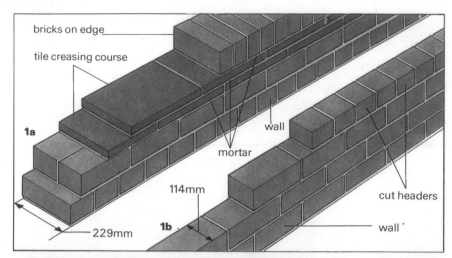

1a Brick wall with staggered tiles laid below the brick coping to give extra protection against the weather
1b Single thickness brick wall with a coping of cut headers
2 By incorporating a honeycomb bond into a brick wall you can provide an attractive screen within the garden without cutting off the view completely

Labels on diagram 1a/1b: bricks on edge; tile creasing course; mortar; wall; 114mm; cut headers; 229mm; wall

inherently busy pattern and a surfeit can quickly become boring. As a general rule use them in a controlled way; a single run is more effective than being enclosed on all four sides by walls of this type. Planting can be used to good effect to soften their rather mechanical looking outline; for example, a screen block wall showing through the foliage of a willow tree could be most effective.

The 'landscape bloc' is a well-designed and practical material which has recently become available. It has a flattened 'U' shape and can be put together in a variety of ways to make walls and screens with differing characteristics. It is sufficiently adaptable to be used to form raised beds, seats and tables as well as retaining walls and steps.

Precast concrete slabs Paving slabs, which can be used in certain situations for walling, are usually cut in half to conserve material. In design terms they provide a useful link between the surface used in a terrace or patio and a low retaining wall. Paving slabs can be used as coping on a low wall – a row of 600 × 600mm (2 × 2ft) slabs provides a useful long seat at minimal cost.

Concrete cast on site Rather than buying individual modules, you may decide to cast the concrete on site; this method is particularly suitable for low and retaining walls. You can finish off the surface in a variety of ways – for example with attractive board marking used in the shuttering, or with various exposed aggregates.

Stone walls

You may decide to use stone, a traditional walling material which is now relatively expensive. As a general rule you should try to use local stone; the wall will not look out of place and you will avoid the cost of long distance haulage.

Walls in the country are often built dry with the stones placed one on top of another and no mortar between the joints; this operation requires considerable skill. In a rural situation stone can be teamed with rammed earth to form a combination of a wall and a bank with the stone acting as a weatherproof face.

Rectangular blocks These are far easier to lay than random shape ones and the resulting wall will look less rural and more architectural, a point worth bearing in mind in an urban situation where a link

between house and garden is important. Sawn blocks look the most architectural but they are expensive to buy.

Small stones In some areas small stones such as cobbles and flints are used as a decorative feature within a framework of some other material such as brick. Flint-knapping is a highly skilled traditional craft; a wall finished with flints in this way can be an excellent feature so long as it is in keeping with its surroundings.

Constructing walls

The procedures you should follow when constructing a garden wall will depend partly on the type of material you have chosen. Building a brick wall has been covered in detail earlier in the book. There are, however, several factors you will have to consider when building a garden wall, whatever the type; these, together with the construction of walls from materials other than brick, are described below.

Building foundations

The foundation or footing you build will depend upon the site conditions. The main object of the footing is to carry the wall above without move-

3a Garden wall with a bitumen damp proof course which is stepped to suit the sloping site
3b To give a wall in an exposed position greater strength, two layers of engineering bricks can be used as a damp proof course
3c Alternatively the damp proof course can consist of two staggered layers of slate with mortar in between

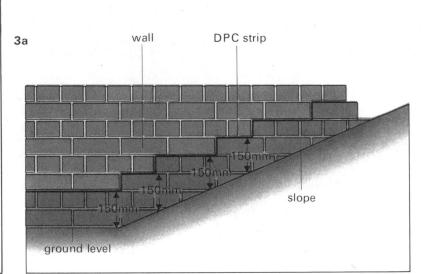

3a

wall   DPC strip

150mm
150mm
150mm
150mm
slope
ground level

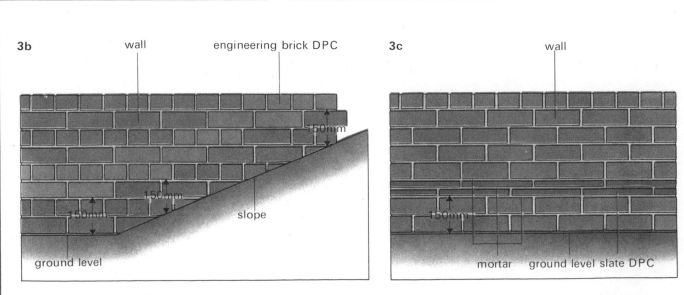

3b   wall   engineering brick DPC

150mm
150mm
150mm
slope
ground level

3c   wall

150mm
mortar   ground level slate DPC

ment or subsidence; this means the footing will have to be taken down to a point where there is no frost penetration or movement due to water in the ground. Where there are shrinkable clays, ground movement due to a fluctuating water table' is common; if there are young fast-growing trees such as willows or poplars in the vicinity, the problem can be aggravated. Mature trees which have reached their adult proportions will rarely be a problem close to a wall or building since their root system will have become established and little further development is likely; in most cases it is a young tree which is likely to cause damage as it develops. On poor ground under these conditions it may be appropriate to excavate to a depth of 1m (3ft) to make sure a wall has the best possible chance of stability. As a general rule a free-standing wall is less prone to damage due to settlement than a wall which is an integral part of a larger structure.

In most garden situations a footing depth of 600mm (2ft), 450mm (1½ft) or even less is usually quite adequate. For a 229mm (9in) thick brick or concrete block wall approximately 1.8m (6ft) in height a concrete foundation mix of one part sand to two parts cement and five parts aggregate is suitable; the dimensions of the footings will be between 450mm (1½ft) and 600mm (2ft) wide and between 150mm (6in) and 600mm (2ft) in depth. As a guide, the minimum width of the footings should normally be twice the width of the finished wall. If you are dealing with a sloping site, remember the footings will have to be stepped to accommodate the fall.

Keeping out weather
You will have to prevent weather penetrating the wall at the top and bottom. In certain situations, ground water may contain sulphates which can attack the brickwork and must be counteracted.
Damp proof courses A horizontal dpc should be laid 150mm (6in) above ground level; if you are working on a sloping site, this should be stepped with the fall. In very exposed situations a wall can become weakened along the line of a horizontal dpc so the whole structure is liable to be blown over. In this case a dpc consisting of two courses of engineering bricks laid 150mm (6in) above ground level is suitable. Other types of dpc can be constructed from lead, copper or at least two courses of slate laid to a breaking, or staggered, bond with each slate bedded in a mortar mix of three parts sand to one part cement; mastic asphalt or bitumen roll can also be used. Metal dpcs are usually expensive, while bitumen is satisfactory in most cases.
Installing copings Coping will keep the weather out of the top of the wall as well as shedding water off its face. Copings can either be flush with the wall, when some streaking of the surface is likely from drip down, or they can project from each side, so the drips fall clear to the ground. With a projecting coping a shadow will be cast and this can give an attractive and definite end to the vertical wall line.

Some copings are constructed from the same material as the rest of the wall – for example brick over brick or stone over stone. Whatever type of material you use for the coping, remember to keep the detailing relatively simple so you do not spoil the straightforward line of the wall.

Limestone and slates are easier to work than other types of stone and are therefore particularly suitable for use as coping materials. Sandstone can undergo shrinkage and thus open up the joints between the stones. To ensure a completely weatherproof seal, a dpc is often inserted under a

4 A screen block wall gives some privacy and provides support for climbing plants, while simulated stone blocks and concrete coping make an attractive raised bed
Types of coping:
5a Metal sheet
5b Bull-nosed bricks
5c Stone or concrete
5d Precast concrete with drip channels
5e Precast concrete slabs

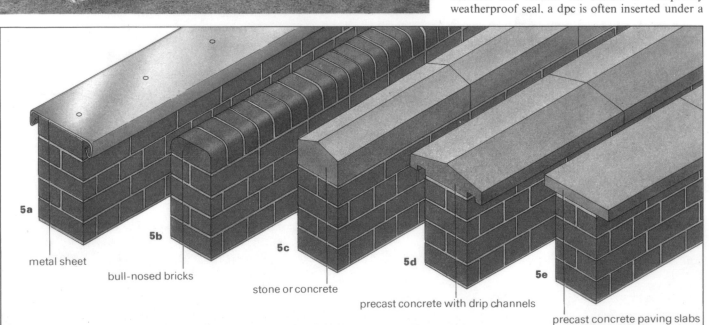

5a metal sheet
5b bull-nosed bricks
5c stone or concrete
5d precast concrete with drip channels
5e precast concrete paving slabs

stone coping although in the case of slate, which gives a particularly crisp finish, there is no need for this since it is virtually impervious.

Precast concrete copings are available in a wide range of finishes and sizes and can provide an ideal finish for a reasonable price. If they overhang the wall, it is worth including a throating to keep drips clear of the wall. Copings can be flat or weathered so they slope downwards in one direction or on both sides.

If you are using a tile 'creasing' course with a coping of bricks on edge, it should consist of two courses of plain tiles laid to a breaking bond. There is no need for the tiles to project beyond the face of the wall; if this is done and the projection finished with a cement fillet, the cement will often crack away and allow water penetration.

Metal copings can often give a very precise finish to a wall. They are impervious to water and you can extend the line of a metal roof by using a similar material to that used in the roof for the coping of the garden wall. The three metals most commonly used are copper and aluminium, which are expensive but long-lasting, and zinc, which is considerably cheaper but will not last as long.

Apart from metal copings which are usually screwed or clipped into position, all the other types can normally be bedded on a mortar mix of three parts sand to one part cement. Make sure the mortar layer is not too thick, particularly where a dpc is used; as a guide, a layer of the same thickness as the joints used in the general construction of the wall will be suitable.

Counteracting wall movement

If a free-standing wall is of any length, it will be subject to expansion and contraction due to temperature changes. Where a wall extends out from the house, there should be a 13mm (½in) gap between the wall and the building since the garden wall will be susceptible to movement. Along the length of an extensive wall expansion joints should be positioned not more than 9m (30ft) apart. If you want to avoid an obvious gap which shows daylight, you can stagger the joint so one side overlaps the other.

Building retaining walls

Walls over 1m (3ft) high are often used for retaining levels on sloping sites. They require considerable strength and complicated construction work, although a wide variety of materials can be used. Since the back of the wall will be permanently wet, there is little point in incorporating a horizontal dpc; the back of the wall could, however, be protected with a water-proofing compound. To relieve pressure from ground water you should leave an open vertical joint between the brick or blockwork at 1m (3ft) intervals along the length of the wall. This joint should be one course above ground level since if it is any lower it is likely to become blocked by dirt and weed growth. On very wet sites, sections of land drainpipe may be built into the wall; you can make sure they are kept clean by angling a slate against the inside.

Building concrete walls

For garden walling, concrete blocks measuring 229 × 229 × 457mm (9 × 9 × 18in) are generally the most suitable size to use. They are usually available with hollow cores which can be filled with concrete and strengthened with steel reinforcing rods tied

into the footings; with a wall less than 1.8m (6ft) high, however, this is not usually necessary. Each block constitutes the thickness of the wall so you can use a simple stretcher bond and cut the blocks to form the ends of each course.

Using screen blocks These blocks, which are more delicate in appearance and strength, are usually 114mm (4½in) thick. Short runs of walling are built between specially detailed pilasters and corners which have a keyway into which the blocks can be built. The pilasters and corners are hollow and can be built round steel reinforcing rods which have been bedded into the footings of the wall in the same way as for concrete block walling. As work progresses concrete is poured into the pilasters around the rods to provide strength and support for the wall as a whole. There is usually a purpose-made coping available for this type of wall. Since the wall is pierced, there is less wind resistance than with a solid wall of the same dimensions; so although the wall is only 114mm (4½in) thick, it has reasonable mechanical strength.

Building stone walls

These tend to be expensive and difficult to lay and construction is often best left to a local craftsman. Rubble walls, which are most commonly seen, can be of a number of different types. Regular and irregular courses can be used where the stones are rough-faced and roughly rectangular. With irregular courses, several stones can make up the depth of a course. In walls built of random rubble, there are no courses; each stone is selected to interlock with its neighbour.

Traditionally, all these types of stone walls were laid dry, but using mortar makes construction easier. If you are using this technique, make sure you keep the joints as small as possible so the mortar does not mar the appearance of the wall.

Most stone walls are laid to a batter so the wall is wider at the bottom than the top to give the wall stability and strength. Coping is usually traditional and it is best to copy coping used on stone walls in your area. This may be stones on edge or flat; some walls have no coping at all. In areas where stone is used for building, there is often a layer of rock just beneath the surface so foundations can be kept to a minimum; if there is a layer of soil, you will have to excavate for foundations.

6 To give a stone wall stability and strength, lay it to a batter or angle: use large stones at the bottom and smaller ones on top
7 A natural stone wall can double as a planting ground and is ideal in rural situations

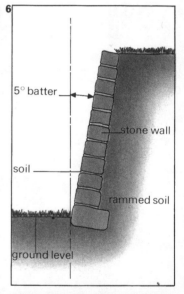

6

5° batter

stone wall

soil

rammed soil

ground level

7

Garden steps

Steps can cause more problems in design than virtually any other feature in the garden. A flat garden can be relatively easy to plan, but as soon as there is a change in level the difficulties begin. One of the hardest things is to think of the garden in three dimensions, particularly when converting it to a plan – which is two dimensional. Nevertheless the scope for planning a sloping garden is immense and the result can be much more interesting than a level garden.

Designing the steps

Think carefully about siting steps to make the most of the steps themselves and to ensure they enhance the garden. Placing steps right down the middle of a garden chops it in two, making both sections seem smaller than they really are; but if the steps are placed down the side or diagonally across, you will achieve a feeling of space and movement which disguises the rectangular boundaries.

Choosing materials

The materials from which steps can be made all have different characteristics; some such as brick and stone look best close to the house, while timber and earth are more suited to the back of the garden.

Natural stone, one of the most expensive types of paving available, can be one of the most attractive if used correctly. Rectangular concrete slabs should be used closer to the house in conjunction with stone or brick for a riser. With both natural stone and concrete slabs it is best to have the tread overhanging the riser by about 38–50mm (1½–2in); this creates a shadow which gives the impression the steps are floating.

Brick steps on the other hand usually have a flush riser, for which special bull-nosed bricks are ideal. The tread can be completely surfaced in brick or the riser can act as a frame for another surface such as aggregate concrete or asphalt if it is at the front of the house leading to the drive.

Gravel can be useful, particularly for filling hexagonal or circular steps, while grass always looks attractive and can be used how you like. If you live in the country, you can make good use of timber; even diseased elm, once the bark has been stripped, is ideal for the garden.

Planning first level

Since the first step in most gardens is down from the house itself, it should set the tone for the whole garden. Here you need a wide, generous platform which extends the full width of the house doors and more; the tread can be 600mm (or 2ft) deep and is a good place for plants or statuettes.

This step is an important link between the house and garden, so choose your materials carefully; if your house is brick, a brick step will form a visual bond. If you are lucky enough to have stone floors inside, stone would look superb as a step or a terrace. If there is no obvious linking material, use precast concrete slabs or concrete steps. Try to keep things near the house rectangular; curves and stronger shapes look better further down the garden. Above all keep things simple to create a feeling of space.

Basement access A problem you might encounter close to the house is gaining access to a basement well. What you need here is a feeling of lightness and stone or brick steps could prove too cumbersome in an area where space is often at a premium. A wrought-iron staircase which allows light to filter through could be ideal; alternatively timber steps with the risers kept open to admit the maximum amount of light would do just as well.

Planning second level

The next major change in level is from the terrace down to the main lawn and a good idea is to turn the flight of steps at 45 degrees to the house to link with a diagonal path. Don't treat the steps as an isolated feature, but link them to the overall design of the terrace and garden by interlocking them with

1 These slate steps provide an attractive visual link between the house and the garden

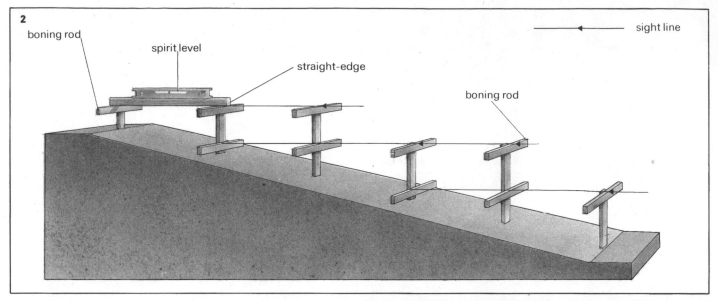

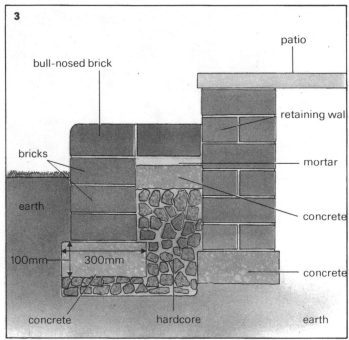

raised or split level beds – with perhaps a pool or herb garden at the top or bottom. Keep the steps deep and wide; an overall width of 2.4, 3 or 3.6m (or 8, 10 or 12ft) is not too much. If you have room, treat the steps as a series of platforms on which to place statuettes, pots or a garden seat. Steps do not have to be regular in size and a flight can even turn through 90 degrees if you wish to save space or descend a slope more quickly.

Different patterns Curving shapes often look more effective at the back of the garden and components and methods of construction can be more informal. A steeply sloping site will allow for several changes in level, each of which will have to be accessible by means of steps closer to the house or a ramp at the back of the garden; try to be original and not merely copy what is nearer the house. Railway sleepers can look good in a steep garden and are best laid in a staggered pattern and not one above the other. You can vary the pattern with long lengths of timber sliding into planting on each side, with the odd boulder placed to give a bit of shape.

Hexagonal and circular steps look attractive in the middle of the garden; you can fill a large hexagon of bricks with aggregate concrete or grass and have them butting together up a slope.

Tree trunks can be used to build a more permanent flight of steps and are held in place by stout stakes driven into the ground. The space between the risers is filled with rammed earth, hoggin and gravel – or even chamomile which smells lovely when crushed underfoot (plant the prostrate variety since the ordinary type will grow too tall).

Cantilevered steps suit a really sharp slope and can be built with natural stone, each step projecting from the vertical face of a wall. It is important to build them properly with the slabs having at least half of their overall length bedded into the wall; estimate your calculations for each step to take a far heavier load than usual. This horizontal construction set against something vertical like a tree can look very striking.

If you have a large garden, you might build circular steps which can have a diameter of anything up to 300mm (or 12in). The riser of each step should be in brick with turf set just above this so the

2 Using boning rods to plot the slope; you can then relate the change in level to the number of steps required
3 Section showing brick steps formed at the end of a patio; hardcore is used as infill and a bull-nosed brick gives a neat finish
4 Brick steps can be used effectively in a formal garden and here blend in with the watercourse which runs alongside them

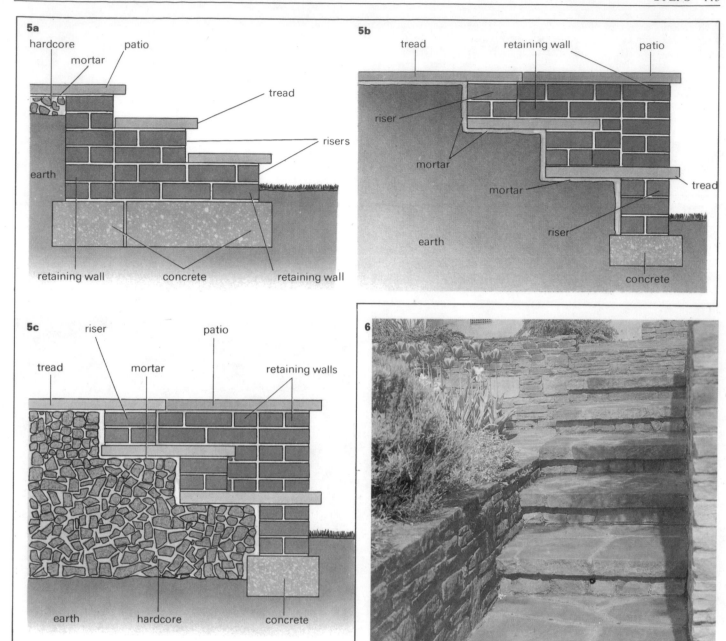

5a
hardcore   patio
mortar
tread
risers
earth
retaining wall   concrete   retaining wall

5b
tread   retaining wall   patio
riser
mortar
mortar
tread
riser
earth
concrete

5c
riser   patio
tread   mortar   retaining walls
earth   hardcore   concrete

6

mower can run smoothly over the top. The circles should overlap one another in a staggered pattern – and you can add plants if you like. The treads can be of grass, concrete, brick or stone; all are equally good and will make for different effects.

Constructing the steps

Once you have decided what type of steps best suits your design, you can start constructing them. Whatever steps you use in your garden, sound construction is essential if you want them to provide years of trouble-free service.

Plotting slope

You must first plot the slope involved accurately to relate the change in level to the number of steps required. If the site is complicated with a number of steep falls, you may need a qualified surveyor to give an accurate set of figures.

Usually, however, you will be able to plot the slope yourself using home-made boning rods; these are T-shaped stakes driven into the slope at regular intervals so marks can be lined up and heights added together. Drive in a short boning rod at the highest point of the slope and place one end of a straight-edge on the edge of this; drive in a longer boning rod down the slope to support the other end of the straight-edge. Lay a spirit level on top of the straight-edge and adjust the second boning rod until the bubble is at dead centre. This means the tops of the two boning rods are level and by taking a sighting across them you will be able to drive in a third rod further down the slope without needing to use the spirit level or straight-edge.

If the slope is steep, it will be impractical to make boning rods tall enough to maintain the original level. Instead measure an identical distance down the last two rods, nail on additional cross pieces at this new lower level and continue as before. The sum of the height adjustments made in this way, plus the difference in height from soil level to the top of the first boning rod and to the top of the last boning rod, is the difference in level from the top to the bottom of the slope.

You can often estimate small changes of level,

5a Section showing how steps can be formed at the end of a patio; retaining walls are built out onto the lower level to support the treads
5b Section showing how steps can be built into the patio area; the rough shape is cut into the soil and the treads are laid on mortar (the treads can be used as footings for the retaining wall on each side)
5c Section showing how steps can be built into the patio area where the soil is soft; a retaining wall is built each side and the area behind the risers is backfilled with hardcore as the steps are laid
6 Overhanging stone steps built between retaining walls

such as low banks and retaining banks, by eye or with a measuring tape. Existing brickwork can also be a good guide if you remember each course of bricks measures 75mm (3in).

Once you have this information, transfer it to a scale drawing which will be the basis of your subsequent design. The levels must be related to a fixed point or 'datum' which makes the rest of the garden either above or below that point. Manholes are often useful as fixed points; alternatively you can take the finished level of your terrace or patio as a suitable starting point.

Garden steps are very often too steep and small, whereas they should be broad with ample treads to make them easy to walk on. As a rule a 150mm (6in) riser is ideal and it is easy to divide your slope or change of level by this figure to work out the number of steps required. The tread should be at least 300mm (12in) deep, although 450mm (18in) makes for a more comfortable step. The width of the tread determines the amount of ground the steps need; the wider the steps the greater this will be.

Setting steps

Once you know the overall dimensions of the steps you can prepare for the flight. On normal ground which is relatively stable, start by digging a trench for the bottom riser. The riser can be made of stone, brick or concrete section and the footing will need to be approximately 300mm (12in) wide and 100–150mm (4–6in) in the ground, depending on the type of soil.

Use a mix of one part cement, two parts ballast and three parts sand on a base of hardcore and fill the trench; build the riser from this, remembering the thickness of the tread needs to be taken into account when calculating the measurement of each riser. If using precast concrete treads, lay the treads on a 25mm (1in) bed of mortar made up of three parts sand to one part cement. The treads can be flush with the riser, giving a clean, crisp line, or overhang by about 50mm (2in), producing a shadow which gives a softer feel. If you are using brick for the tread, pick a hard, well-fired variety to stand up to weather and frost. The engineering type is the hardest, although a good facing brick is usually adequate.

For the edge of a step a special bull-nosed brick gives a rounded finish which can look most attractive. Subsequent risers can be built off the back of each tread and should be checked constantly with a spirit level. When positioning the treads, make sure they have a slight fall to the front

to prevent the formation of puddles, which can be especially dangerous in frosty weather.

Retaining walls If instead of building a flight of steps up a slope you want to link an abrupt change in level, such as between a paved terrace and a lawn below, the procedure is much the same. To build the steps out onto the lower level you will need a retaining wall on a concrete footing each side of the flight to give it support. These walls can be in stone, brick or concrete, depending on the design of the steps; fill the area between the walls with well consolidated hardcore or concrete as work progresses, allowing the treads to be bedded on the normal layer of mortar.

If you wish to cut the steps into the higher level, you can cut out the rough shape of the flight and build the steps from the bottom up as before; the treads of the steps can be used as footings for the retaining walls on each side.

If you are working on soil which is too soft or unstable to form the shape of the flight, excavate the entire section, build retaining walls on concrete

7 These circular steps provide a stylish feature linking the house and garden
8 Section through hexagonal steps, showing the materials used and a plan of how the steps are linked (**inset**)
9 Section through circular steps and a plan of how the steps are linked (**inset**)
10 Section through steps formed with sleepers laid at an angle; the area behind each sleeper is backfilled with hoggin and rammed soil
11 Section through log steps held in place by stakes and backfilled with rammed soil
12 Section through a stepped ramp formed by laying granite setts at an angle on mortar and hardcore

7

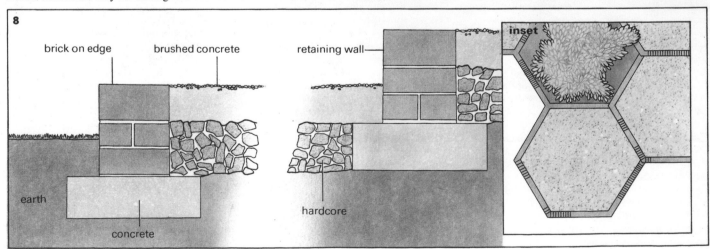

8

brick on edge   brushed concrete

earth

concrete

retaining wall

hardcore

inset

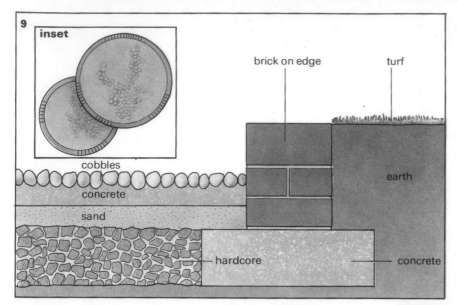

brick on edge · turf

cobbles

concrete

sand

earth

hardcore · concrete

the bank at each end of the log to hold it firmly in position. The stakes themselves should preferably be of hardwood and both the logs and stakes should be soaked in a suitable preservative – not creosote which is poisonous to plants – before use. If the slope is steep, one step can follow immediately above another; but with shallower gradients you can use quite deep treads slightly ramped if necessary. The tread can be rammed soil, gravel bedded on hoggin or even planting, with stepping stones. Rows of stakes can also act as risers, the diameter of each stake being 50–75mm (2–3in).

Stone steps If you can get hold of them, large sections of stone roughly shaped or preferably sawn can be used in much the same way as sleepers. They can be laid one above the other to form a continuous flight or used at intervals with a wide tread between each.

Warning Whichever type of material you decide to use to make steps in the garden, remember the steps must be laid securely or accidents could arise if people do not have a firm foothold.

footings and build the flight between them; backfill with hardcore as the work proceeds.

Large steps With larger steps which might measure anything up to 1.8–2.4m (6–8ft) square, the procedure is the same as for the paved surfaces on the terrace or patio. Falls are particularly important with large steps, so keep a close eye on the levels as you work up the slope.

Large circular or hexagonal steps are usually suitable for a gently sloping site and need careful setting out. Find the radius point by scaling off your design drawing and calculate the length of the radius itself. Drive a stake into the middle of the proposed circle and swing a line from this to mark out the curve. For a hexagon or other multi-sided geometrical patterns, divide the circle into regular sections, driving stakes into the circumference to mark them; join the points together working round the circle until you have the required shape.

With large steps, the treads can be constructed from any material or combination of materials, while drainage is ensured either by using porous materials such as gravel or grass or by making weep holes. Weep holes are incorporated into the brickwork by building a wide joint between two bricks and making sure it is kept free of mortar and pointing; they should be at the bottom of the wall and spaced approximately 1m (or 3ft) apart.

Cantilevered steps These can be attractive and useful, but have to be carefully constructed since they have no riser to act as a support. The strength depends on the material used and the depth to which the step is bedded into the supporting wall. Natural stone is often used, as is concrete which has to be reinforced. The retaining wall which supports the steps must be built at the same time with each step having at least half of its overall length bedded and securely anchored into the wall. If you are in any doubt over the construction, call in a qualified engineer or builder.

Timber steps Railway sleepers make useful and informal steps and can be bedded dry. Simply cut a platform for them and lay each sleeper in position, making sure it is slightly angled back into the slope.

Logs can be used in a similar way. Having first stripped the bark, particularly if the timber is elm, place the section in a shallow depression cut out of the bank. Being circular, logs will tend to move more easily than sleepers, so drive two stakes into

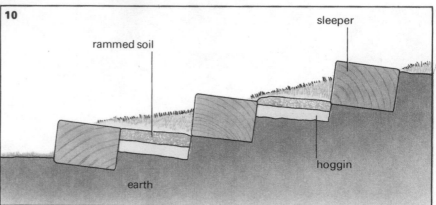

rammed soil · sleeper · hoggin · earth

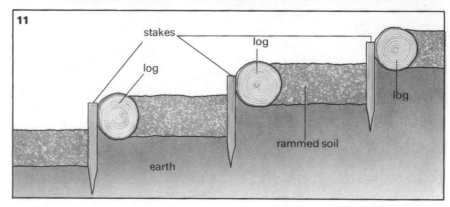

stakes · log · log · log · rammed soil · earth

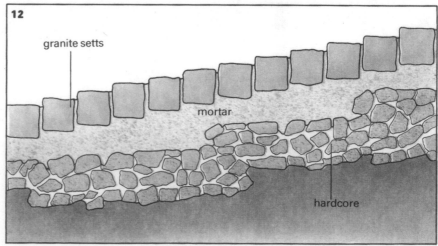

granite setts · mortar · hardcore

Garages and carports

As with any extension, a garage or carport should be chosen carefully to blend in with the shape and style of the house and garden. If you decide to design your own garage and have it built privately, you should choose the same brickwork and roofing materials as those on the house. Building a brick extension is being covered later in the book. A custom-built garage can be expensive, however, and will take time to complete, particularly if you build it yourself.

Garages are usually bought in prefabricated form; kits are supplied by several manufacturers and have the advantage of being quick to put up and less expensive to buy. From the wide range of garages available in this form, you should be able to choose one which suits your requirements.

A carport is useful in providing a covered area for a vehicle; it can also be used as a play area for children or for hanging out washing on a rainy day. Carports are simple constructions which you can

Above Single flat-roofed garage with glass fibre door and aggregate-finished walls with brick-pattern front posts
Right Pitched roof garage with partially glazed timber doors
Putting up a typical prefabricated garage:
1 Having laid a concrete base, fix the first layer of wall panels all round
2 Go back to the starting point and build up the wall panels, fitting door and window frames as required; fix roof trusses in position as you work
3 Fit the remaining roof trusses and fix the fascias before bolting the purlins and ridge beam in place

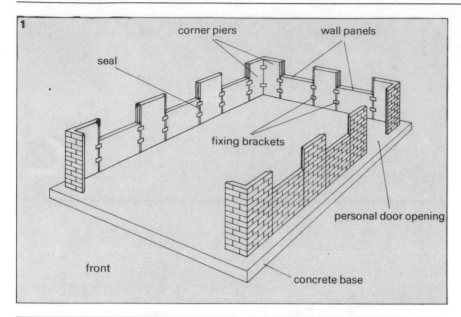

1 corner piers, wall panels, seal, fixing brackets, personal door opening, front, concrete base

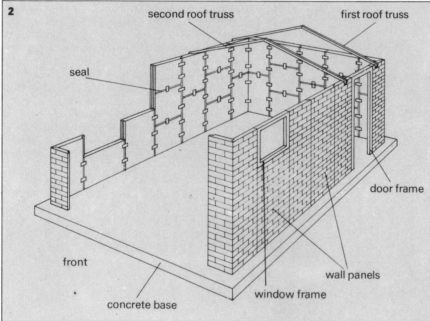

3 roof trusses, ridge, front fascia, purlin, concrete base

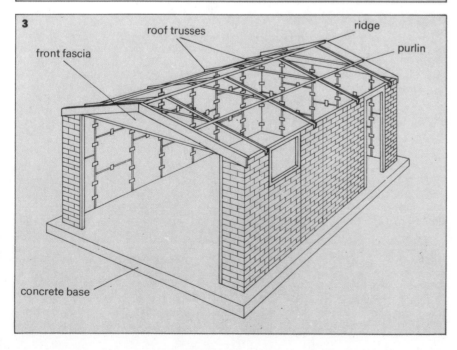

2 second roof truss, first roof truss, seal, door frame, front, wall panels, window frame, concrete base

buy in kit form or build yourself using timber supports and roof framework.

Planning permission This will be required before you begin to build a garage; it applies even if you are taking down an old garage to build a new one. You will need to submit at least three plans of the building to your local authority planning department. Most prefabricated garage manufacturers will give advice and supply you with plans free of charge since they produce their garages to comply with current Building Regulations.

Choosing garages

Obtain as many catalogues as possible and study the information and prices offered. Before you apply for planning permission you should know exactly the style and size of garage you want to build. Most manufacturers will supply single and twin garages; widths range from 2.5m (8½ft) for a single to about 5m and 7m (16½ and 23ft) for a double. The specified dimensions are usually internal and the outside dimensions in length and width will naturally be larger. The internal dimensions are important in relation to the size of your vehicle.

Length Prefabricated garages are available from 4 to 7m (13–23ft) in length, although some models can be supplied in up to 8.5m (28ft) or over 9m (30ft) lengths. It is worth considering building a long garage if you have the space; the extra area will be very useful for a workbench, gardening equipment or household appliances. You could add a carport to the front or rear of the garage since this will serve as a covered play or work area. Some manufacturers supply small annexes which can be built onto the end of a garage to form a workroom.

Roof The roof can be flat or pitched, the latter being more expensive. A pitched roof does give extra height inside the garage and this can be useful if you need to store ladders or long pieces of timber. If you intend garaging a high vehicle, such as a motorized caravan, you will need the extra height of a pitched roof.

The roof is supported on steel trusses and purlins and is usually clad with corrugated asbestos roofing boards. You can order a tiled roof for the garage, but this will increase building costs considerably. Building Regulations specify garage roofs must be built using asbestos or tiles to comply with fire resistance requirements; you can fit translucent roofing sheets for extra light, but they must have asbestos boards on each side. Some prefabricated garages are supplied with standard fascia boards, while other kits offer a choice between timber and steel fascias.

Doors There are three types of door generally available for prefabricated garages – softwood, galvanized steel and glass fibre. All can be up-and-over in operation and softwood doors can also be supplied hinged. If there is not enough natural light in your garage, you could fit partially glazed timber doors. If you decide to fit an up-and-over door, bear in mind it will take up a small amount of the floor-to-ceiling height when it is open.

Personal door This can be a standard feature or an optional extra and is usually fitted into a side or rear wall. The door normally takes the place of one prefabricated wall panel and can be either steel or timber. If you have a wide item, such as a concrete mixer, to store in the garage, you can fit double versions of the personal door.

Rear doors You can choose full-width rear doors

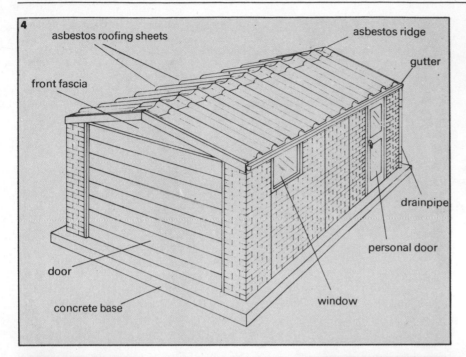

4

- asbestos roofing sheets
- asbestos ridge
- gutter
- front fascia
- drainpipe
- personal door
- door
- window
- concrete base

4 Complete the garage by
fitting the roofing sheets
and asbestos ridge sections,
glazing the window and
installing the main and
personal doors
Above Traditionally styled
double garage with tiled roof
brick-pattern front posts and
aggregate-finished side and
rear walls

with some prefabricated garages; these allow a
vehicle to be driven through the garage – to a
covered maintenance area at the back, for example.
Windows Windows can be supplied as standard or
as optional extras. You can fit more than one
window if required and they can be fixed or
opening.
Walls Prefabricated garages are usually supplied
with concrete panels which slot together to form
the walls. There is a wide variety of finishes, from a
stippled concrete effect to a decorative brick or
stonework pattern; all can be painted to match the
external decorations on the house. Some manufacturers offer a garage with a decorative brick
pattern on the walls each side of the garage door.
Accessories You will need guttering on both sides
of a pitched roof or at the rear of a flat roof. Several
manufacturers supply guttering as an optional extra
or you can buy your own elsewhere. Some manufacturers also supply brackets for shelving inside
the garage; again you can accept these or provide
your own.

Building a garage

A prefabricated garage is supplied with full building
instructions and you should always follow them
closely to ensure good results. The instructions
given below should be taken only as a guide to
construction since the details will vary from make
to make.
Concrete base Once you have obtained the
required planning permission, the base can be laid.
The size of the base differs between manufacturers;
some stipulate one which is only slightly larger in
length and width than the garage, while others
stipulate a base which has a 300mm (12in) overlap
in length and width. Laying a slab of concrete has
been covered earlier in the book. Check your
formwork is square and the top edges are horizontal
in all directions; the finished slab must be smooth
and level since any unevenness will make it very
difficult to build the garage.

One prefabricated garage manufacturer recom-
mends a finished hardcore and concrete base level
of 300mm (12in). Lay at least 100mm (4in) of
hardcore – and up to twice this depth if the soil is at
all loose or unstable. The layer of concrete should
be 100–150mm (4–6in) thick; use a mix of one part
cement, two parts sharp sand and four parts gravel.
Cover the concrete with polythene and allow it to
cure for two or three days.
Assembly Once the garage has been delivered, read
the manufacturer's instructions carefully. Start
building at one of the rear corners, slotting the
panels and piers together and clamping them with
the fixing brackets supplied. Fix one panel layer all
round the base of the garage, return to the starting
point and build up the wall section. Fix the first
steel roof truss in position and continue to build the
wall panels to full height, adding more trusses as
work proceeds. Once you reach full height, the
panels will be quite heavy to handle; it is best for
two people to lift them into position and a third
person to fit the clamping brackets and bolts. Fit
the front fascia and roof purlins before bolting the
roofing sheets and ridges to the roof trusses.
Finally, fit barge boards, windows, doors, rainwater goods and accessories.

Another type of prefabricated garage requires a
similar concrete base with an overlap of 100mm
(4in) in length and 50mm (2in) in width. First
assemble the corner panels, which must be set at
right-angles to the rear and side walls. You can
then add further side and rear wall panels, including
a window if required. Bolt the remaining rear walls
panels into position and build the rest of the side
walls; ensure the walls remain parallel and add the
roof rafters as work proceeds. Fit the metal
brackets to the front rafter and the top of the side
wall panels so you can fit the fascias. Fix the roof
panels to the rafters and rear wall panels using the
bolts provided and add flashings to complete the
garage roof. Check the front opening is square and
hang the garage door. You can then add any
accessories you have chosen, such as a side door.
If the garage walls are of decorative pebbledash, you
will usually have to conceal the joints between
panels. Rub a sand and cement mix into the joints
inside the garage; the joints outside should be filled
with the special mastic and pebbledash granules
supplied with the garage.

Replacing a garage door

If you want to change the appearance of an existing
garage or replace a rotted timber door – timber

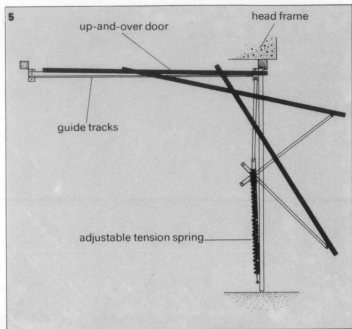

5
up-and-over door

head frame

guide tracks

adjustable tension spring

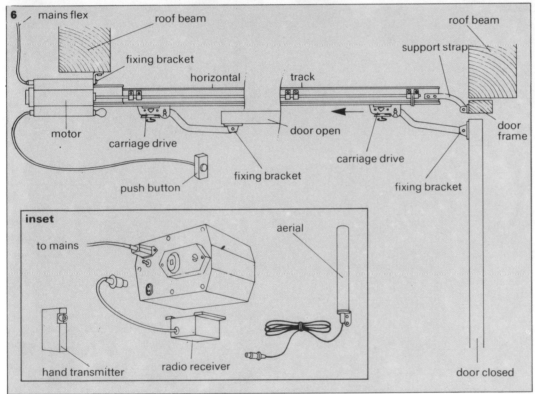

6 mains flex

roof beam

fixing bracket

horizontal

track

roof beam

support strap

motor

carriage drive

door open

carriage drive

door frame

push button

fixing bracket

fixing bracket

inset

to mains

aerial

hand transmitter

radio receiver

door closed

Above left Single garage
with aggregate finish to all
walls and fascias; also
available in multiple form
5 Opening/closing action
of a typical up-and-over
garage door
6 Cutaway of an up-and-
over door fitted with an
electric operator; the
mechanism can be operated
from a wall-mounted push
button or radio transmitter
in the car (**inset**)

garage doors are notorious for rotting from the
base upwards – you can fit a new garage door.
Hinged timbers doors for garages are not widely
available so choice will be limited and you will
probably have to fit an up-and-over door.

Most up-and-over doors are made of aluminium
or galvanized steel and are either flat faced or
corrugated. Some doors are faced with wood or
textured plastic simulating wood; glass fibre
imitation period doors are also available.

The most common type of door track is fitted
inside the garage, just below the roof; the door is
lifted onto this with counterbalanced springs or
weights. When the door is opened, it will usually
slide fully back into the garage. When fitting an up-
and-over door, follow the manufacturer's instruc-

tions very carefully; this job is sometimes difficult
and you may prefer to have the door installed by a
professional.

Door sizes Before ordering a replacement garage
door measure the height and width of the opening
at several points and check the diagonals to ensure
the opening is square. Study manufacturers'
brochures to find a door of the correct size. Some
companies will give actual door sizes, while others
will give the size of opening their doors will fit. If the
door size is specified, you will have to allow for a
clearance round the door.

Standard door sizes are usually exact multiples of
305mm (1ft) and between 2.1m and 4.3m (or 7 and
14ft). There are some odd sizes available, such as
2.3m (or 7½ft). If your opening is 25 or 50mm (1 or

Left Vinyl-coated galvanized steel carport with translucent corrugated plastic roof

2in) too narrow or too wide for the standard door, you can reduce or increase the width of the timber frame to suit. Some doors can be fitted directly to the walls, in which case you can remove an existing timber frame to suit the size of door.

Most door heights are 2 or 2.1m (or 6½ or 7ft); anything higher than this becomes difficult for most people to operate. If the opening at the front of your garage is high, fit a suitable fascia – of timber, for example – to reduce the height so a standard door will fit.

Electric operators Most up-and-over doors can be fitted with an electric operator which enables them to be opened and closed from a wall-mounted push button or key switch or from a radio transmitter. A typical operator incorporates an automatic garage light, a safety clutch and a manual release lever. It is powered by an electric motor, protected by a circuit breaker, and has a six point switch which you adjust according to the size of door – although you should always select the lowest possible power setting.

Full instructions for installation are supplied with the equipment and these should be followed carefully. The power to the unit should be supplied from a 13amp switched socket outlet near the motor. All push buttons or key switches should be wired in parallel using bell wire and connected to the low voltage supply from the transformer in the operator unit.

Building a carport

A carport is a simple construction which can be free-standing, with pillars on both sides to support the roof, or a lean-to structure using a house wall as a fixing point for the roof.

All proprietary carports are very similar, comprising galvanized steel supports under a simple roof framework of steel or PVC; the roof itself can be of translucent corrugated PVC sheets. You can sink the steel supports into the ground and concrete them in place or fix them to existing concrete slabs

with special brackets. The usual heights are 2–2.5m (6½–8ft) and widths are 1.75–3m (6–10ft); lengths are from 2.1m to over 9m (7ft to over 30ft).

If you prefer, you can devise your own carport using timber supports and roof framework to accept corrugated plastic sheets.

Below Spacious double garage with extra wide main door for easy access for two cars; this model is also available with a full width door opening at both ends

Laying paths and drives

Laying concrete blocks and concrete paths and drives have been covered earlier in the book. There are several other materials you can use and many require the same preparation as for concrete.

Drives

Drives are more expensive to lay than paths and they require far more preparation. Make sure the foundations are stable; they may have to withstand heavy delivery vehicles and would otherwise be prone to cracking and subsidence. A sloping site should be made as smooth and shallow as possible since a steep slope would cause problems – especially in winter when snow and ice could block your drive.

Bitumen A versatile and easily laid drive surface, bitumen is a mineral pitch which resembles tar; but unlike tar it does not crack with shrinkage. Cold bitumen emulsion can be laid using a watering can and hired spreader; you will need a well compacted 100mm (4in) thick hardcore base blinded with ash. The base is the same as required for a concrete drive, covered earlier in the book. Apply the emulsion in quantities of 5.5lit per sq m (1gal sq yd). Cover this immediately with stone chippings; roll them well in and after 24 hours roll the surface again. Leave the drive for about two weeks and apply a second layer of cold bitumen emulsion in quantities of 1.8lit per sq m ($\frac{1}{3}$gal sq yd). Spread a second layer of smaller stones over the surface; washed pea shingle provides an ideal finish. This top dressing must be well rolled at intervals over a week or more; if not rolled thoroughly, the drive may deteriorate rapidly.

If the drive is to take very heavy traffic, lay the bitumen on a concrete base. Lay a 100mm (4in) thick hardcore base, blinded with ash, and add a 75mm (3in) layer of concrete. The bitumen coats are laid on top of this as before.

Asphalt A mixture of crushed stone or pea shingle and bitumen, asphalt can be applied hot but is easily applied cold. Cold asphalt is available in bags supplied by builders' merchants; the stone is already mixed so an asphalt drive is slightly easier to lay than a bitumen one. Prepare the hardcore base, blinded with ash as for a bitumen drive and rake cold asphalt to a depth of 13 to 19mm ($\frac{1}{2}-\frac{3}{4}$in) over the surface. Roll the drive immediately; if asphalt sticks to your roller, apply water to the roller. Add decorative chippings if required and roll the drive once more.

If the drive is to take heavy traffic, lay a concrete base as before. You can form a camber for both asphalt and bitumen drives; this will ensure rainwater dispersal.

Gravel Criticism of this material often derives from bad laying techniques; if laid properly, a gravel drive will give years of service. However, gravel does not lend itself to a sloping site; the surface tends to migrate to the lowest point. The surface must be thoroughly rolled during all stages of laying. Unless this is done, the covering surface will loosen and form a treadmill effect; puddles will form, leading to rapid deterioration. Try to keep the shape of a gravel drive as simple as possible; this will enable you to roll its entire area thoroughly.

Above Using a roller to compact the base for the marked out path
Left The finished precast concrete paving slab path laid with mortar on a hardcore base; make sure your foundations are stable – if one slab lifts or moves, your path will look untidy and could be hazardous

There will be many local specifications relating to a gravel drive, but the following instructions will cover most eventualities.

Lay a base of hardcore and roll it to a finished thickness of 100–150mm (4–6in). Using a 50mm (2in) screen mesh as a gauge, lay a layer of coarse gravel to a depth of 50mm (2in). The third surface should be fine gravel with hoggin acting as a binder; roll this to a thickness of 25mm (1in). Hoggin is simply a clay dug from the same pit as the fine gravel and acts as a binder for the surface. The final dressing should be 10mm ($\frac{3}{8}$in) thick washed pea shingle. Spread and roll it onto the surface; it should simply cover the surface since it will migrate to the lowest point of the drive if you make it too thick. If you are laying the drive in dry weather, you can water the roller to prevent it picking up gravel; avoid laying the drive in very wet weather.

1 To lay a paving slab path through a lawn, prepare the base thoroughly and rake over the sand. **2** Roll the sand flat. **3** Lay the slabs on a bed of mortar, tap them into place with a mallet and check with a spirit level. **4** Fill the joints with mortar. **5** Section through a bitumen drive or path. **6** Asphalt drive. **7** Gravel drive. **8** Brick path. **9** Stepping stones laid across a lawn

Brick The best bricks to choose are engineering bricks; an ordinary brick will break up under heavy wear or frost damage. You will need to lay hardcore at least 100mm (4in) thick as the base; for extra durability this can be covered with 75mm (3in) of concrete as described earlier in the book. The bricks should be bedded on a 3:1 mortar mix and you can either butt join the bricks or point the joints using a mix of one part cement, two parts lime and six parts of washed builder's sand. Pointing is preferable since it seals the surface and protects it from heavy vehicles and weathering.

Paths
Paths are more delicate features than drives, but the laying operation is straightforward. The range of materials for paths is similar to that for drives, although there are additional materials such as stepping stones which cross a second surface such as grass or planting. Make sure you lay your path correctly. If you do not, it will soon deteriorate and become a hazard; a wobbling paving stone could very easily cause a broken ankle.

Concrete, ashphalt & gravel The method of laying paths using these materials is the same as for a drive, except the base layer blinded with ash is not so thick – 50mm (2in) should be sufficient. Falls and levels along the path are critical; puddles are dangerous when frozen and they will also allow water to undermine the path, leading to deterioration.

Brick You can lay bricks for a path, flat or on edge, on a bed of mortar; they can be butt joined or pointed and rubbed back. Engineering bricks are particularly suitable for butt joining and are normally laid on wet mortar. Second-hand bricks are usually laid on a 5:1 dry mortar mix which can be easily raked out to the correct fall; lay the bricks with a 10mm (⅜in) gap between them for pointing. Brush more mortar into these joints and spray the path with water. Granite setts and stable pavers can be laid in a similar manner.

Stepping stones The base for this material is less critical since the stones are usually expected to take less wear. Lay the slabs or stones out across the grass, slice the turf round each one and remove the stone. Lift the turf with a spade and remove a thin layer of the soil underneath; this will ensure the stone sits just below the level of the grass when you reposition it, making it easier to mow the grass without striking the stones. If the stones are to receive heavier wear, you can position them on a base of hardcore; bed the stones on mortar and remember the finished path should be level with the surrounding surfaces.

Timber More unusual paths can be made from timber railway sleepers, logs and other associated materials. The weight of a railway sleeper will be sufficient to hold it firmly in position. Logs can be used to form stepping stones if you use sections cut from tree trunks. The stepping stones are laid as described above.

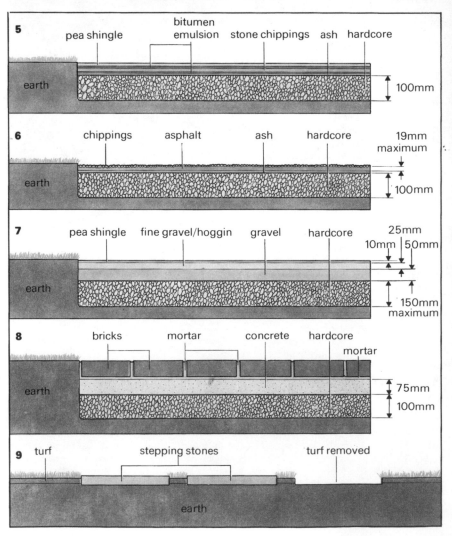

Making a porch

There are several good practical reasons for building a porch enclosing a front or back door; it will form an effective heat trap and cut down draughts, keeping the hall and the house warmer. A porch is also a useful place for storing muddy boots and shoes; if you make it large enough, you can also use it is a pram park or cloakroom.

A porch can provide shelter for visitors and add to the value of your house, and because a porch can be well insulated and give additional security, you can change your front door to a glass one – improving the light level in your hall. In this case fit a good quality mortise lock, with deadlocking function, to the porch door.

Legal requirements

Before you begin building a porch, whether prefabricated or otherwise, you will need local authority approval; this includes planning permission and Building Regulation approval.

Planning permission This is mainly concerned with the visual impact of the porch on your house and its impact on the surrounding area. However, if the porch has a floor area of less than 2sq m (or 22sq ft), is situated more than 2m (or 6ft 6in) from a main road and has a height of less than 3m (or 9ft 10in), planning permission is not required – even if the porch comes in front of the building line. A porch exceeding one or more of the above dimensions will require planning permission unless it is built on the side (not fronting a main road) or at the rear of the house; in this case it is classed as a home extension and planning permission is not currently necessary, as long as it does not exceed 50cu m (or 1750cu ft) in volume.

Building Regulations These are intended to ensure the porch meets a satisfactory standard of building with regard to such aspects as foundations, damp proof course, roof construction, drainage and fire resistance. All porches must conform to these regulations, whether built at the front, side or rear of a house. Therefore in all cases you will have to submit a Building Regulation application to the local authority.

Procedure The relevant forms for Building Regulations applications are available from the building control department of the local authority; planning permission forms can be obtained from the local authority planning office. Officers from both departments will give advice about an application and it is well worth talking to these people at an early stage in the planning of a porch, especially if you are uncertain about approval by the local authority. Some manufacturers of prefabricated porches will supply free drawings of the proposed porch which you can submit to the local authority; some will make the application on your behalf for an extra charge.

Types of porch

A porch designed to form an integral part of the building can improve the appearance of the house.

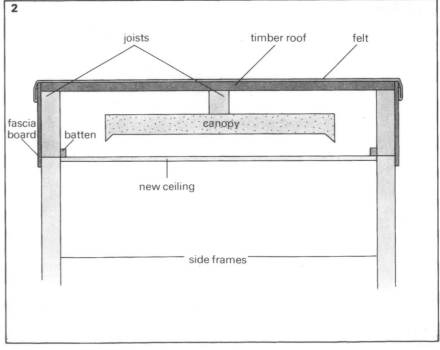

The simplest porch is a canopy roof over a front door, although this type gives little more than rudimentary protection from light rain. Enclosed porches are far more useful and these can be divided into two basic types – built-in and built-out.

Built-in This type of porch is the cheapest and easiest to install. You can fit it if your house is built with the entrance door set back from the front of the building, thus forming an open porch. If this opening is rectangular, you may be able to choose a suitable proprietary front frame. Otherwise the frame can be made to measure by a specialist porch manufacturer or a skilled joiner.

If the existing open porch has an arched top, you will probably require a made-to-measure porch; these are available from some manufacturers. The DIY alternative is to fill the curved section with an exterior grade plywood panel to enable a fan light window to be fitted into a frame underneath. If your arch has a large radius, you may be able to shape softwood to follow the line of the arch and form a frame for a shaped piece of glass to act as an infill panel; a glass merchant will cut the glass to shape if you take a paper template of the exact shape of the arch frame.

Built-out This type of porch is basically an extension to the building, projecting in front of the doorway and comprising front, side and roof sections. It is the most common design of porch and various types are available. Timber framed prefabricated glazed sectional porches are very popular and come in both modern and period styles to suit most houses. This type is available in a range of standard sizes, although you can have a porch tailor-made at an additional cost. Many prefabricated porches are glazed to ground level; some have decoratively finished reinforced concrete under-sill sections; and some are designed for building on top of an existing or proposed brick or stone low wall base.

The alternative to a prefabricated porch is an individually designed and built unit. In this case, the porch can match the style of the building exactly. Unless you intend designing and building the porch yourself, however, the cost of employing an architect and builder can be high. You may already have a large canopy roof and a side wall, in which case you can use these by filling in the front and sides to form an enclosed, built-out porch. You may also be able to infill a porch area using the standard size frames sold by joinery and sectional porch manufacturers; they can be adapted slightly to suit your particular porch. If this is not possible, made-to-measure frames can be obtained from a specialist manufacturer. You can also use made-to-measure frames if the porch is to be joined to an adjacent bay window.

Some houses have concrete canopies over the front door which are not large enough or suitable for the porch roof. In this case, either remove the canopy (which can be difficult if it is made of reinforced concrete) or build around it. This is done by building the new roof to enclose the old canopy; the porch ceiling is underneath the canopy and the exposed sides of the cavity thus created are enclosed with a fascia board.

Designing a porch

Before you decide to build, it is important to plan the porch carefully; the size can often be critical since if it is built too small, you may find it does not meet your requirements. If it is to be used as a cloakroom, it should have a minimum floor area of about 3sq m (32sq ft). Should you need to store a pram, push chair or children's garden toys, the floor area should be increased to about 5sq m (54sq ft). By increasing the floor area to about 6.5sq m (70sq ft), it is possible to divide the porch into two parts with a linking door in the dividing wall. Use one half as a conventional porch and the other as a separate cloakroom or pram store. In this case, consider the possibility of fitting a WC and/or a wash-basin; if you can lay on only the cold water supply, you could fit an instantaneous electric water heater.

Door Try to ensure the doorway of the porch is as wide as possible, and both doors open on the same side, so large items of furniture and other goods can be taken in and out of the house easily. A doorway directly opposite the front door is also useful.

Previous page

1 Enclosing an existing open porch which has an arched top with a wide span; shape softwood to follow the line of the arch and form a frame to take a glass infill panel

2 Section through a porch built round an existing door canopy

3 Proprietary built-in porch; the door opens inwards and flush with the existing wall

4 Made-to-measure built-in porch; the doors open outwards because of restricted space

5 Designing a porch for a passage; if the wall is less than 1m from a boundary, it should have at least half an hour fire resistance from both sides. If the porch is to to be used for storage, the doors should open outwards

6 Proprietary built-out porch in period style

7 Exploded view of a porch kit. To assemble, fit one side frame, the front and then the second side frame, finishing with the roof

3

4

5

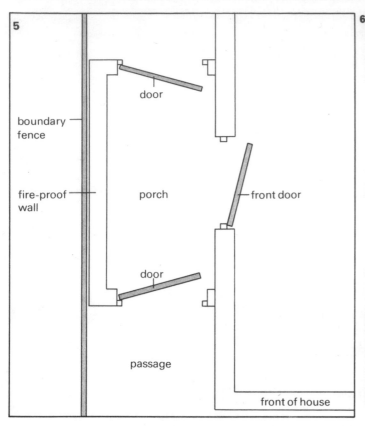

boundary fence

fire-proof wall

door

porch

front door

door

passage

front of house

6

7

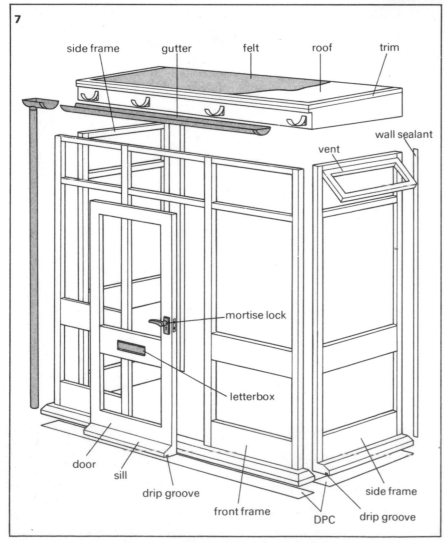

side frame   gutter   felt   roof   trim

wall sealant

vent

mortise lock

letterbox

door

sill

drip groove

front frame

DPC

drip groove

side frame

On the other hand a side door can give better protection from the wind and reduce draughts if your house is particularly exposed.

If the porch is too narrow for the door to open fully inwards, fit a pair of doors or build the door to open outwards; alternatively you can fit a sliding door. If there is restricted access to your garden and the front door is in a narrow passage between houses, you could fit a porch with doors in both side walls. If the wall of your porch will be closer than 1m (39in) to a boundary, Building Regulations require this wall has at least a half-hour fire resistance from both sides. A full height brick or building block wall, of course, would be suitable in this case; manufacturers of prefabricated porches will supply full height, fire-resistant walls to satisfy the regulations.

Electrical wiring Any roof wiring should be laid as the porch is built. Take a fused spur from a convenient circuit for lighting the inside of the porch – and possibly for an exterior light. It may also be useful to have a socket outlet in the porch, run as a spur from a ring circuit. If you are not competent at electrical wiring, it is essential that this part of the job is left to a qualified electrician.

Partitions Partitions can be used inside the porch to divide the area. These can be made with a frame of timber studs and a covering of plasterboard, chipboard or tongued and grooved boards (as described earlier in the book).

Insulation You should consider insulation before the internal walls are covered; a layer of insulating material will conserve heat in winter and help to keep the porch cooler in summer. You can either use thick glass fibre matting in the cavity behind the ceiling or wall lining or fix insulating plasterboard to the wall surface.

Floor coverings These must be hard-wearing and easily cleaned, although a door mat set into a well by the door will take much of the dirt. Quarry tiles

8 Built-out porch, incorporating the existing step and canopy
9 Tailor-made, built-out porch adjoining a bay window
10 Built-out porch on brick base
11 Section through the base of a porch adjoining a house with a solid floor; a mat well has been incorporated
12 Section through the base of a porch adjoining a house with a suspended timber floor. A pipe from the airbrick passes through the concrete base to a grille under the sill; the dpc should be wrapped round the pipe where it joins the airbrick

or glazed ceramic floor tiles are a practical choice or you could use good quality cushioned sheet vinyl or vinyl floor tiles. Properly sealed parquet flooring blocks, which look attractive, are also suitable for a porch. If you prefer carpet, a sensible choice would be heavy-duty loose-lay carpet tiles; these can be lifted for cleaning and are easy to replace when worn. The most important point to remember is that floorcoverings must be practical.

Building a porch
Building a porch to your own specifications using traditional building materials will involve many techniques: concreting, bricklaying, roofing, installing window and door frames, glazing and weatherproofing; make sure you are able to handle all these. It is simpler to erect a prefabricated porch, which should take only two or three weekends to build, including laying the concrete base. The following building hints are for a prefabricated porch; but always make sure you read the manufacturer's instructions carefully. Many of these hints will also apply to a porch being built of traditional materials.
Foundations In some cases you may be able to use an existing step or path for the foundations, but often the building control officer will require a new concrete base to be laid. He may specify the depth of the foundations and possibly insist on an extra depth of concrete around the edge of the slab where the walls will be. In the majority of cases, 100mm (4in) of concrete over 100mm (4in) of well-packed hardcore will be adequate for the main slab, but the overall depth at the edges supporting the porch should be 600mm (or 2ft). Some prefabricated porches are sealed at the base with a sand and cement screed and you may need to reduce the depth of the concrete by about 50mm (2in) to allow for this.

If you do lay a new base, make sure you insert a

damp proof course, which must be linked with the damp proof course inside the house to make sure the latter is not bridged. Ensure the excavation for the foundations is adjusted so the finished base is at least 150mm (6in) above the level of the outside ground. A sheet of 1000 gauge polythene will form a good damp proof membrane. Lay it onto a layer of sand rolled into the surface of the hardcore to cover all sharp protrusions. Allow any surplus polythene to come up the sides of the formwork used to hold the wet concrete; also allow it to lap against the wall of the house to prevent the concrete bridging the existing damp proof course.

To finish the base use a concrete mix of one part Portland cement, two-and-a-half parts damp concreting sand and four parts coarse aggregate. Lay the concrete onto the membrane and cut off surplus polythene when the concrete has set and the formwork has been removed.

After the porch has been built, place a second dpc and another layer of concrete on top of the base to bring it level with the door sill; allow about 3mm ($\frac{1}{8}$in) for a self-levelling floor screed. It is worth bearing in mind the door position when laying the second slab since a mat well could be incorporated. To make the well, cut a sheet of hardboard to the size of the mat and nail a timber surround around its edge to the depth of the mat to form a tray. Use bricks to hold the tray at the correct level in the wet concrete, so the top edge of the surround is level with the concrete surface.
Slope If the ground slopes away from your house, you may need to build a thicker concrete base to compensate. It is usually best to build the floor of the porch at the same level as that of the house floor, so any steps are kept outside the building. This will ensure the damp proof course is not bridged.
Low eaves Bungalows, for example, have low eaves which can make the addition of a porch difficult. Building Regulations currently require a minimum

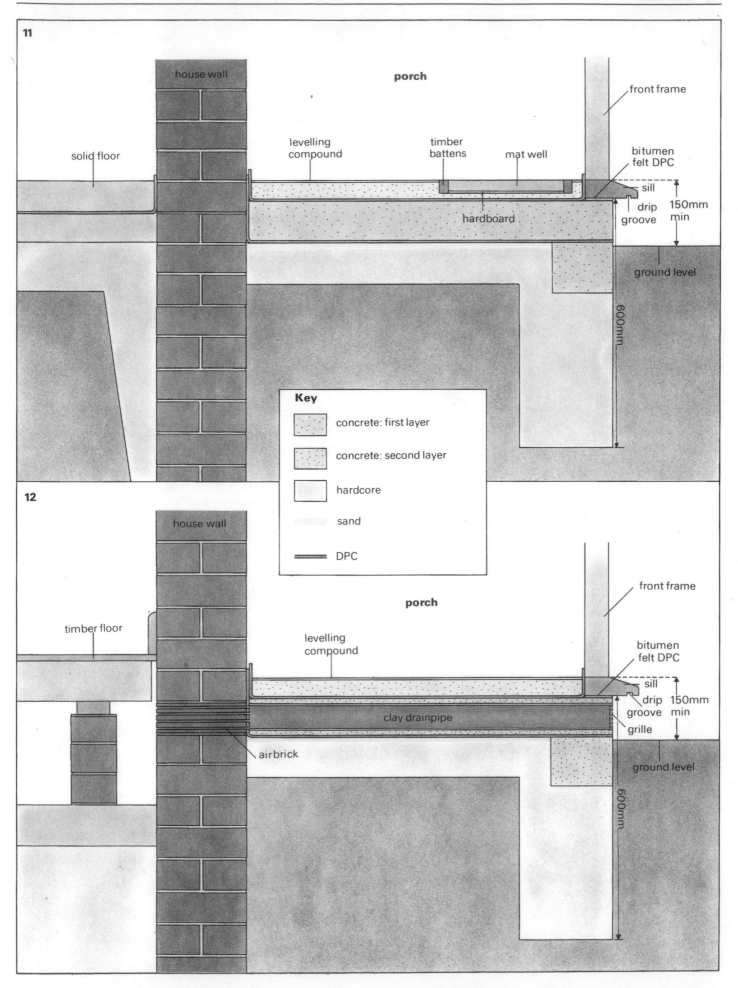

11

house wall

porch

front frame

solid floor

levelling compound

timber battens

mat well

bitumen felt DPC

sill

drip groove

hardboard

150mm min

ground level

600mm

Key

concrete: first layer

concrete: second layer

hardcore

sand

DPC

12

house wall

timber floor

levelling compound

porch

front frame

bitumen felt DPC

sill

clay drainpipe

drip groove

150mm min

grille

airbrick

ground level

600mm

internal headroom of 2.28m (or 7ft 6in); so, allowing for the thickness of the roof, the overall height of the porch should be at least 2.41m (or 7ft 11in). If the eaves of your house are too low to allow for this, you will have to excavate soil so the base can be fitted at a lower level. In this case you must have one or two steps from the house floor level down into the porch. Also, the wall between the surface of the concrete base and the damp proof course must be coated with a waterproof sealant.

Manholes Drain inspection covers which fall in the proposed porch area can also cause a problem. Make sure the wall of a porch will not cover one, although you can build the porch so a manhole is enclosed inside – as long as a screw-down (double-seal) inspection cover is fitted. When laying the base, brick round the chamber so the cover's surround can be brought up to the level of the base.

Airbricks Whenever possible do not cover the air-bricks in the house wall when laying the concrete base. You can lay clay drain-pipes inside the base to link the existing airbricks to the outside of the porch base, but you will have to fit a new grille in the porch base to prevent rodents or dead leaves entering the pipe.

Wall frame After the concrete base has hardened, you can fit the frame of the prefabricated porch section by section. Each section of the frame must stand on a strip of bitumen damp proof course; if a hardwood sill is fitted, the drip groove in it should overhang the edge of the concrete base. There is usually a flexible strip which fits between the side sections and the wall of the house to form a water-proof seal. The sections can be fixed at the base with expansion bolts, and the manufacturer may recommend you to seal the base, after the sections have been erected, with a 50mm (2in) sand and cement screed; the final 3mm ($\frac{1}{8}$in) of this can be a self-levelling screed.

Drill clearance holes into one of the side sections, following the manufacturer's instructions; hold the section against the house wall and mark the drilling positions through the clearance holes. Drill and plug the wall with wall plugs, which are usually supplied, and screw the section into place. Check the section is exactly vertical with a plumb line or spirit level.

Fit the front section to the section already fitted then fit the second side section in the same way as the first. Check the three sections are square and vertical and make any necessary adjustments. Apply a bead of mastic along both vertical edges of the side sections so the joints are sealed, then lay the inside base as previously described.

Roof After the frame sections are fitted, the roof can be added. The roof is normally bonded and felted, but you can use wired glass or corrugated PVC sheeting. Often the roof is supplied as a ready assembled chipboard deck which is screwed to the side and front frame sections; in this case the roof covering is fixed to the decking with special adhesive. The covering usually consists of two layers of felt; the top layer is asbestos-based and the surface is coated with mineral chippings. Use self-adhesive flashing strip to seal the joint between the porch roof and the house; sometimes the kit includes an aluminium trim which forms a neat seal around the edge of the porch roof. You may have to shape the new roof around obstructions, such as a drain pipe or chimney (although it may be more practical to reroute a drain pipe). Some porch manufacturers will shape the roof before your porch is delivered. If not, cut the roof covering to form a neat collar around the projection and seal the surface with self-adhesive flashing strip.

Doors In some cases, the door or doors may be supplied ready-glazed and primed, often with letter boxes and locks fitted or the door may be supplied as a primed frame only. You can hang doors to open inwards or outwards as required and they can be left or right-hinged. Once you have decided their position, fit the hinges; to prevent draughts nail the door stops in place so they touch all round the edge of the door when it is closed. Other fittings, such as the lock and letter box, can be fitted later where necessary.

Glazing The glass is almost always supplied cut to size, so glazing is not too difficult. You can usually choose either patterned or clear glass. It is worth considering sealed unit double glazing, especially in a porch in a particularly exposed position; but check the frames are suitable before you buy.

Ventilation A glazed porch can provide problems of ventilation on a hot day. Top vents which open can either be supplied as standard or as an extra. Opening glass louvres are slightly more expensive, but as long as they are of good quality they can be less of a security risk than top-hung vents.

Gutters These essential items are one of the last to be fitted to the exterior of the porch. On some prefabricated porches, the gutter is hidden by a fascia board. You can link the rainwater downpipe to your existing system or to an underground soak-away; check this with the building control officer.

Painting Prefabricated porch frames are usually supplied primed; you must apply undercoat and two coats of gloss paint as soon as the building work is finished. Some hardwood or western red cedar porches are supplied in natural timber; these types can be varnished with a clear preservative or polyurethane varnish.

13 Assembled prefabricated porch kit, complete with guttering; you can link the rainwater downpipe to the existing system or build a soakaway in accordance with Building Regulations

Extensions

Sooner or later you will almost certainly find the place in which you live is no longer large enough; and there may be many good reasons why you do not want to move. The alternative is to improve the existing facilities and you can do this by putting on an extension. This can be an extra room added to the outside of the house – either prefabricated or purpose-built – or a two-storey extension with access from both the ground and first floor. In each case you should consider very carefully exactly what accommodation you need, how much it will cost and whether it will conform to current Building Regulations.

Planning an extension

You may decide to build an extension to gain more space and avoid the expense, aggravation and frustration of moving house. There is another real advantage to adding an extension; the extra space you gain can provide new scope for planning the other rooms, which can be organized to serve other purposes. An extension could enable part of your house to be converted into a self-contained flat; alternatively you could use the extension as a dining room and convert the existing dining room into a study or bedroom.

It is therefore important not to think solely of the extension providing the extra room you require. For example, if you need another bedroom, it may not be feasible to build an extension to serve that purpose; you could, however, build the extension so it forms part of the main living area, thus releasing another room for the desired bedroom.

Building one yourself The easiest and cheapest extension to build is a single-storey one at ground level. However, if you have an attached garage, you can build an extension on top provided the garage is built with sufficient foundations; this location can be ideal for an extra bedroom. You could also build a two-storey extension, but this is not a simple job and is best left to a specialist.

Planning its function This must be one of your first considerations when planning an extension. Some types of extension are more suitable for occasional daytime use, such as a conservatory or sun room. These are not suitable, however, for a habitable room, defined as any room used for dwelling purposes – living, sitting, eating and dressing – but not (except where so expressly provided) any room used only as a kitchen or scullery. Building Regulations discussed below ensure your extension meets certain minimum standards of construction. These regulations are often less stringent for a sun room than for a habitable room; for example, a prefabricated home extension with a corrugated plastic roof can be used as a sun room but not as a dining room or bedroom.

Choosing types

Having clearly defined the function of your proposed extension, you can choose the type of construction. Your choice will be between a purpose-made brick-built extension and a prefabricated extension. Both types of extension are being discussed in detail later in the book.

Brick-built extension

This is the most flexible type since it can be designed exactly to your requirements with regard to shape, size and appearance. It will take longer to build than a prefabricated extension and it will probably cost 30–50 percent more if you hire a builder to do the work. This is the only type of extension you can build over an attached garage.

Prefabricated extension

These extensions fall into three basic types; in each case the building is supplied in sections, ready to be

Above A simple, flat-roofed extension can often work better than one which is more elaborate; here features of the house have been repeated on this new brick building for a harmonious effect

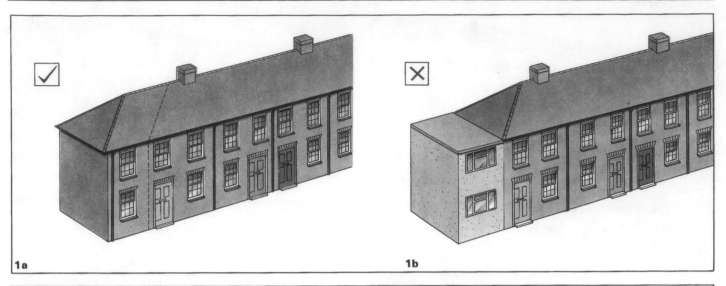

1a

1b

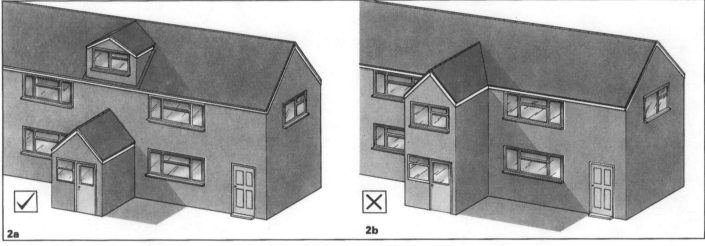

2a

2b

bolted together on a concrete foundation slab which you lay before the extension is built.

The simplest type of prefabricated extension forms a lean-to or conservatory which has a sloping roof to admit plenty of light. You can use it as a sun room, plant house or even as a utility room to help clear the kitchen of a washing machine or other large appliances.

Another type, which is slightly more expensive to build, is the occasional room with a clear corrugated plastic roof and a deep fascia to hide the slope of the roof. This type will probably have low wall panels designed to blend in with many types of house. It makes a useful lounge extension for summer use, but has insufficient insulation to be used as a living room all the year round.

The third type complies fully with Building Regulations, especially with regard to thermal insulation and minimum ceiling height. It can thus be used all the year round as a habitable room – a living room, bedroom, dining room or dressing room, for example. This extension is often designed to match closely the finish of house walls.

There are several advantages in choosing a prefabricated extension. You have the manufacturer's experience behind you with regard to selecting a suitable design, ironing out minor problems such as drainpipes which seem to be in the way and applying for the necessary local authority approval you will require. Many manufacturers are able to arrange finance and nearly all will guarantee their buildings; the latter is something a local builder,

putting up a brick extension, may be reluctant to do.

The building of a prefabricated extension is straightforward; but if you decide to put it up yourself, under current legislation you will have to pay tax on the building; this will not be the case if you decide to let the manufacturer put it up for you. It is well worth costing both methods before you order your extension from the manufacturer.

Making plans

Once you have decided on the function and basic type of extension you require, it is best to give some thought to preliminary planning, particularly with regard to the external appearance of your extension. Early planning such as this can reduce the risk of having a planning application turned down; this is a waste of both time and money. Formulate your rough proposals and discuss your plan in general terms with the local authority before you draw up detailed plans or have them drawn up for you; then submit your planning application as described below.

Character of design
Your extension should as far as possible be of a design in character with the house and neighbouring properties. This will not only help get your application passed by the local authority, but it will also help good neighbourly relations; it may prevent neighbours sending in objections to your proposal, which must be taken into account by the

1a The design and proportions of this two-storey extension are completely in character with the existing building; the line of the roof has been continued and the same type of windows and brickwork as in the rest of the terrace have been used
1b An example of an unsympathetic extension to the same house; nothing is in keeping with the rest of the terrace
2a A single-storey extension at the back of the house, together with a loft conversion, provides almost as much floor area as a two-storey extension and will not overshadow the neighbouring house
2b This large two-storey pitched roof extension shows inconsiderate planning; it causes shadows to be cast on the adjoining property and restricts the neighbours' view — which could cause them to send in objections to your proposals, delaying the passing of plans

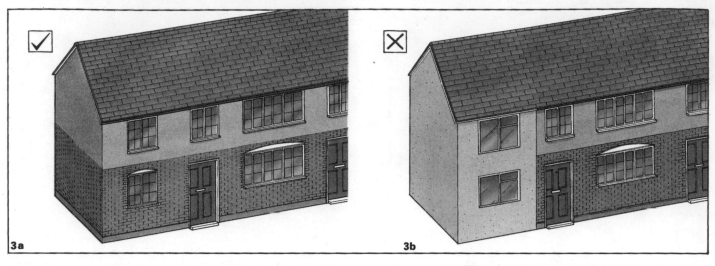

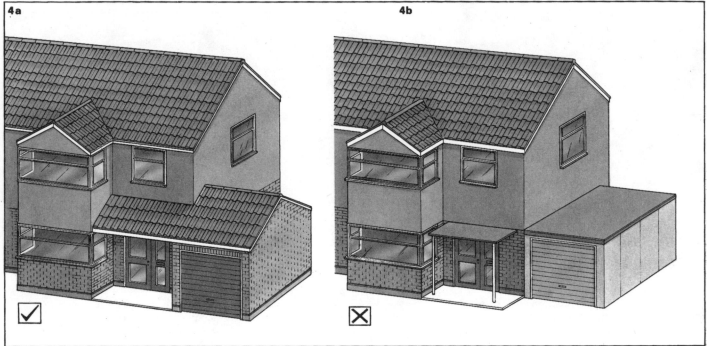

local authority when they consider your planning application.

Ensure the possibility of overlooking or over-shadowing neighbouring properties is kept to a minimum. For example, instead of building a large two-storey pitched roof extension on the back of a house, you should be able to have the equivalent floor area by building a single-storey extension and adding a loft conversion. The extension should not be so big it changes the scale and character of the building already in existence; if you do choose a large extension, keep its shape and proportion in scale and style with the existing building. If possible you should retain existing natural features such as trees and make the best possible use of other features such as a good view or a sloping site.

Extension materials
Where appropriate, use materials which match those already in existence; for example, roofing tiles, doors, windows and wall treatment (such as the type of bricks used) should match those used on the main building. Although flat roof extensions are popular since they are relatively cheap and easy to build, try to avoid them if your house has, as is

likely, a pitched roof. If you cannot avoid using a flat roof entirely, at least try to incorporate elements of a pitched roof into the design. Also try not to make the extension too plain and functional; many houses have some sort of design detail and it is often possible to incorporate a matching style into the design of your extension.

At this stage it is a good idea to turn your attention to the inside of your extension. Decide where electrical sockets should be and also where lighting points, central heating pipes and the water supply are to be sited.

Shape of plot
In most cases your extension will be built like the house – in a rectangular or square form when seen in plan view. It can, however, be acceptable to build the extension in an irregular outline according to the shape of your plot, the proximity of neigh-bouring buildings or general lack of building space.

If the extension is to form a separate room, you may have to make a new doorway from the existing building (as covered earlier in the book); but if the extension is to form part of an existing room, you will probably need to demolish the wall be-

3a Use of the same materials makes this a successful extension; the tiles on the roof, the brickwork and facing on the walls and the style of window all match those on the existing house
3b Although the shape of this extension is correct, the materials do not match the existing ones
4a A garage extension which blends in well with the style of the house; again, the materials used match those on the house and the tiles continued over the porch bring the house and extension together
4b Here neither the shape nor the structure of the extension is in harmony with the house — and the stainless steel garage door only draws attention to the fact

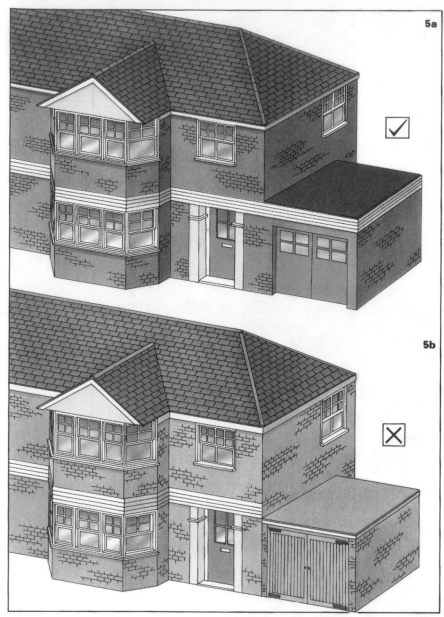

5a

5b

5a With careful planning a flat-roofed garage extension can be made to blend in with a pitched roof house; here decorative moulding has been continued along the garage and painted white for emphasis and the walls on both buildings have been painted in the same colour to disguise any differences in the brickwork
5b Here no attempt has been made to give the extension a feeling of unity with the house; it appears to be simply a square box tacked onto the building
Right A typical self-assembly extension available in a wide range of sizes; the walls can be brick-based as here or you could use a timber base or full length glazing

tween the two. It is likely this wall will be a load-bearing outer wall and the upper part of it must be carefully supported with a new lintel or RSJ before you make the opening; always seek professional advice in this case.

Getting approval

Before you begin work on any type of extension, you will need local authority approval as already mentioned. Once you have drawn up a preliminary plan, it is best to discuss your proposals with the local authority planning and building control departments. Officers from both of these departments will tell you which forms to complete and the drawings and plans you need to supply. Local authority approval falls into two sections – Building Regulation control and planning permission; you will need the former in all cases, but planning permission is not always required.

Building Regulations

These regulations lay down minimum standards of construction the extension must meet, as already mentioned. They cover such items as the materials you use, fire resistance, ventilation and insulation. There are many regulations applicable to a home extension and your extension must comply with them; the building control officer will probably outline the main requirements. You can also buy a copy of the current Building Regulations published by HMSO; this will also be available at your local library. There are also several books available which present the current Building Regulations in an easily understood form. The following is a basic guide to current Building Regulations applicable to a home extension; make sure you get detailed advice before you start any work.

Structure The floor-to-ceiling height in the extension must be at least 2.3m (or 7½ft). The Building Regulations also lay down minimum standards of fire resistance, thermal insulation, ventilation and damp proofing. A well-built extension should automatically conform to the regulations; but problems can arise if walls are less than 1m (or 3ft) from a boundary, in which case they must be fire-resistant. A brick wall without doors and windows conforms with the regulations and can be built right up to the boundary; the foundations and overhanging gutters should not cross the boundary, however, since this is considered as trespass.

Ventilation Regulations must be carefully considered if your extension is built across the windows of an existing room. Habitable rooms, kitchens and sculleries not fitted with mechanical ventilation (such as an extractor fan) must have ventilation to the outside of at least one-twentieth of the floor area. This ventilation will invariably be an opening window and the regulations state the top of this window must be at least 1.75m (or 6ft) from the floor. If the extension covers the only windows of an existing room, the ventilation area of the extension must be one-twentieth of the total floor area of the two rooms.

Zone of open space To ensure the extension has sufficient light and ventilation, the Building Regulations lay down a minimum zone of open space. This must be outside any one or divided between all the windows of your proposed extension. Difficulties over open space are only likely to be encountered if you build an extension close to

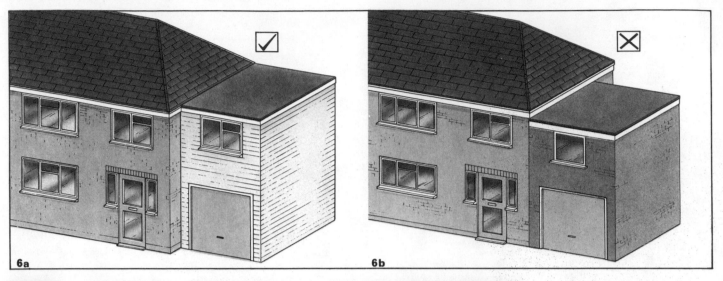

6a

6b

6a Where it is not possible to match styles and structures, good results can be obtained by contrasting the extension with the house, although some continuity is still desirable. In this example the building is set back from the house and the roof is flat rather than pitched; however the fascia boards are in line and the cladding on the extension is painted gloss white to match the woodwork on the house

6b Neither matching nor contrasting, this extension fails on all points; the dropped roof line creates an awkward junction, the window is out of character and even the brickwork is different

Above left This is the simplest type of prefabricated extension; the roof and glazing materials admit plenty of light, so you could use it as a sun room or a conservatory

neighbouring buildings; but the requirements to determine zones of open space are quite complicated, so ensure you consult the local building control officer or the Building Regulations.

Sanitation Existing or proposed sanitation can be important in your plans and affect them, although existing house drains, for example, can normally be built over as long as you protect them adequately from the weight of the extension. Try to avoid having drain covers or inspection chambers inside your extension; if this is unavoidable, the chambers must be fitted with screw-down, double seal, airtight covers. You can also use sealed, back-inlet waste gulleys inside the extension provided the cover is airtight and screwed down. If you intend installing a WC inside the extension, its door must not open directly into a habitable room, kitchen or scullery. The door can open directly into a bedroom or dressing room however, as long as your house has another WC. If you do not have another WC, then this one must be fitted with another door so you can enter it without passing through a bedroom or dressing room.

Fire resistance Using conventional building materials and building techniques will ensure your extension is as resistant to fire as the rest of the house. There are special fire regulations which apply to houses of three or more storeys; your local building control officer will advise you in this case.

Planning permission

This deals with the effect of your extension on the local environment and ensures any building fits in with local planning policy. In general your extension will require planning permission since it increases the size of your house.

Permitted development In some cases your extension may be classed as permitted development. This will require Building Regulation approval but not planning permission, which is automatically given without formal application in this case. The building must not be listed for special architectural or historical interest and the extension must not increase the overall size of the house by more than 50cu m (or 65½cu yd) or one-tenth of the size of the house, whichever is the larger. Measurements must be taken externally and the original building taken to be as it existed in July 1948 or as it was built if built after that date.

You will have to apply for planning permission for an extension larger than 115cu m (or 145cu yd) and for an extension which increases the height of the existing building or projects beyond the house frontage to the road. Remember any estimates for areas qualifying for permitted development are cumulative; so after building a 20cu m (or 26cu yd) extension, a further extension exceeding 30cu m (or 39cu yd) will require planning permission. Address any questions on planning permission to your local authority's planning officer.

Building a prefabricated extension

Building a prefabricated extension is relatively straightforward in many cases since manufacturers supply ready-glazed wall and door panels with ready-hung doors.

Prefabricated extensions fall into three basic categories, as already outlined. The traditional extension is usually framed in red cedarwood and makes extensive use of glass; used as a sun room or conservatory, this extension can be glazed to the ground. It is usual to build a low base wall round the perimeter of the planned extension and the panels are mounted on the wall for a degree of privacy inside the finished extension. Low base walls are normally built of brick or stone.

Walls Apart from glazed wall panels suitable for sun rooms, other panels are available in reinforced concrete with a decorative finish of stone chippings or simulated brick or stone to match the finish of the house. Prefabricated extensions used as habitable rooms, as described earlier, require substantial and well-insulated wall panels and it is usual to reduce the amount of glass in this type. Some wall panels are based on a module size, which means you can use standard door and window frames to match those fitted in the rest of the house. Walls can be clad with chipping or brick-finished concrete panels, bricks, cedarwood or concrete tiles which clip onto aluminium battens. You can fit aluminium frame doors and windows (which can be double-glazed) to match those already fitted.

Roofs The roof you choose for your extension will depend upon usage; habitable rooms require roofs which are boarded and it is usual to fit insulation material such as glass fibre between the boards and ceiling. The boards are normally of 18mm ($\frac{3}{4}$in) chipboard waterproofed with two or three layers of roofing felt running along the length of the roof. Some boards are supplied with the first felt layer already fitted; as soon as the boards have been nailed into place and you have applied bituminous solution and tape, the roof will be waterproof. Later you can apply the second and third felt layers and seal the joint between the roof and the house with self-adhesive flashing strip.

If you require good light transmission through the roof, use translucent corrugated PVC panels fixed to a framework of timber roof joists. Some manufacturers offer a translucent suspended internal ceiling with their prefabricated extensions; this will help to reduce condensation.

Laying a concrete base

The manufacturer will build the prefabricated extension for you, which will under current legislation save tax payable on the building. All prefabricated extensions are built on a concrete slab foundation; some manufacturers offer a timber floor, but most extensions have a floor finished with either cement mortar or a self-smoothing screed. If you decide to contract the manufacturer to build the extension, make sure the quote includes laying the base slab and check on this

when comparing prices; the manufacturer may require you to lay the slab yourself or to hire a builder to do the work. If you lay the concrete base yourself, the techniques required are similar to those described for a porch earlier in the book.

Excavating Digging out the area for the slab and laying it are probably the most difficult parts of the job. The manufacturer of the extension will specify the dimensions of the required slab and the building control officer will specify its depth, with regard to local soil conditions. The main floor area usually consists of 100mm (4in) of concrete over 150mm (6in) of rammed hardcore; laying a slab of concrete has been covered earlier in the book. Around the edges of the slab the overall depth, including hardcore, should be at least 600mm (2ft) and you should lay at least 200mm (8in) of concrete. Position formwork round the perimeter of the proposed slab and ensure the top edges are perfectly square and level.

Concreting Remember it is often very convenient to use ready-mixed concrete. As you mark out the area of your slab, change any waste water gullies for sealed-trap versions and replace drain inspection covers with screw-down covers. You must include a

Above A typical prefabricated extension using timber cladding and exterior tiles secured to aluminium battens for a maintenance-free finish; this extension features large double doors for easy access to the garden

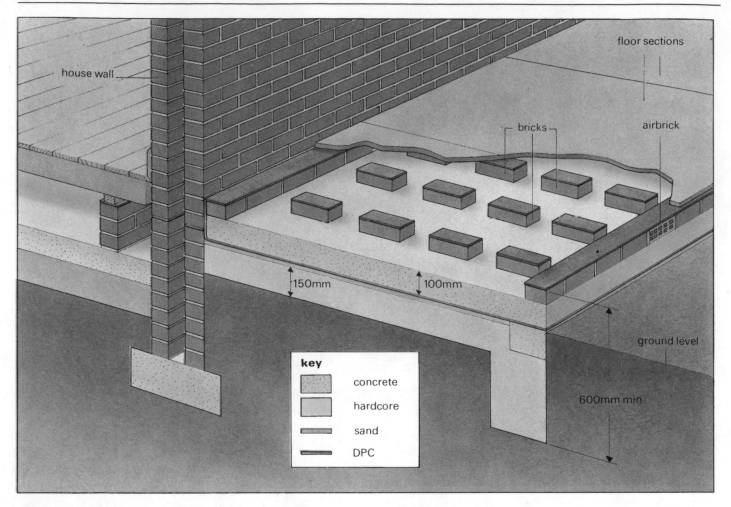

house wall

floor sections

bricks

airbrick

150mm

100mm

ground level

600mm min

key

concrete

hardcore

sand

DPC

damp proof membrane, as described earlier in the book; it should link with the damp proof course of the house and not bridge it. Once the slab has been laid and left to cure you can begin to build your extension.

Putting up components
Using the manufacturer's building service, a medium-sized extension can be built in about a day. If you choose to build it yourself, you will need an assistant; a competent handyman should be able to build and weatherproof the exterior in a weekend. You can leave the interior until it is convenient. All manufacturers provide detailed fitting instructions which should be followed very carefully; the basic steps in building a typical prefabricated extension are outlined below.

Making a timber floor If you choose to lay a timber floor, you will probably have to lay a course of bricks round the edge of the base slab and at regular intervals over it; this is to provide good underfloor air circulation. Add a number of airbricks to the course round the slab and lay strips of bitumen damp proof course material over all the bricks before laying the floor sections. In some cases the floor is supported with tanalized timber battens instead of bricks. Floor sections are held together by skew-nailing; if they cover drain covers or sealed trap gullies, you will have to leave access traps. Timber floorboards must be laid across and fixed onto floor joists.

Fitting wall panels Fit the end panel first; this butts against the house wall. The usual fixing method is to fit a post to the house wall using screws and wall plugs and screw the panel directly to the post. In

other cases the panels may fit directly onto the wall using plugs and screws. In both cases carefully check the wall post or panel is vertical using a spirit level. Lift the end panel into place and make sure the bottom edge slightly overhangs your timber floor; it should rest on a strip of damp proof membrane if you have a concrete floor. Once the first panel has been secured you can fit subsequent panels, working away from the house; use screws or bolts (usually provided) to fit them together. Before finally tightening wall panel fixings, check they are square and correctly located on the base.

Fitting the roof The main roof beams run from the front wall panels to the house wall. The wall panels may accept these beams direct or you may have to fix a front wall plate to their tops. Some manufacturers supply special fixings to enable the roof beams to be fixed directly to the house wall; if not, you will have to fit a wall plate to the house wall to support the beams. This plate must be level and securely fixed with large screws and wall plugs or expanding bolts. The beams may be notched so they rest inside the plates, but it is more likely they will be fixed to the plate using galvanized nails and galvanized steel brackets. It is usual to fit purlins between the beams to give additional support and to provide fixings for the roof and ceiling panels. Once the beams are in position you can cover them with roofing material; use clear or white corrugated plastic sheets for a sun room and felted chipboard for a habitable room.

Fitting corrugated sheets The sheets should be drilled through their corrugations and fixed to each purlin with the screws supplied. Manufacturers will provide full fitting instructions.

Above Section through an extension floor, showing the concrete base, support bricks and dpc; the timber floor sections are mounted on the bricks to provide air circulation underneath

Above right Section through an extension roof, showing wall plates with notched roof beams; some extensions use slotted beams and galvanized 'T' brackets screwed to the house wall (**inset**)

Right Laying the concrete base for a prefabricated extension

Far right Lifting the first wall panel into position on a dpc strip laid round the edge of the base; the panel is then screwed to the wall post

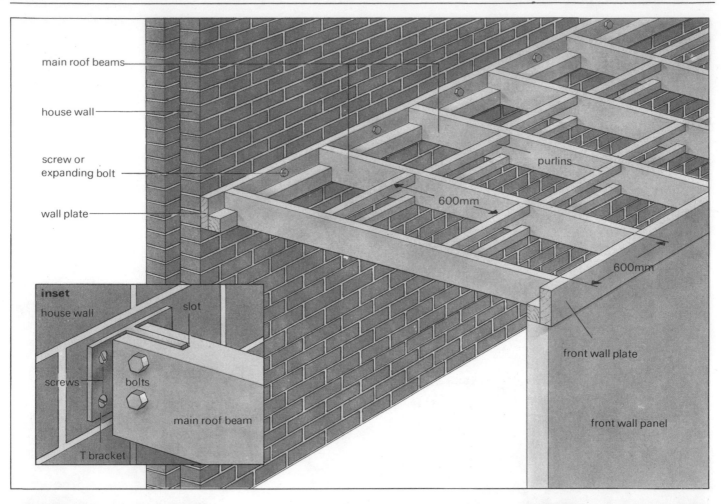

main roof beams

house wall

screw or expanding bolt

wall plate

inset

house wall

slot

screws

bolts

main roof beam

T bracket

purlins

600mm

600mm

front wall plate

front wall panel

Fitting felted boards You can nail felted boards to the beams and fit the second and third layers of felt over all of the roof. Where necessary, fit gutters and fascia boards as supplied. The joint between the extension roof and the house wall should be weatherproofed with a band of self-adhesive flashing strip; use a similar strip to weatherproof along each of the side fascia boards.

Using exterior cladding Some prefabricated extensions use exterior cladding tiles or strips which are fixed to the non-glazed areas of the wall panels. Insulate the panels with glass fibre and cover with waterproof building paper before nailing battens into place to support the cladding.

Finishing the interior
Once the outside is complete, you can finish the extension inside, provided the wall and roof panels were not supplied ready-finished. Add electrical cable runs and fittings, water pipes and central heating pipes as required. The ceiling and solid areas of the walls can be covered with sheets of plasterboard, which can be fixed to battens or directly to the panels with gap-filling adhesive. All roof and wall cavities should be filled with glass fibre insulation material as you fit the plasterboard lining to ensure the temperature in the extension is comfortable throughout the year. Check carefully with any instructions from the manufacturer.

Below left Fitting the subsequent wall panels together and onto the base dpc with the screws or bolts supplied
Below Fitting the fascia framework and front wall plate to receive the beams
Bottom left Using glass fibre to provide thermal insulation
Bottom Fixing purlins between the roof beams using the clips supplied

Building a brick extension

Although every brick-built extension will vary, the basic building stages are the same; planning extensions and building prefabricated extensions have already been discussed in the book, as have many of the basic building techniques required for brick-built extensions.

Planning the extension

Once you have satisfied the Building Regulations and obtained the necessary planning permission, you should cost the project – if you have not already done so. You may find it worth employing a local builder to do the work for you if time is a definite cost factor. In most cases, however, the cost of the materials (the amount you will pay to build the extension yourself) will be about one third of the amount a builder will charge. A compromise is to sub-contract parts of the work such as bricklaying and plastering; this will speed up the building and ensure a professional finish. Make sure you hire only tradesmen who have been well recommended to you or who can show examples of recent work in the neighbourhood; this avoids the possibility of sub-standard work.

Two-storey The work involved in building a two-storey brick extension is similar to a single-storey one. However, you will need to hire scaffolding to build the upper storey and work on the roof; the foundations will need to be dug to a greater depth and a suspended timber floor will have to be built. It is not advisable to attempt this type of construction without specialized assistance.

Ground floor extension

The first job is to buy all the materials you will need. If you look around local builders' merchants, you may be able to obtain all the materials from one supplier; this should entitle you to some discount.

Buying materials Your extension should match the house as much as possible, although you may find it difficult to match the bricks used on the house – especially if the house is more than 30 years old. Demolition yards often have stocks of used bricks and you may be able to find the type you require there; make sure the bricks are free from old mortar and not cracked or flaking. If the extension is to be built of stone, you may be able to buy matching stone locally; alternatively use reconstructed stone blocks. These blocks consist of natural stone aggregate and coloured concrete; sometimes they look rather bright when you buy them, but they will tone down in colour with weathering. If the extension walls are to be rendered, build them from common bricks or lightweight load-bearing building blocks. The latter material should,in any case be used for the inner leaves of the cavity walls and internal partitions in any extension of this type.

Remember to order window and door frames which match those used in the house. You will also need to order sand, aggregate. cement, damp proofing materials, wall ties, timber for joists and floorboards, roof boards and felt (or battens and roof tiles if you choose to build a pitched roof extension), gutters and downpipes, nails and hardware, insulation material, plasterboard and plaster, and plumbing, electrical and decorating materials.

Marking out You will need to mark out the site using string lines, pegs and profile boards. You will also need a builder's square to ensure right-angles; this should have measurements in the ratio of 3:4:5. You can make one from planed softwood or hardwood and it should be as large as is practicable.

Digging foundations The trenches should be dug to the width of your string guidelines; the depth of the trenches will be specified by the local building control officer, with regard to local soil conditions. Take measurements from your string lines to ensure the trenches are of an even depth and their bases are level. To avoid having to dig excessively deep trenches if the extension is being built on sloping ground, you can step the depth of the trench. The height of each step must be a multiple of the height of a brick course to make the bricklaying easier.

Laying concrete Concrete is poured into the base of the trenches, usually to a depth of 250mm (10in). The trenches should have pegs inserted to the required height; these must be level with each other and should be checked with a spirit level and straight-edge. At about this stage the building control officer will probably make an initial inspection of the work.

Once you begin laying concrete, you should try to lay it all in one operation as far as possible; this avoids joints in the footings which could later cause cracks in the base. Make sure the concrete is well compacted and level with the tops of your pegs. The concrete should cure in about four days.

Building the floor

Once the concrete has cured you can begin laying bricks up to ground level. Lay the bricks using lines, steel pins, a spirit level and the stretcher bonding method. Maintain a 50mm (2in) cavity between the outer and inner leaves of the wall and link them at regular intervals with metal wall ties. The bricks should be laid up to damp proof course level; make sure this level matches that of the damp proof course in the house. The cavity between leaves should be filled up to ground level with fine concrete. Once you have built the walls to this level,

Above Building a first floor extension over an existing garage. Bricks have been chosen to match those of this modern semi-detached house, the roof line has been continued and the windows are in the same style as those in the original building; one window has been fitted into the rear wall of the garage. To build this type of extension you will need specialized advice and proper equipment, such as scaffolding

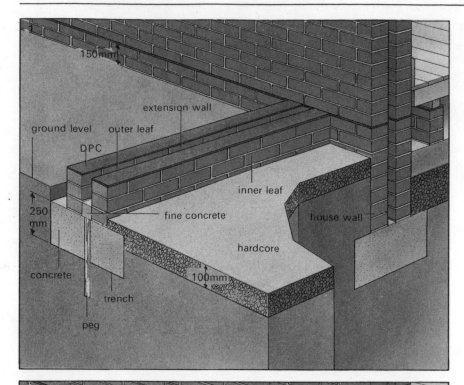

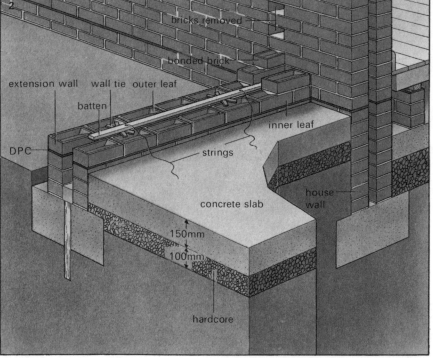

but to leave the installation of the dpc and surface screed until you have finished the main structure of the extension.

Bricklaying
You can now build the walls up to window sill height. Remember to position door frames; they are usually set on a bitumen felt dpc laid on a bed of mortar and held upright with props made from scrap pieces of timber.

The extension walls must be properly bonded to the house walls. You can use a cold chisel to remove alternate courses of house wall bricks so the inner and outer leaves of the extension walls can be built into them; some local authorities require bonding of both leaves of the extension wall, others of the outer leaf only. For accuracy you should adjust mortar joints in the extension walls so the brick courses align; this is done with the help of a gauge rod. The corners are usually built first; stretch a builder's line between the corners and lay the intermediate bricks.

As the cavity walls are built, you have to insert metal wall ties at regular intervals; take great care not to allow any mortar to fall inside the cavity. You could make a timber batten which fits inside the cavity and catches any mortar which falls; thread loops of string through holes drilled in the batten so it can be lifted as you build the brick courses.

When you come to the door frames, build galvanized frame ties into the mortar joints; four ties each side will usually be sufficient. Fit them to the door frame with galvanized screws or nails.

Once the walls have been built to window sill level you can fit the window frames. Hold the frames upright with the help of timber props as before; the props should be fixed into the ground at each side. Both window and door frames should have the cavity at each side sealed with strips of dpc; position the strips vertically and under the sill to prevent damp transmission from the outer to inner wall leaf.

Warning The traditional brick cavity wall, while structurally stable, alone no longer meets the Building Regulation requirements on insulation. This means you must either fill the cavity with insulating material or insulate the inside of the wall.

Fitting lintels Door and window frames will require some type of lintel above them. The size of lintel you use will depend upon the span involved and the amount of brickwork above it. Pressed galvanized steel lintels are a good choice since they are easy to lift into place and do not require a dpc. Concrete lintels are very heavy and are best used only for short spans; they require a separate dpc.

Building the roof
Once the walls have reached eaves level on the extension you can begin to build the roof. Most extension roofs will be flat and are built by taking timber joists from the house wall and resting them on the opposite extension wall. The joists are usually 50mm (2in) thick; their depth will depend upon the span involved, but should be at least 100mm (4in). Space the joists at 400mm (16in) centres.

Supporting joists on new wall It is usual to fit a timber wall plate on the inner leaf of the new wall to support the roof joists; this should be at least 100 × 50mm (4 × 2in) and bedded on mortar. Treat the ends of the joists with timber preservative and

1 Foundations for extension showing bricks laid to dpc level, peg marking top of concrete base and 50mm cavity between leaves filled to ground level with fine concrete; when laying hardcore for floor, allow for final layer of concrete and surface screed
2 Extension walls are bonded to house wall above dpc level; insert wall ties between leaves and use timber batten inside cavity to catch falling mortar

the building control officer may again wish to make an inspection of the work.
Laying concrete slab You will now have to excavate soil from the centre of your site so 100mm (4in) of rammed hardcore and 100–150mm (4–6in) of concrete with a 50mm (2in) surface screed can be laid. Adjust the excavations so the final floor level comes just above the damp proof course levels in the house and walls of the extension. You must lay a damp proof membrane over the concrete so it links with the other damp proof course; this can consist of two coats of a heavy bitumen damp proofing liquid or a heavy gauge polythene sheet. The damp proof membrane will be protected by the surface screed which is laid on top of it. It is usual at this stage to lay the over-site concrete for the floor,

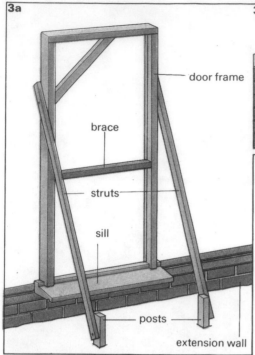

3a

door frame

brace

struts

sill

posts

extension wall

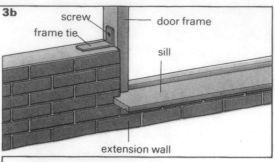

3b screw

frame tie

door frame

sill

extension wall

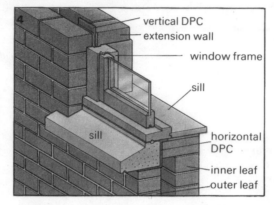

4

vertical DPC

extension wall

window frame

sill

sill

horizontal DPC

inner leaf

outer leaf

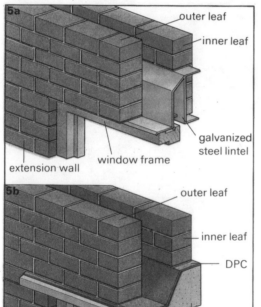

5a

outer leaf

inner leaf

galvanized steel lintel

window frame

extension wall

5b

outer leaf

inner leaf

DPC

window frame

concrete lintel

extension wall

build up the outer leaf of the cavity wall so the joists are held firmly between the brickwork. If you require eaves which are flush with the extension wall, you can trim the ends of each joist flush with the outer leaf of the wall.

Supporting joists in house wall There are several methods of fixing the joists to the house wall in this case. The commonly used method is to secure the ends of the joists with galvanized joist hangers fixed to the house wall. Another method involves resting the ends of the joists on a timber wall plate; each plate is screwed and plugged to the house wall and the ends of the joists are notched and secured with large galvanized nails to prevent any movement. A third method – which is rarely used – involves cutting bricks from the house wall so the joist ends rest on the outer leaf of this brickwork.

Making a fall for the roof It is normal to set the roof joists so they are horizontal; this gives a level ceiling after you have nailed plasterboard directly to the joists. It is important, however, to create a slight slope to disperse rainwater; this is achieved by using tapering pieces of timber known as firrings. These pieces are fixed to the top edge of each joist; use galvanized nails and make sure they are secure. The minimum fall for a two or three layered felt roof should be about one in sixty.

3a When building in door frame, rest sill on wall at dpc level, fit timber brace to hold frame square and use struts nailed to posts in ground to support frame while you build wall up each side

3b As you build wall round frame, insert galvanized ties to secure frame to outer leaf; four ties per side will normally be enough

4 When fitting window frame, build wall to sill level and fit strips of dpc material horizontally and vertically round frame; use timber struts to support frame

5a Fit galvanized steel lintel, without dpc, above window frame

5b Alternatively insert concrete lintel with dpc strip above

6 Support roof joists on extension wall using timber wall plate and metal ties; place tie every two or three joists

7a Support joists on house wall using galvanized steel joist hangers set into raked out mortar joints

7b Alternatively use timber wall plate screwed to house wall; cut notch in joists and secure to plate with large galvanized nails to prevent movement

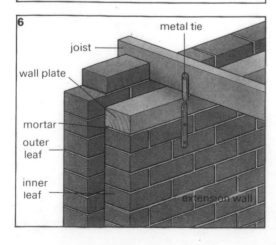

6

metal tie

joist

wall plate

mortar

outer leaf

inner leaf

extension wall

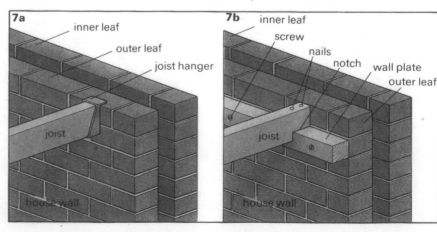

7a

inner leaf

outer leaf

joist hanger

joist

house wall

7b inner leaf

screw

nails

notch

wall plate

outer leaf

joist

house wall

Depending on the direction of the fall of the roof, firrings may be fitted along or across the joists.

Fixing roofing boards Once the firrings are in place, you can nail the roofing boards onto the joists. Roofing boards can be pre-felted chipboard panels, standard chipboard panels, compressed straw-board, 19mm (¾in) timber boards, plywood or other materials.

Fitting upstands These strips of triangular timber, which form a fillet under the roofing felt, must be fitted to prevent rainwater running off the verges. A gutter should be fitted along the lowest portion of the roof; upstands are formed for the other edges. Nail them round the edges and fit drip rails and fascia boards; the tops of the drip rails should be level with the tops of the upstands and the fascia boards.

Fitting gutters Where the roof falls towards the edge, nail a fascia board for the gutter so its top edge is flush with the roofing boards. Fit a drip rail so there is nothing to prevent rainwater flowing directly into the centre of the gutter and remaining clear of the brickwork.

Waterproofing roof You will have to waterproof the roof with two or three layers of roofing felt. If you use pre-felted boards, speed of waterproofing is not essential since the boards are already rain-proofed. Unfelted boards are usually waterproofed by fixing the first layer of underfelt with 19mm (¾in) galvanized clout nails at 150mm (6in) intervals. Each layer of felt should overlap the adjacent layer by 50mm (2in); the second and capping layer should be fixed with roofing felt adhesive. Make sure you stagger the joints between sheets and avoid trapping air underneath the felt. Fix the sheets with galvanized clout nails at the edges and fold them back on themselves to form water drips. Where the extension joins the house wall use roofing felt and a timber fillet to form a felt flashing; tuck the top into a raked-out mortar joint.

The final job is to paint the roof with chipping or roofing felt adhesive and spread 13mm (½in) stone chippings over the surface. This will protect the roofing felt, improve fire resistance, give a non-slip surface and increase solar reflection – keeping the roof cooler in summer.

Finishing off the exterior Complete the weather-proofing by fitting downpipes, glazing the windows, fitting the doors and painting the exterior wood-work the colour of your choice; make sure the surface is fully prepared for the best results.

Finishing interior

If you have not already done so, paint or lay on the damp proof membrane inside the extension and

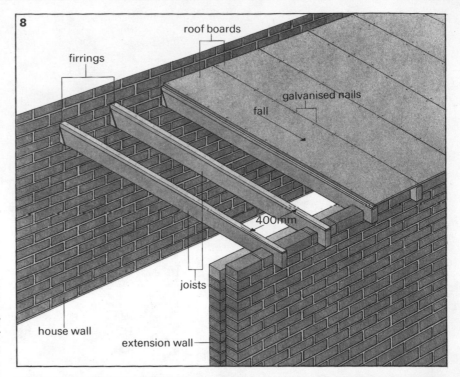

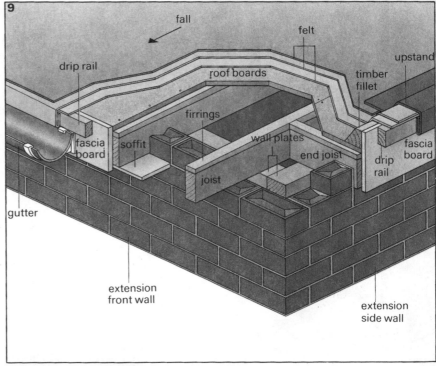

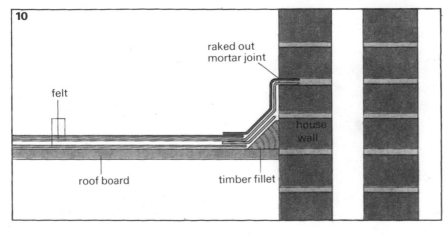

apply the 50mm (2in) cement screed. Fit electric cable runs and socket outlets, as well as plumbing pipe runs if required. Form the ceilings by nailing plasterboard sheets directly onto the joists and include insulation material in the cavities formed, with a vapour barrier if necessary.

You can line the walls with plasterboard or plaster them direct. Fit skirting boards, door archi-traves, ceiling cove and finally decorate the interior to complete your extension.

First floor extension

This project will require specialist advice. In many cases a first floor extension will be built over an existing attached garage. Access to the new room can be made by opening up a new doorway or converting an existing window into a door.

Foundations The usual problem with this type of extension is wall thickness; most garages are built with only single thickness walls and to support the weight of the extension you would have to reinforce them. There are several methods of doing this and much depends upon your local authority's interpretation of the Building Regulations. There must be a great deal of planning and discussion before you begin to build a first floor extension.

One method of support is to dig down to the garage wall foundations, widen them and build new external single brick walls alongside the existing ones. These walls must be bonded together by raking out mortar joints and inserting wall ties, as mentioned earlier. You should then use 100mm (4in) lightweight building blocks for the inner leaf of the extension wall above garage roof level, having cut back the roof covering and joists. You could form an inner leaf for each garage wall; use 100mm (4in) lightweight load-bearing building blocks and leave a 50mm (2in) cavity between the old and the new walls. Use an exterior cladding to hide the ends of the joists. This construction can be continued upwards to form the walls of your new room. In both cases the wall above the garage door may require further support in the form of an RSJ; seek specialist advice before you begin any work.

Flooring The existing garage roof may be too low to form the new floor and you will have to build a raised timber floor above it. This is usually constructed from softwood timber joists of at least 125 × 50mm (5 × 2in). The depth of the joists depends upon their span. The joists are usually laid across the shortest span at 400mm (16in) centres and the floor can be of 19mm ($\frac{3}{4}$in) tongued and grooved flooring grade chipboard. Joists can be supported on joist hangers or wall plates or built into the brickwork.

Warning This type of extension requires specialized knowledge and there are several restrictions you will have to take into account. Consult the building control officer at an early stage to avoid making any dangerous or costly mistakes.

8 When fitting roof, lay firrings in required direction of fall and nail roof boards in place; firrings can be laid across joists instead of along them

9 Before finishing roof with layers of felt, nail end joists in position and fit fascia boards, upstands, drip rails, soffits and guttering

10 Where extension roof joins house wall, use felt and timber fillet to form flashing inserting top of felt into raked out mortar joints

Building first floor brick extension:

11a Plan view showing existing garage wall; new outer leaf and RSJs

11b Elevation, including new foundations and building block inner leaf on first floor

11c Detail showing roof joists and roofing material cut back to accept new outer leaf and floor joists fitted to new block wall

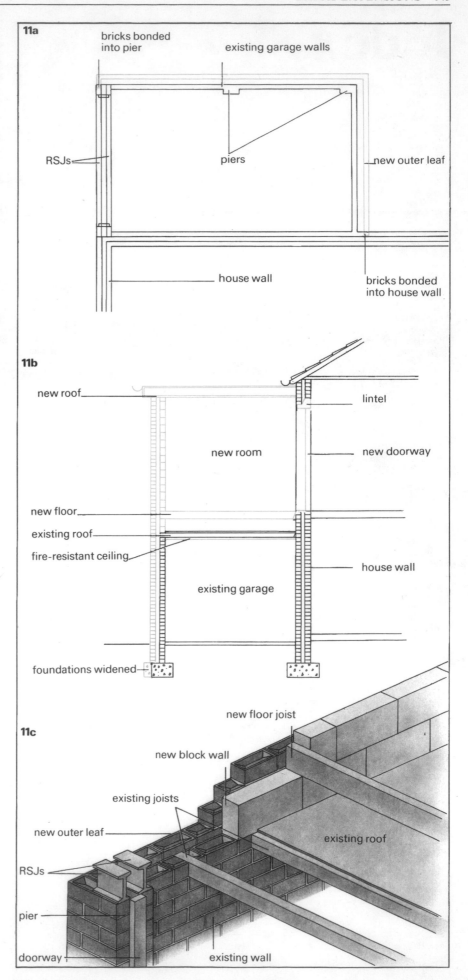

Index